ROUTLEDGE LIBRARY EDITIONS BROADCASTING

Volume 38

WESTERN BROADCASTING OVER THE IRON CURTAIN

WESTERN BROADCASTING OVER THE IRON CURTAIN

Edited by
K. R. M. SHORT

Taylor & Francis Group
LONDON AND NEW YORK

First published in 1986 by Croom Helm

This edition first published in 2024
by Routledge
4 Park Square, Milton Park, Abingdon, Oxon OX14 4RN

and by Routledge
605 Third Avenue, New York, NY 10158

Routledge is an imprint of the Taylor & Francis Group, an informa business

© 1986 K.R.M. Short

All rights reserved. No part of this book may be reprinted or reproduced or utilised in any form or by any electronic, mechanical, or other means, now known or hereafter invented, including photocopying and recording, or in any information storage or retrieval system, without permission in writing from the publishers.

Trademark notice: Product or corporate names may be trademarks or registered trademarks, and are used only for identification and explanation without intent to infringe.

British Library Cataloguing in Publication Data
A catalogue record for this book is available from the British Library

ISBN: 978-1-032-59391-3 (Set)
ISBN: 978-1-032-60335-3 (Volume 38) (hbk)
ISBN: 978-1-032-60337-7 (Volume 38) (pbk)
ISBN: 978-1-003-45863-0 (Volume 38) (ebk)

DOI: 10.4324/9781003458630

Publisher's Note
The publisher has gone to great lengths to ensure the quality of this reprint but points out that some imperfections in the original copies may be apparent.

Disclaimer
The publisher has made every effort to trace copyright holders and would welcome correspondence from those they have been unable to trace.

WESTERN BROADCASTING OVER THE IRON CURTAIN

Edited by
K.R.M. SHORT

CROOM HELM
London & Sydney

©1986 K.R.M. Short
Croom Helm Ltd, Provident House, Burrell Row,
Beckenham, Kent, BR3 1AT
Croom Helm Australia Pty Ltd, Suite 4, 6th Floor,
64-76 Kippax Street, Surry Hills, NSW 2010, Australia

British Library Cataloguing in Publication Data

Western broadcasting over the Iron Curtain
   1. Radio broadcasting 2. International
   broadcasting 3. Radio in propaganda
   I. Short, K.R.M.
   385.54'09171'3   PN1991.55

ISBN 0-7099-4438-1

Printed and bound in Great Britain by
Biddles Ltd, Guildford and King's Lynn

CONTENTS

Preface

Chapter 1: The Real Masters Of The Black Heavens: Western Broadcasters Over The Iron Curtain by K.R.M. Short, Westminster College, Oxford 1

PART ONE: NORTH AMERICAN BROADCASTING OVER THE IRON CURTAIN

Chapter 2: Radio Canada International And Broadcasting Over The Iron Curtain by Frank Ward (formerly Eastern European editor) and Helen Koshits (supervisor, Russian section), Radio Canada International 27

Chapter 3: International Broadcasting And US Political Realities by Frank Shakespeare, former chairman of the Board for International Broadcasting, Radio Free Europe/Radio Liberty 57

Chapter 4: Radio Free Europe/Radio Liberty In The Mid 1980s by William A. Buell, vice president, US Operations, RFE/RL 69

Chapter 5: The Voice Past: VOA, The USSR
And Communist Europe by Alan Heil,
director, VOA Broadcast Operations
and Barbara Schiele, research analyst,
VOA Broadcast Operations 98

Chapter 6: The Voice Present and Future:
VOA, The USSR and Communist Europe by
Edward Mainland, chief, VOA European
Division and Mark Pomar, chief, VOA
Russian Service and Kurt Carlson, staff,
VOA European Division 113

PART TWO: EUROPEAN BROADCASTING OVER
THE IRON CURTAIN

Chapter 7: The BBC External Services:
Broadcasting to the USSR and Eastern
Europe by Peter Fraenkel, controller,
European Services, BBC External Services 139

Chapter 8: Deutsche Welle's Russian
Service, 1962-85 by Botho Kirsch, head
of Eastern Service, Deutsche Welle 158

Chapter 9: Deutschlandfunk: Broadcasting
to East Germany and Eastern Europe by
Jürgen Reiss, director, Europa-Programm,
Deutschlandfunk 172

Chapter 10: Radio in the American Sector,
RIAS Berlin by Donald R. Browne,
University of Minnesota, Twin Cities 185

Chapter 11: German Democratic Republic
Censorship and West German Broadcasting
by Gerhard Wettig, Bundesinstitut für
ostwissenschaftliche und internationale
Studien, Cologne 204

PART THREE: IRON CURTAIN AUDIENCES AND
PUBLIC OPINION

Chapter 12: Soviet Area Audience and
Opinion Research SAAOR at Radio Free
Europe/Radio Liberty by R. Eugene
Parta, director of SAAOR, Paris 227

Chapter 13: Public Opinion Assessment
and Radio Free Europe's Effectiveness
in Eastern Europe by Mary McIntosh,
chief, Statistics, Analyses and
Attitude Research, East European
Audience and Opinion Research,
Radio Free Europe, Munich 245

BIBLIOGRAPHY   264

CONTRIBUTORS   267

INDEX   272

Everyone has the right of freedom of opinion and expression: this right includes freedom to hold opinions without interference and to seek, receive and impart information and ideas through any media and regardless of frontiers.

                UNIVERSAL DECLARATION OF HUMAN RIGHTS

PREFACE

This collection of essays dealing with the broadcasting of western governments to the USSR and its eastern European satellites originated in a conference on 'Broadcasting Over the Iron Curtain' held at the Freedoms Foundation at Valley Forge, near Philadelphia, Pennsylvania, at the end of September 1984. The essays have been brought up to date wherever necessary. The conference was organised by The Historical Journal of Film, Radio, and Television and sponsored by the Freedoms Foundation. The editor of this volume, on behalf of the participants, would especially like to thank the Foundation's vice president for programmes, Dr Franz Lassner, for his support and hospitality during the three days of meetings on the Foundation's campus.

Unfortunately it has not been possible to include all of the papers given during the several seminars. These include 'The BBC and the Beginnings of the Russian Service' by Judith Hammond of the London School of Economics; 'Historical Issues of the Voice of America Broadcasts to Austria 1945-55 and the McCarthy Attacks on the VOA' by Robert A. Bauer of the Brookings Institution, Washington; 'The Iron Curtain Will Roll Back: The USA and the Hungarian Revolt' by the late Paul Nadanyi; 'Broadcasting Between the Two Germanies: An Update' by Douglas A. Boyd of the University of Delaware; 'Influences on the Development of Radio Liberty, 1946-85' by Jon Lodeesen; 'Kol Israel and the Jews of the Communist Diaspora' by Victor Grajewski; and, finally, 'The Evolution of Policy at Radio Free Europe and Radio Liberty, 1949-84' by Sig Mickelson, former president of Radio Free Europe. The conference, composed of some 30 people, including a group of active observers, also heard presentations from Patrick Nieburg, former director of RIAS Berlin and now at the Voice of America; from Allan Familiant, director of programme operations, Radio Canada International; and from Alan Heil of the VOA (see extracts in Chapter 1). The other conference participants were Elzbieta Olechowska of Radio Canada International, David Culbert, Allan Baker, Brian Hammond, Nien Sheng-Lin, Harold Fisher, Turki Bahashwan, Mari Johnson, Susan Fronterhouse and Harold Rhoads.

Finally, the editor would like to record his gratitude to the former president of Radio Free Europe/Radio Liberty, James Buckley who, when approached with the idea of such an international gathering of the free world's broadcasters, gave it his support and ensured the fullest cooperation of the Radios. The editor would also like to thank Cedric Tate of RFE/RL Munich for his help concerning the history of the two Radios and James Brown, former director of Radio Free Europe for freely sharing his views on international broadcasting with the editor. Various broadcasting organisations and universities provided for travel funds and the editor especially wishes to thank the British Academy.

K.R.M. Short, Westminster College, Oxford

Chapter One

THE REAL MASTERS OF THE BLACK HEAVENS: WESTERN BROADCASTERS OVER THE IRON CURTAIN

K.R.M. Short
Westminster College, Oxford

Ten years ago this month (August 1985) the leaders of the 35 states, participating in the Conference on Security and Cooperation in Europe (CSCE), signed a document called the Final Act. Although the leaders have changed, those men and women who gathered again in Helsinki had good reason to ask if anything else had changed and particularly if the good intentions of the Helsinki meetings had in any measure been realised. What was particularly noticeable was that there was a new Soviet treatment of the international press. For the first time, Soviet officials made themselves available in places ranging from the conference halls to the coffee shops and provided a remarkably more interesting press conference than the United States on the results of the Secretary of State Shultz - Foreign Secretary Shevardnadze meeting.
   Although the new Soviet look initiated by Mikhail Gorbachov gives the appearance of liberalization, it is liberalization applicable only to the western media and the manipulation of western public opinion. Gorbachov's recent revitalization of Soviet foreign propaganda efforts, after its failure to mobilize Western European public opinion adequately against the siting of cruise missiles in western Europe, is a logical response; for the Final Act of Helsinki is not, as The Times (3rd August, 1985) points out, the final act but 'just the first act of an immense and open-ended play, featuring countless diplomatic, military, economic, scientific and cultural exchanges, follow-up meetings and review conferences'. Gorbachov's new public relations-propaganda look also includes the revitalization of the Soviet Union's domestic propaganda machinery which includes the propaganda department, state television and radio, the press and

publishing houses and the Ministry of Culture. The end product of this reorganization could well be an even greater tightening of the censorship under which the Soviet people have lived since 1917 and represents a complete negation of the so-called 'basket three' of the Helsinki Accords.

Ten years ago, 'basket three' was seen as an important step in building bridges across the Iron Curtain by encouraging the free flow of information, ideas and people; what has been achieved is very little. The people of the Soviet Union have not benefited from the following clause (2. Information/The participating States), to 'make it their aim to facilitate the freer and wider dissemination of information of all kinds, to encourage cooperation in the field of information and exchange of information with other countries, and to improve the conditions under which journalists from one participating State exercise their profession in another particular State.' (1)

The restraints on western journalists are still pronounced and anyone who transgresses the Soviet taboos will meet with a deaf ear to a subsequent visa request, if not immediate expulsion if they are already in the USSR. Of course much of the problem lies in western reporting of what is going on in the Soviet Union, particularly in that most sensitive of areas, human rights. Although the 'third basket' does not concern human rights in particular, the two matters are inextricably linked. Thus there are still enormous difficulties in extracting relevant news and information from the Soviet Union and the Soviet-dominated states of central and eastern Europe because the communist leadership does not want such material used against it in the world struggle between communism and capitalism. In the same fashion, the Soviet government, be it that of Stalin or Gorbachov, is not going to allow the ideology of the 'capitalist imperialists' to corrupt the right thinking and ideologically proper living of its communist citizens. It is impossible for a free flow of information to take place under such ideological restrictions. George Shultz has commented with some justice on the 'gap between hope and performance ... Despite the real value of the Final Act as a standard of conduct, the most important promises of a decade ago have not been kept'. That is clearly so in respect to the promise to 'respect human rights and fundamental freedoms' made in the opening Declaration of Principles.

This is not to say that, despite Soviet

obstructionism, the western signatories to the Accords are powerless to achieve some its aims. Great Britain, the United States, the Federal Republic of Germany and Canada amongst the signatories, support important broadcasting programmes to provide those people who live east of the Iron Curtain with the news of the day and information relating to the broadcasting nation's history, culture and foreign policy views. Additionally there are surrogate broadcasting organizations such as The Federal Republic's Deutschlandfunk, the United States's Radio Free Europe/Radio Liberty, and RIAS Berlin, funded jointly by the two nations, which seek to provide an alternative domestic radio service for the German Democratic Republic, Hungary, Czechoslovakia, Bulgaria, Poland, Rumania, (the Baltic republics are the responsibility of the VOA) and several of the Republics of the Soviet Union.

These western broadcasting organizations, dubbed by a correspondent from the Novosti news agency as the 'real masters of the black heavens' at the time of the invasion of Czechoslovakia, circumvent the communist information stranglehold and do more for the free flow of information from west to east than all the official channels and exchanges sponsored over the past few years under the Helsinki Final Act. A brief survey of standard allegations raised against these western democratic voices indicates how seriously the communist leadership takes the threat that such broadcasting can undermine the socialist state. Eastern European and Soviet newspapers and magazines regularly carry articles detailing the cunning devices of western intelligence, which are the cause of virtually all the grievances and failures of communist society, ranging from racial and national tension to youth rebellion, social unrest and the encouragement of the human rights movement.

The reason for the communist response to such broadcasting is closely related to the necessary defence of its monopoly power over society, which involves the Party's monopoly on information. Botho Kirsch of Deutsche Welle's Russian Service reminded the conference at Valley Forge on Broadcasting Over the Iron Curtain that only three days after the victory of the Bolshevik revolution, Lenin signed the General Decree on the Press and re-introduced the press censorship that had been abolished by the revolution. The decree of 9th November, 1917 promised that, 'As soon as the new system has been consolidated all administrative intervention will be rescinded, and the press will enjoy complete freedom in accordance with a law formulated as widely and as progressively as possible.' (2)

Seven decades after the Bolshevik revolution, the hopes of the General Decree on the Press remain unfulfilled for there is still no 'complete freedom' for the press in the USSR or those eastern and central European nations which came under Soviet domination. Today these people are protected from knowing those facts and ideas judged to be of a counter-revolutionary nature. A leading Belgrade newspaper has commented, 'People in the Soviet Union are in an absurd situation. Despite their high standard of general knowledge and a strong intelligentsia unequalled anywhere in the world, they have a press which seeks to eradicate their desire for individual responsibility and to instil them with the belief that their leaders are infallible.' (3)

Leading Soviet dissidents like Alexander Solzhenitsyn and Andrei Sakharov have appealed in vain to the Soviet authorities to abolish what they see as preposterous censorship which has stifled the intellectual life of the country. In a samizdat protest document smuggled to the west in early 1980, the dissident writers Viktor Nekipelov and Feliks Serebrov made a passionate plea for freedom of information before being sent back to prison: 'we do not even have a "wall of democracy" on which to put up our "wall newspapers" as is done, or at least was done until recently, in China ... today the voices of western radio are not merely a primary source of information and inspiration for millions of our fellow-countrymen today but a unique school of democracy, a door to the Russia of tomorrow.' (4)

It is estimated that more than 70,000 censors watch over the so-called state secrets in the Soviet Union. According to a list which found its way to the west and cited by Botho Kirsch, press publication of the following types of newsmatter is forbidden without the censor's explicit approval:

> Information about earthquakes and other natural disasters, diseases and epidemics within the territory of the USSR.
> News about fires, explosions, train or plane crashes, naval and mine disasters, criminal statistics or statistics for numbers of prisoners, beggars, tramps and prostitutes.
> Reference to the existence of labour camps, including the number of prisoners and

'special occurrences' such as riots and suicides.
   Reports of food shortages in the USSR.
   The names of the members of the State Security Committee (KGB), apart from that of the chairman and his deputies; data on the salaries of the Party and government officials, the special privileges enjoyed by them or reference to their personal lives.
   Any reference whatsoever to the censorship organs or to the jamming of foreign radio stations. (5)

The limitations on the communist media are quite clear and although some of the items on the list above might seem unexpected, for the most part it could have been written by any experienced Kremlinologist. References to foreign radio stations, which are made regularly, are not initiated by newspapers or magazines; efforts to destroy both the citizen's desire to listen and the credibility of the stations is a centralized function of the Party's propaganda machinery. There is no reason to refer to the 'real masters of the black heavens' if they cannot be heard - hence the longstanding and ever increasing communist commitment to jamming foreign radio stations.
   Jamming takes either the form of transmitting a continuous 'buzz saw' noise on the same frequency as the unwelcome station, or a complex mixture of speech, music and atmospheric noise (Mayak jamming), designed in both instances to overwhelm the incoming programme. Mayak jamming is most commonly used by the eastern bloc and appears to be designed to promote the illusion that the western-originated signal is being blotted out by the sort of atmospheric and station interference common to shortwave broadcasting. Every major city has local ground-wave jamming stations; the rural areas are protected from western penetration by sky-wave jammers. These broadcast a Mayak or buzz saw shortwave signal to the east of the target area (say from part of Poland) on the same frequency as that of the Voice of America or Radio Free Europe programme transmitted to the west of the target area. Radio Free Europe's transmitters are in Spain and Portugal, to allow for the required angle to bounce the shortwave signal off the ionosphere down to the Polish target area. The signal bounces off the earth and back to the ionosphere and thence to earth on its 'second hop' and continues to do so with steadily diminishing strength. Soviet jamming

is helped by the publication of western broadcasting times but the system locks onto the right frequencies so quickly that the process is probably computerized.

Local jamming and sky-wave jamming can be overcome to a certain extent with specialized aerials. It is fairly common for those keen to listen to western views to have shortwave receivers secretly modified to receive the higher frequencies which provide better reception. Increased western signal strength and better tuned antennae increase the ability to penetrate the jamming. The timing of broadcasts is also important, because the twilight hours of morning and evening are the most ineffective for Soviet-originated sky-wave jamming. This is because the western broadcasts can take advantage of the ionosphere's 'solid' condition at these times, while the eastern jamming broadcasts have difficulty in achieving a reasonable reflection in their 'broken' section of the ionosphere. This creates a time-related gap in the Soviet defences. Jamming is estimated to employ 15,000 people, as many as 3,000 powerful transmitters and to cost more than $150 million a year. The simple way of avoiding the impact of local ground-wave jamming is to take a bus or drive into the country with a shortwave radio, and to listen at twilight. Some individuals record and sell western popular music or circulate the tapes to friends.

An important point developed in the following articles is that the Soviet policy of jamming has followed the ebb and flow of East-West tensions and crises, internal and external. The USSR intermittently jammed western broadcasts in English from 1948 to 1973 and stopped in 1980; jamming of the VOA and BBC was renewed as the Solidarity movement in Poland gained strength and western criticism mounted of the Soviet occupation of Afghanistan. The surrogate stations of Radio Liberty (targeted on the USSR) and Radio Free Europe (except Romania) were jammed during the entire period; Kol Israel is subject to blanket jamming, together with all international stations that broadcast in the language of the communist target area. All-India Radio may be the only exception. The practical effect of such massive blockades of noise is that, during peak evening listening hours, up to 80% of all usable shortwave frequencies in Europe are affected by jamming. All that you have to do to confirm that estimate is to turn on a shortwave receiver on any given night.

The histories of the radios represented in this

Figure 1.1

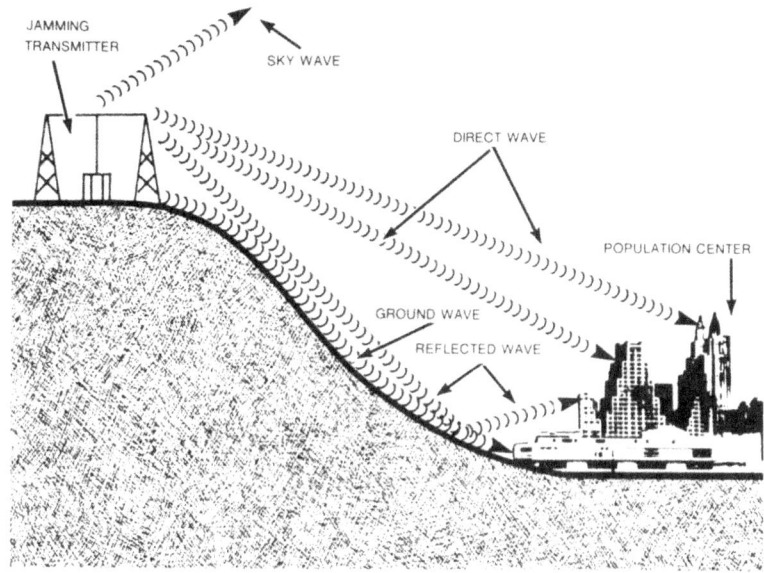

LOCAL JAMMING consists primarily of a direct wave and a reflected wave.

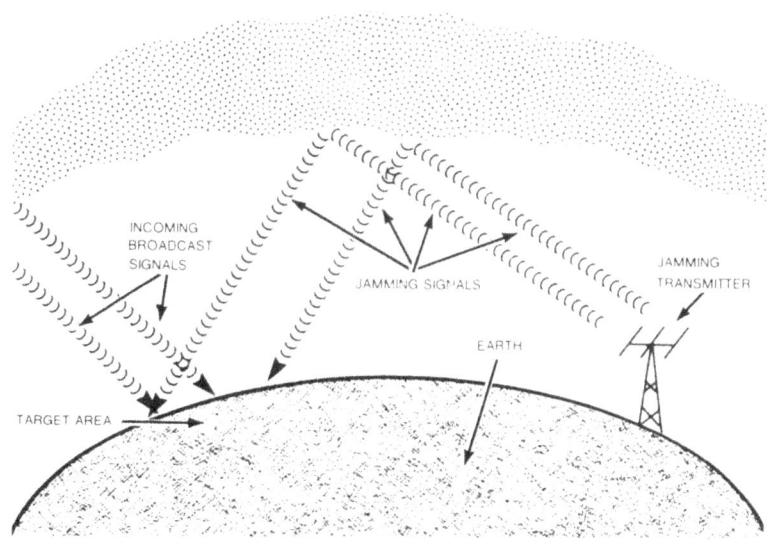

SKY WAVE JAMMING uses the ionosphere to propogate jamming signals over great distances.

Source: Courtesy of the Board for International Broadcasting, Washington DC

The Real Masters of The Black Heavens

Figure 1.2

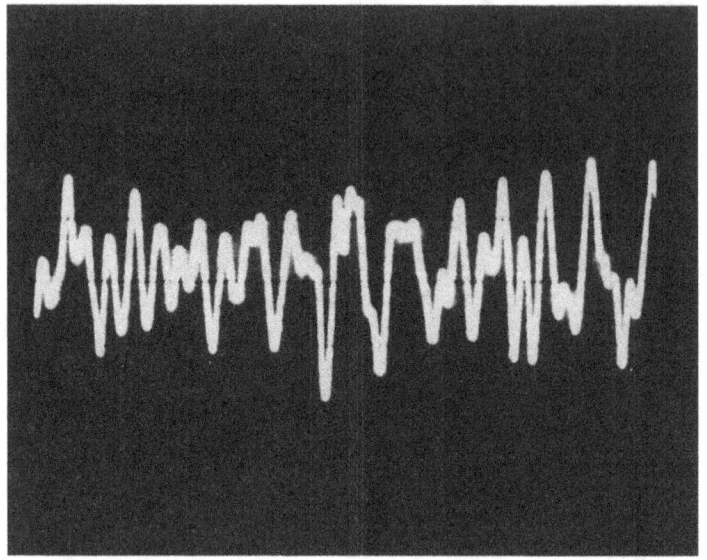

OSCILLOSOPES show a clear broadcast signal (above), jamming (below)

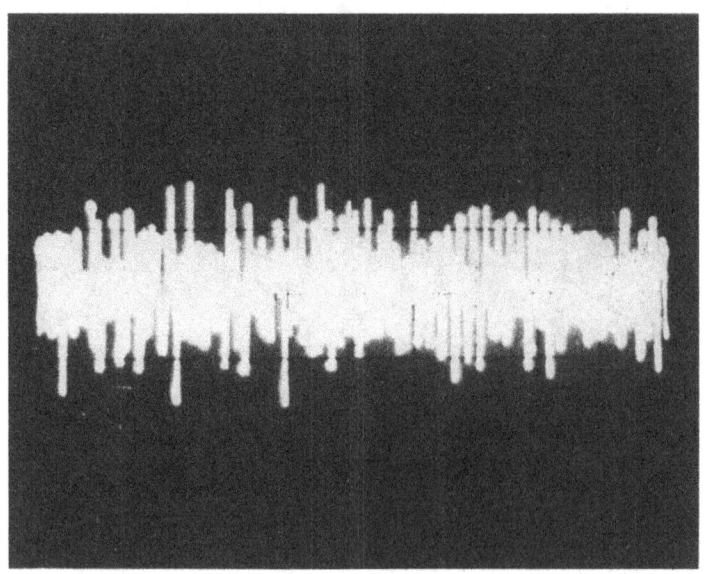

Source: Courtesy of the Board for International Broadcasting, Washington DC

book indicate that they are strongly affected by the perceived national interests of the moment. Radio Canada International came close to extinction in late 1967. The two Munich-based surrogate stations, Radio Free Europe and Radio Liberty, were brought near to close-down by the forces of détente led by Senator William Fulbright; this was in the wake of the public disclosures that the bulk of their operating funds came, not from private contributions, but from the US Central Intelligence Agency. Although the break with the CIA came some 15 years ago, both radios continue to be accused of being CIA voices by communist critics. Deutsche Welle and Deutschlandfunk, along with RIAS Berlin, have a less fraught history. The BBC External Services have never been threatened by closure; periodically the Foreign Office, which funds the External Services, (as opposed to BBC domestic radio and television which are funded by licence fee), obeys the government of the day and drops or adds language services along with the usual budget trimming which inhibits the development of the service's interests. As of 1985, the BBC has received the go-ahead to site new °20 million transmitters at Orfordness which will be directed to East Europe and the Soviet Union.

The BBC External Services were recently faced with demands from the Foreign Office to make in-house economies of °1.2 million; the total budget was raised from °86 million to °90 million, which barely reflects the impact of inflation. On the other hand, after long years of comparative famine, the Voice of America, benefiting from President Reagan's style of foreign policy, was given an extra $1.5 billion in 1985 to invest in new services and transmitters, bringing its total broadcast hours by the end of 1985 to 1,298 hours in over 60 languages. The Soviet Union is currently transmitting 2,169 hours in 84 languages. If Radio Free Europe and Radio Liberty are added to the American commitment the American figures are roughly the same as those of its superpower opponent (see Appendix 1 to this chapter for comparative broadcasting and listening statistics). RFE/RL, which spent the post-CIA years in a political wilderness, are also benefiting from the sympathetic climate at the White House, a process described with insider's knowledge by Frank Shakespeare in Chapter 3.

The extent to which political climates control the vitality and message of these radios is a major issue which surfaces in most of the following articles and played an important role in the discussions which surrounded them at the time of presentation. Frank Shakespeare claims that in his years of association with VOA and RFE/RL, Presidents Nixon, Johnson and Reagan never interfered with the operations or sought to use the radios for propaganda. The radio respresentatives at the Valley Forge conference saw themselves as journalists, not as propagandists; Alan Heil of VOA said that all of them were determined 'to protect and wisely employ (their) autonomy and decision-making on news and programming content'. While there is no doubt that the voice of any Eastern Bloc radio is that of its government's information or dis-information services, the western radios have freedom of action. This is typified by the objectivity characteristically attributed to the BBC. The Federal Republic of Germany's two services are similarly protected by their enabling legislation, while the VOA makes a clear distinction between its general programming and the VOA Editorial, which is an official statement of US policy.

RFE and RL offer a different problem because of their current funding and management. Sig Mickelson's recent study of these two radios reports their genesis in the early days of the Cold War, their alleged nurturing without interference by the CIA, attempted abolition by Senator Fulbright, and, after the public revelations of CIA funding, their reorganization into RFE/RL under a presidentially appointed Board for Internation Broadcasting (BIB) and funded by Congress. Mickelson's continuing concern is that the radios could become politicized and lose their credibility and influence throughout Eastern Europe and the Soviet Union. He concluded that, 'Self-serving political interference from members of the Congress began to surface when the CIA ceased to serve as a buffer between Capitol Hill and the radios. Radio executives in the future could find themselves in the position where they devote an inordinate share of their time to protecting themselves from ill-informed attacks from individual congressmen or in seeking evidence to reply to petty, politically-motivated questions. Serving under a board of directors appointed by the President could conceivably lead to political pressures and encouragement to alter policy to conform to the political interests of the party in power in the White House.' (6)

Mickelson's fears seemed to have foundation, in the light of two incidents which occurred after the appearance of his book. The first was in the summer

The Real Masters of The Black Heavens

of 1983 when the director of Radio Free Europe, the widely respected broadcaster and East European scholar, James Brown, resigned over his fears that the radio was going to be politicized under the direction of former Republican Senator, RFE/RL President James Buckley. Brown's case was taken up by The Times (18 June, 1983) under the heading The True Voice of Freedom. Noting that under Brown (a British citizen) the station had developed a reputation for 'reasonably careful and accurate reporting of East and West', the editorial warned that, 'If the more extreme voices in Washington get their way with RFE, it will be bad for the radio and bad for the West. It is not that they will provoke uprisings in eastern Europe. The more likely result is that they will lose audiences by destroying the fragile credibility which the radio has built up'. Echoing the BBC philosophy of broadcasting, the editorial concluded: 'The peoples of eastern Europe are more sophisticated and well-informed than is sometimes supposed. Surveys by RFE confirm that listeners do not want to hear incitement and propaganda. They want accurate news and responsible comment. They are highly sensitive to propaganda because they live with it all the time. If RFE starts to give them a mirror image of their own distorted media they will switch off. The West would then have lost a valuable line to the ears of the East Europeans. Only the regimes of eastern Europe would gain. The best persuasion the West can offer is truth.'

Brown was replaced by the Hungarian-born George Urban, whose reputation was as hardline as Brown's was softline, although both descriptions include the assumption of anti-communism. There was no evidence that either Urban or his opposite number at Radio Liberty, another hardliner, George Bailey (now retired) were tampering with policy or giving greater emphasis to the emigré groups calling for a more strident anti-communist line in broadcasting. Then came President Reagan's appalling gaffe in 1984 when he told an off-air, off-the-record joke to assembled newsmen concerning the best way to deal with the Soviets, which was to 'bomb them'. The leaked story stole headlines across the world and all radio stations carried the news, including RFE and RL. The next morning the RFE and RL radio directors ordered the story to be dropped, which was done only with reluctance by the staff. Radio Moscow used the embarrassing silence to state once again that the radios were controlled by the CIA. The Sunday Times (2 September, 1984) quoted one veteran producer as saying, 'Our credibility suffered a damaging blow because of the clumsy attempt to suppress what, in essence, was a pretty minor story'. Reagan's gaffe was described by the world's press in terms ranging from bad taste to a Freudian slip by a megalomaniac cowboy. RFE/RL were the losers in the international broadcasting game, where credibility is the prime commodity. James Buckley of RFE/RL and Frank Shakespeare of BIB strongly reject any notion that the radios are less objective than before and critics are hardpressed to prove otherwise, but the fear remains.

On 7th August, 1985, the BBC External Services went silent for the first time since Britain began international broadcasting 53 years earlier, when the journalists of the BBC's domestic and overseas networks joined those of Britain's independent radios and television to protest over the Thatcher government's successful pressure on the BBC's Governors to ban the showing of the television documentary on Northern Ireland, <u>The Edge of the Union</u> (this was finally broadcast with small amendments in October 1985). Letters sent to the Home Secretary and the Governors by the External Services staff said that the ban, which was widely covered by the communist media as an illustration of government control of the BBC, had 'handed a weapon to regimes which openly practise political censorship' (<u>The Times</u>, 8 August, 1985). Claims that the External Services and the English World Service have had their credibility significantly weakened smacks of over reaction when one realises that there has never been any official communist doubt that the BBC is the tool of the Foreign Office. What the BBC has always been given credit for (see chapter 7) is that it is such a marvellously devious propaganda organ that it always, and to everybody, appears objective. Its broadcasting is often described by communist commentators as the 'most dangerous'.

Soviet listeners to the BBC normally get their advance notice of programmes by listening to the service; late in 1981, the BBC placed programme listings in the London Communist Party paper <u>The Morning Star</u>, because it was the only English paper widely available in the USSR; out of its circulation of 12,000 copies, four out of every six are airlifted by Aeroflot every day into the Soviet Union. The External Services bought a week's advertising highlighting its programmes. The ad ran for three days before <u>The Morning Star</u> cancelled the booking and returned a cheque for £90 without explanation, to cover the remaining three days. Clearly, the Soviet censors had not been looking in the right place.

At the Valley Forge conference, Alan Heil of Voice of America noted that each of the stations has a unique personality, style, format and mission. He continued:

> As broadcasters of the free world, our common points far outweigh our differences in approach. Much more united us than divides us. First of all, we share a commitment to informing through facts; more, I think, than persuading, in the international broadcasting of the 1980s. Even in closed societies, it is up to the listener to sift the facts and determine where the truth lies, in the manner of free men. In the private sanctuary of the human mind, enslavement is impossible. We (broadcasters) array the facts. The listener, in wisdom, distils these and concludes.
>
> Secondly, we all have a determination to protect and wisely employ our autonomy and decision-making on news and programming content. Several speakers pointed to the remarkable degree of latitude (coupled, to be sure, with a deep sense of responsibility) we western broadcasters enjoy. By broadcasters, I mean the professional writers and editors who transcend the changes in what were called 'publishers' (the political leadership). Sometimes we lose perspective about just how much freedom we have. Four years ago, a delegation from Radio Beijing paid a first visit to the VOA. We briefed them thoroughly over a period of several weeks, showed them the copy tasting and other editorial processes in the VOA Newsroom, taught them about interviewing, how Washington news bureaux work, etc. At the end, the course proctor asked the visiting Chinese if there was any aspect of operation they had missed, or if they had any questions. One responded, 'But you didn't show us the secret room where policy is applied to the news.'
>
> Third, western broadcasters try to reflect reality. We do not second guess confirmed facts. Ed Murrow, after returning to the United States from London at the end of World War Two, put it best: 'Radio,' he said, 'if it is to serve and survive, must hold a mirror up to the nation and the world. The mirror must have no curves and it must be held with a steady hand.'

Finally, I think all of us have reached a consensus about the necessity of building a reliable resource base to do our jobs. We are, and have been, critically underfunded over the years. Some have suggested that there is a price being paid (or yet due) for additional resources to the radios ... that with these resources, we must pay a promissory note in the form of cold war propaganda. I don't, myself, think that's possible in the 1980s. We in international broadcasting in the west are larger than that, by leagues. In the Voice and in the United States Information Agency, there is an unshakeable commitment to our legislative charter. News and current affairs content is the province of VOA and VOA alone. Eight years ago, when the VOA Charter became a public law, we erected the legal framework for news as accurate, objective and comprehensive as competent editors can make it. Even the 'publisher' stands by this. (7)

Other themes which emerge in this book include the significant difference between broadcasting to the USSR and to Eastern Europe, a comparative newcomer to communist ideology and information control. There is strong evidence (cited by Mary McIntosh of RFE in Chapter 13) to support the contention that a significant percentage of the populations of Poland, Bulgaria, Romania, Czechoslovakia, Hungary and the German Democratic Republic are in sympathy with western democratic ideas and some form of mixed economy, if not with capitalism. The leakage from Austrian and West German medium wave radio must have a measurable influence on the changing patterns of expectation and aspiration in countries like Hungary and Czechoslovakia and the influence of West German radio and television on the German Democratic Republic is even greater. Efforts by the GDR to limit that influence are discussed by Jurgen Reiss, Donald Brown and Gerhard Wettig in Chapters 9 to 11. The Soviet Union is entirely different. Whereas many in Eastern Europe depend on the surrogate stations based in Cologne and Munich to provide them with a 24-hour alternative radio service, the Soviet audience is more difficult to please, as the SAAOR research indicates (see Chapter 12). Some programmes beamed on the USSR are criticised for being too negative or offensive to the Soviet sense of patriotism; others say the same programmes are too soft and that the Russians need to be reminded that they are the 'last great predatory empire on earth' (Philip Nicolaides, former VOA deputy programme director), or in President Reagan's terms the 'empire of evil'.

The theme of empire leads western broadcasters to encourage nationalism, including culture and language in the USSR, along with religion for which there seems to be growing interest. Nationalism and religion are part of western broadcasting strategy to both the Soviet Union and Eastern Europe. The Soviets attack such programming as illegal intervention in their domestic affairs and have become vigorous advocates of the New Information Order. This is part of their defensive policy to prevent western radio exerting a destablising influence within their multinational, multi-lingual, multi-racial and multi-religious state.

Is the Soviet fear of destabilisation justified? and is it actually a goal of western radio? It is, if one accepts M.M.'s assessment in the Warsaw review The Democratic Journalist (no. 5, May 1984) of the book Radio Free Europe: An Instrument of Propaganda Aggression (1983, no stated authors, Prague). M.M. claims that the 'United States highly proclaimed concept of the free flow of information strongly resembles the Goebbels methods of Nazi propaganda. The diversionist character of both these espionage transmitters (RFE/RL), their programme intent and organisational structure, created during the Cold War, have persisted with all these fundamental features until the present day.' (8) If broadcasters are asked whether they are seeking to overthrow the communist state, they answer that it is not a realistic goal, but they do see the possibility of stimulating important changes which could contribute to the evolution of a more humane form of communism. Evolution, not revolution, seems to be the hope.

Is it the responsibility or the right of western nations to adopt such a role towards another sovereign state? This question was addressed by the Report of the United States Advisory Commission on Public Diplomacy, published in 1982. It outlined what Soviet propaganda sought to achieve (see the Appendix to this chapter) while stressing that an important function of foreign policy was to support public diplomacy. In the words of the report, public diplomacy has the task of providing 'other peoples with a better understanding of the policies, values, institutions and culture of the United States; and ... to enhance understanding on the part of the government and people of the United States of the history, culture, attitudes, perceptions and aspirations of others.' Although the International Communication Agency whose mission this document was defining has again become the United States Information Agency, the first half of the information mission is still very much alive and, to judge from people like Walter Reich, of Washington's Kennan Institute for Advanced Russian Studies, very much needed. In a nationally syndicated column in July 1983, Reich gave the opinion of his Moscow taxi driver that Soviet leaders wanted only peace and their American counterparts wanted only war. At a Russian dinner party Reich asked the guests how much Soviet people believed what they read and saw. 'Fifty per cent of them', one guest replied after consulting with his friends, 'believe fifty per cent of it. A smaller percentage in the big cities, a greater percentage in the countryside. But many believe it. They really do.' Reich asked: 'they really believe we're evil?' The answer was, 'They really do.' So much for establishing a case for public diplomacy, but is it possible to achieve meaningful change in a nation where there is no real public opinion - that is to say, opinion that can be mobilised to effect change? According to the Jewish 'refusnik' scientist, Aleksandr Lerner, there are only private opinions in Russia.

Even if the possibility for encouraging change is minimal should that make a difference? Is there a responsibility that the democracies cannot evade - any more than the materially blessed nations of the west can ignore African famine? The responsibility is argued strongly by former US Ambassador to the United Nations, Jeane Kirkpatrick. In an interview conducted in 1983 by the current director of RFE, George Urban, Kirkpatrick argued that, 'It is very important that we always recognise and affirm the legitimacy of resistance to tyrannical governments, of whatever type. We must, as free societies, make clear that we stand on the side of the aspirations of the people to have governments that 'govern by the consent of the governed'. This involves supplying them with information in our broadcasts, and depicting for them alternative images of reality and alternative ways of being and social existence so that the official controls of the symbolic environment are rendered ineffective.' She qualified this statement by stressing that while it was the 'right and duty' of the west to inform, it was not 'for us to tell people in the Soviet Union or Eastern

Europe what particular action they should take or omit taking to further their interests as nations and individuals.' (19)

Broadcasting over the Iron Curtain, it would seem, may save the soul but it will not free the individual; it may assist evolution but it will not feed revolution. Some experts, such as former RFE director, James Brown, suggest that western broadcasting unexpectedly contributes to stability in Eastern Europe because it makes life more bearable. (10) Whatever the future, the broadcasters' expectations, or those of the governments which pay the bills, are that the airwaves of Europe will continue to be crowded with the programmes of the 'real masters of the black heavens', the communist jammers and programmes; the battle is joined between those who would provide the peoples of the east with forbidden information and the communist masters who seek to maintain their information monopoly. It is up to the western democracies to make it possible for people under communist governments to hear the other side of the story; it is up to those people to listen. Whether they do so depends not only on whether they can hear the stations but on whether they find the programming attractive, interesting and, above all, credible. (11)

Notes
1. Conference on Security and Cooperation in Europe: Final Act (Helsinki, 1975), pp. 117ff. The communist media takes the view that it is the true servant of the Helsinki accords and that the west is the violator. This is clearly presented in an article entitled 'The IOJ and the 'Spirit of Helsinki' in <u>The Democratic Journalist</u> (vol. 32, no. 9, September 1985). The Secretary General of the International Organization of Journalists (IOG), Jirí Kubka of Czechoslovakia, is quoted as follows: 'It is obvious that the European agreement on cooperation has always been a thorn in the side of the reactionary and rightist circles. When they failed to torpedo the conclusions of this agreement, certain types of mass communication media launched a vicious campaign attacking the socialist countries and all advocates of the Helsinki document. This campaign falsifies and turns upside down the whole meaning and purpose of the approved clauses, especially those concerning the so-called "third basket". This provocative type of mass communication media in western countries not only works against the strengthening of mutual

confidence and international cooperation, but evokes - especially against the socialist countries - unjustified mistrust and hostility.' A major concern was that the mass media should 'respect the internal affairs of other countries in the sense that one is supposed to withdraw from interfering in them directly'; although not mentioned specifically, western radio was the major culprit.
    2. Botho Kirsch, 'Deutsche Welle's Russian Service, 1962-85', Conference on Broadcasting Over the Iron Curtain, Valley Forge, September 1984.
    3. Kirsch, 'Deutsche Welle', 1984.
    4. Viktor Nekipelov and Feliks Serebrov, 'A School of Democracy: Foreign Radio Broadcasts in Russian - Some Advice and Wishes', <u>Radio Liberty Background Report</u>, RL 70/80 (18 February 1980); the document is dated Moscow, November 1979.
    5. Kirsch, 'Deutsche Welle', 1984.
    6. Sig Mickelson, <u>America's Other Voice: The Story of Radio Free Europe and Radio Liberty</u> (New York, 1983), p.222.
    7. Alan Heil, conference presentation, Conference on Broadcasting Over the Iron Curtain, 1984.
    8. <u>The Democratic Journalist</u> is a monthly published in Prague by the International Organization of Journalists in English, French, Russian and Spanish and is an excellent source for current eastern bloc views on western propoganda and world events. Its cover for September 1985 (vol. 32, no. 9) was drawn by Michal Machon and features an enormous evil serpent tempting the world through its tail fixed to a radio transmitting tower, a curiously biblical allusion for a communist magazine, but such is the force of cultural memory. The magazine's ironical editorial address is Washingtonova 17, 11000 Prague 1, Czechoslovakia.
    9. George Urban interview with Jeane Kirkpatrick, 'American Foreign Policy in a Cold Climate', <u>Encounter</u> (November 1983), pp. 9-33.
    10. Conversation with the author, Munich, September 1983.
    11. I should like to acknowledge the comments of Professor Donald Browne on this introduction. He rightly points out that, 'Certainly it has been confrontation between the political systems that has driven the development of western broadcasting to the east, for the most part, but there have been other factors, especially cultural. It might be well to point out that, even if there had been relative peace between the two systems after World War Two, it's

The Real Masters of The Black Heavens

probable that some of the major broadcasters would have broadcast to eastern Europe and the USSR anyway - to promote trade, cultural understanding, etc.' For a balanced and comprehensive historical view on international broadcasting see Professor Browne's International Radio Broadcasting (New York, 1982).

The Real Masters of The Black Heavens

Appendix 1.1a: Comparison of Western External Broadcasters' Weekly Programme Hours to the Soviet Union

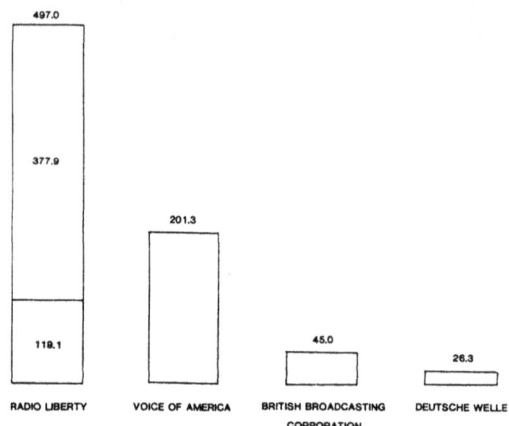

Appendix 1.1b: Weekly Programme Hours to Eastern Europe

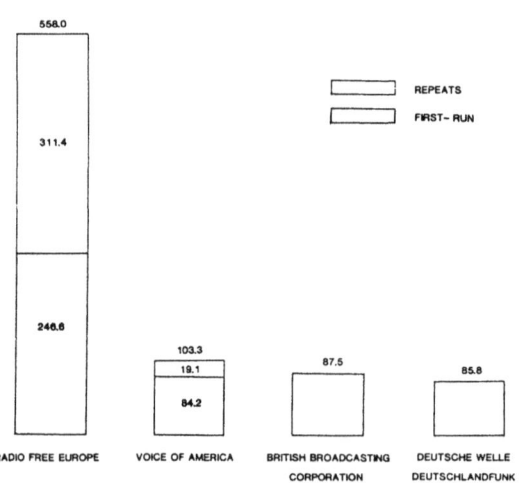

Source: Data are based on current schedules and programming statistics for three quarters of FY 1984. For RFE-RL, The World Radio TV Handbook 1984 and information supplied by the VOA.

The Real Masters of The Black Heavens

Appendix 1.1c: Daily (shaded) and Cumulative Weekly Listener Estimates, in millions.

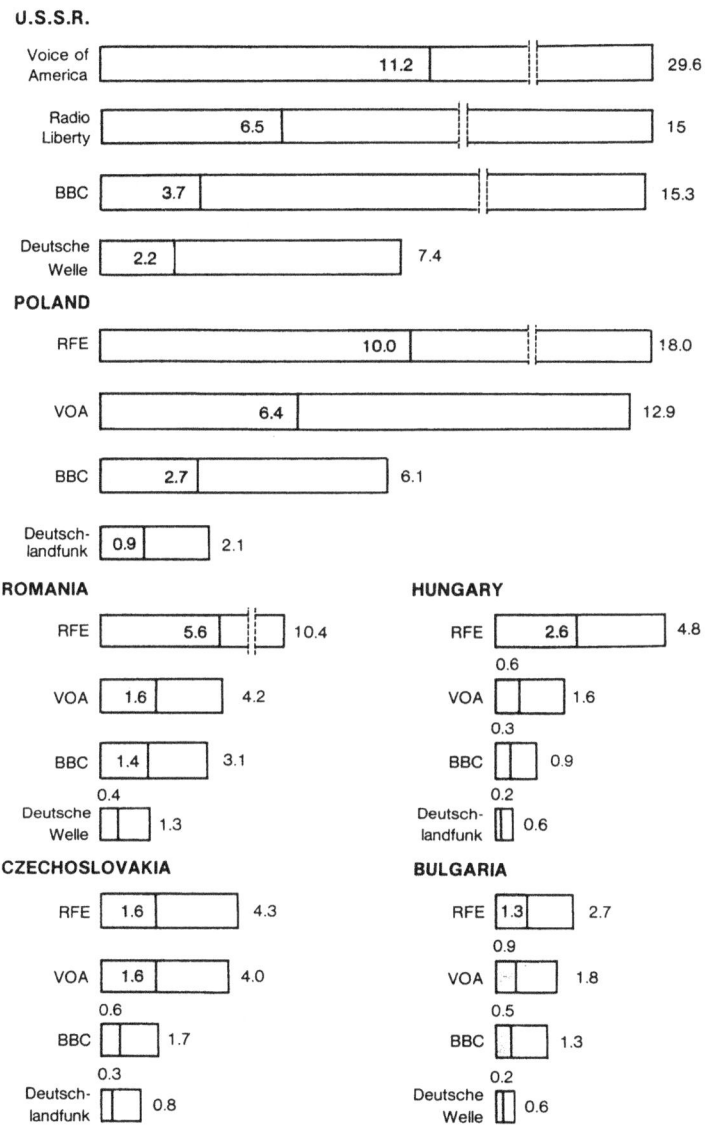

The Real Masters of The Black Heavens

Appendix 1.2 - Soviet Propaganda

Extract from Report of the United States Advisory Commission on Public Diplomacy, 1982. USICA's Soviet Propaganda Alert states that Soviet external propaganda has two principal purposes: (i) to represent the Soviet Union as dedicated to peace and detente; and (ii) to show the Soviet Union as a just, fair, and progressive society, worthy of admiration and emulation.

For these purposes, according to the Agency's analysis, Soviet propagandists follow several basic principles. The first of these is a systematic denigration of the US, its culture, society, political system, and belief structures. The US is portrayed as an unattractive, vicious, exploitative society which has outlived its time. The Soviet Union presents itself as the only alternative: the near-perfect society which has found the answers to the many challenges of modern society. A second key feature of Soviet propaganda is the argument that the US and the West, doomed in their historical decline, present a dangerous threat to the world order. The US is said to be escalating the arms race, provoking conflict, and trying to counter Soviet influence in its effort to regain the military-strategic superiority it once possessed. On the other hand, the Soviet Union is presented as entirely dedicated to the struggle for peace, and its military might is intended only to defend itself and its allies.

Soviet propagandists employ a vast array of techniques, both crude and sophisticated.

> Disinformation is a widespread technique and is usually very difficult to detect. One form is the revelation of false information, usually in a foreign source not directly related to the Soviet Union. Another form is to draw attention to past covert CIA operations and imply American complicity in more recent events.
>
> The technique of indirection includes the inaccurate citation of foreign sources and the citation of western and other non-Soviet sources in an item planted by the Soviets and in support of the Soviet position on a certain issue.
>
> The most effective technique is imputing false motives to US policy. The Soviets point out adverse consequences and offensive features to the countries affected by US actions.
>
> Diversion is used to blunt attacks on the

The Real Masters of The Black Heavens

Soviet Union. When the USSR is criticized, Soviet propaganda responds with countercharges in an attempt to turn the accusation against the accusers themselves.

The following is an example of the wide variety of recent Soviet propaganda attacks on the United States: charges of CIA complicity in and responsibility for the attempted assassination of Pope John Paul II, (and) charges of US interference in the internal affairs of Poland by, among other things, provocative radio broadcasts, 'inhumane' economic sanctions, 'slanderous' declarations, and CIA plotting.

Part One

NORTH AMERICAN BROADCASTING OVER THE IRON CURTAIN

Chapter Two

RADIO CANADA INTERNATIONAL AND BROADCASTING OVER THE IRON CURTAIN

Frank Ward (formerly Eastern European editor) and Helen Koshits (supervisor, Russian section), Radio Canada International

The Past

When the International Service of the Canadian Broadcasting Corporation (CBC) first began regular transmissions to the world in the early days of 1945, it was a world reeling in the shambles of a war already spent. There was no Iron Curtain to penetrate, only a shattered wall of German steel. The Soviet Union was a staunch if battered ally. Nations trampled or still occupied by the Nazis turned toward the west for any word of freedom, and listened for a voice that would talk to them about better things to come. Canada was the newest of these voices. The original purpose of the external service had been to broadcast messages of hope and encouragement to Canadians serving on and beyond the seas, and to reach out, tentatively at first, to foreign friends - those who were still alive to listen.

The early days, for the overseas broadcasting arm of the CBC, were days of vigour, optimism and great plans. The fledgling service attracted the best from both the academic and journalistic professions. They were also days of uncertainty and challenge. No Canadian had ever manned an overseas transmitter on a full-time basis; few Canadians listened to shortwave then or today, unless they are abroad and want news of home. Fewer still were aware of the difficulties and the problems which would beset the International Service for years to come - not only technical and financial, but governmental and bureaucratic as well. We were amateurs in the field of shortwave. But we had motivation and a pair of powerful 50 kilowatt transmitters, located in an ideal site on the east coast, the Tantramar Salt Marshes at Sackville, New Brunswick. So great was the enthusiasm for this new medium that, 18 months after the official inauguration on 25 February, 1945, the first director general of the Service, Peter Aylen, could say with all sincerity:

> There certainly was never a better time for Canada to find a voice. Our war efforts have won a high place and high responsibilities for Canada in the international field. All around the world, the name of Canada is held in high regard. Our mail shows that people are curious and interested and want to know more about Canada. As long as the Voice of Canada is honest and sincere, reflecting without bias or distortion the vigorous young Canada of 1946, I believe we will be making a valuable contribution not only to the welfare of Canada but to the high cause of international understanding. (1)

Mr Aylen was not around to see that high cause brought low. A year later he left to take up the directorship of United Nations Radio. He did not realise that the International Service would be involved in a bitter propaganda war. Canada wanted to talk to the world without ulterior motivation, as Aylen would have said, with honesty and sincerity. The reality of post-war life in Europe, and in other parts of the world as well, lay in wait for his successors. There would be four over the next ten years: Arthur Phelps, Ira Dilworth, Jean Désy and Charles Delafield. Three were academics with broadcasting experience, the other a diplomat, seconded to the International Service.

During the first director's tenure, the emphasis was on broadcasting to Europe in five languages - English, French, German, Dutch and Czech - the last because when the Czechs were under German occupation, they had been a natural target for shortwave, not only from Canada, but Voice of America and the British Broadcasting Corporation as well. By the time of retirement of the second director, the Voice of Canada was also talking to the Scandinavian countries, and operated regular transmissions to the Caribbean, and to Latin America in Spanish and Portuguese. The motivation continued to be to share the Canadian way of life with foreign listeners who wanted to hear. The news was impartial and carefully balanced to present both sides of every event; the ultimate aim was to earn the sort of reputation that had proved so valuable to the BBC, but with a strictly transatlantic flavour. All of this was accomplished, somewhat precariously, from an old building on Crescent Street in downtown Montreal. The three studios and control rooms, a recording room, a master control room, a newsroom and offices were linked by land line to the transmitters at Sackville. If Canada's first shortwave broadcasters felt like pioneers, they had good reason.

When the third director, Ira Dilworth took over, militant communism was beginning to establish itself in many areas of a Europe left leaderless and barren by the war, or shared out to the Soviet Union under wartime agreements. By 1948, a definite pattern was emerging. To quote the <u>Politics of the Atlantic Alliance</u>, by Cottrell and <u>Dougherty (1964)</u> 'Poland, Bulgaria, Hungary and Romania had been completely incorporated into the Soviet empire. Turkey and Iran were under persistent Soviet pressure, and Greece had been the victim of a communist attack that was repelled only with American military assistance provided under the Truman doctrine.' (2)

It was also in 1948 that the Communist Party, clearly in a political minority in Czechoslovakia, waged an effective behind-the-scenes campaign and seized control of the government. Paul-Henri Spaak, later to lead NATO, suggested at the time that the communist takeover in Prague was the key turning point in international politics after the Second World War. These events, thousands of miles from Canadian shores, were to alter the basic structure and thinking of the International Service, with far-reaching consequences for that organisation.

The politics of open warfare with the Germans, the arena in which the Canadian shortwave service first made its appearance, was no preparation for the situation which now faced the Canadian government, the CBC, and the International Service. To understand what followed, it is essential to grasp the overall structure. The International Service had been created by an Order in Council, with the specific mandate - to establish close contact with Canadian troops overseas, to supply the United Kingdom, the rest of the Commonwealth and other countries with accurate and timely information about Canada and the national war effort; to provide an essential means of self defence and counterattack against the continuous flow of propaganda from Germany and Italy directed against Canada; to provide a second line of defence if the enemy were able to put the BBC stations out of operation; and to strengthen the resistance within the occupied countries of Europe. Clearly, much of this mandate was out of date by

1948, but no new one was forthcoming from the government.

While it remained an independent body accountable only to Parliament, which provided funds by annual grants, the International Service relied heavily on the radio facilities of the Canadian Broadcasting Corporation; in addition it was, to some extent, accountable to the Department of External Affairs. Differences in motivation amongst the many masters were to provide elements of future discord. The bedrock of the operation remained unchanged: to reflect Canada, its democratic way of life, its diverse population, its trade opportunities, the culture and interests of its people. Canada wanted to make friends, not grapple with half-understood enemies and their ideologies. But political developments in Europe and elsewhere clearly dictated some reaction from Canada. It was no longer enough to describe the beauty of the Canadian Rockies to foreign audiences, to dwell on cultural diversity, or to write about dog-sled races in the Arctic.

In an interview in 1949, Ira Dilworth said:

> The basic philosophy behind the Voice of Canada, as this service has come to be called, is that in this complicated age, nation must speak to nation, and people to people. The words of John Donne, uttered centuries ago, seem peculiarly true today: 'I am involved in mankind'. This speaking must be simple and straightforward, honest and frank, free from bias and negative propaganda. We feel that the service should be, as far as possible, friendly rather than impersonal, reflecting abroad the true character, the institutions, the habits and aspirations of the Canadian people. (3)

There was an underlying conviction at this time that good example is often the best persuader; that the reflection of a democracy, with all its benefits and many of its flaws, was the most positive propaganda of all. Sir Ian Jacobs, Director of the BBC Overseas Service, put it this way: 'It is evident that any country deciding to embark on a service of broadcasts to foreign audiences does so because it wants to influence those audiences in its favour. All such broadcasting is thus propaganda.' (4) Much later, in 1965, a committee commissioned by the Canadian government and headed by Robert Fowler which, incidentally, strongly supported an external service for Canada, noted that, 'Broadcasting to overseas audiences is still, and will always be, an indirect promotional aid for Canadian foreign policy.' (5)

Canada had emerged from the Second World War with an enviable reputation. Although late into the overseas broadcasting, it had coordinated its efforts with those of the BBC and the Voice of America to penetrate deeply and with telling effect into occupied countries. Canadian troops, returned home with war brides from many nations, and thousands of refugees came with them. More than ever before, Canada was a member of the cosmopolitan, international community. The identification signal of the International Service was a prestige trade mark.

Meanwhile the 'high cause of human understanding' envisioned by the first director general Peter Aylen in 1946 was failing on a global scale. But it left Canada as a leader among middle powers, and as a nation without territorial ambitions, or a history of imperialism, a nation whose voice could be trusted. In Ottawa, trade commissioners looked far beyond their own boundaries, and saw golden opportunities. Canadian diplomats, deeply involved with the United Nations, found themselves pondering the global view with renewed interest. Immigration was vigorous and beneficial, more and more Canadian tourists were venturing overseas, to return with broader outlooks. All these factors pointed the way to a climate in which foreign broadcasting represented a valuable asset. By 1949, more than ninety thousand letters had been received from listeners abroad. There was every reason to believe that the International Service would grow and prosper, with the full support, financial and logistical, of its own government.

By 1948, the International Service had found a new home, the Radio Canada Building on Dorchester Boulevard West in Montreal. These were also the headquarters of the French network of the CBC. In comparison to earlier days, the surroundings were not only sumptuous but technically excellent. Yet by the standards of the day, the structure of the International Service was modest. Primarily an information service, the operation centred on its newsroom, which provided material in English. From this central source, translators were fed a steady stream of news bulletins on a 24-hour basis, with reduced operations on weekends. The policy of the central newsroom was based on the British Broadcasting Corporation which was considered the best model of its kind. A former war correspondent,

Radio Canada International

Paul Barette, headed the service for many years; it was, to all intents and purposes, an autonomous service, run on journalistic lines, where propaganda was outlawed - not by any edict of the government or ruling of the CBC, but simply by the standards set and enforced in the newsroom. Because of the complexity of broadcasting news in eleven languages, a French newsroom was established, but it relied almost totally on the production of the English news service for its material.

News to Eastern Europe came under the supervision of one senior news editor, detached from the regular newsroom for this purpose. This secondary newsroom provided material of special interest to audiences in the iron curtain countries, but of little value to listeners outside that sphere. The news editor in charge of Eastern Europe acted as a filter and a balance; it was his job to see that Eastern European news translators were provided with a balanced and verified version of what was going on, and that minor events which could be magnified into propaganda were not blown out of proportion. The Eastern European news editor had one assistant, a typist, and the services of a policy coordinator, an expert in international affairs with whom he could discuss the output of his operation. Their roles were clear: the editor, who was chosen for his interest in international affairs and his knowledge of Canada's reaction to them, could not in the nature of things be a political expert familiar with all the involved and often contrived nuances of communist rule behind the Iron Curtain. His speciality was news; but it was always necessary to present that news in a way which would not be confusing to either the translator in the section or the listener at the other end.

The policy expert, who was on call at all times during the broadcast periods to Eastern Europe, was not a journalist but a specialist in Canadian foreign policy. His role was consultative. If he felt that the Canadian position on some important issue had been distorted, either by the wire service providing the original story or by the editor's handling of the material, he said so. His main concern was that material emanating from the International Service was factual and balanced, the two major qualities which had made the BBC's external service so admired and trusted. Spot checks were made by a linguist who took air-checks of the outgoing material in its foreign language and re-translated it into English to be certain that it conformed to the original copy. Less than a dozen news editors and assistants were involved, mostly ex-journalists. They had three months in which to measure up to the International Service standards; if they failed, they simply weren't confirmed. Security checks by the Royal Canadian Mounted Police were a matter of course. The precautions had one focal point, to ensure that material emanating from Canada's shortwave system was impartial. This laudable aim was to backfire on the Service later.

By the early 1950s, the Canadian government had decided that in the 'struggle for men's minds', as it became known on Parliament Hill, the Voice of Canada would be a key instrument of official Canadian policy. The International Service, which belonged neither to the government nor to the Canadian Broadcasting Corporation, entered a phase of close liaison with the Department of External Affairs. Managers cleared for access to the weekly ambassadorial dispatches and policy papers were privy to information which gave them a more comprehensive picture of international diplomatic activity than they could have gleaned through normal news channels. A more political atmosphere permeated the structure of the International Service. This was intensified in 1951, when the head of the Service, Ira Dilworth, left to become head of the CBC's British Columbia region. He was replaced by Jean Désy, a former Canadian ambassador to Brazil and Italy, who assumed the title of director general.

Top management in those days consisted of the director general, the assistant director general Charles Delafield, who would soon head the service, and the head of sections - an important post linked directly to the policy coordinator at external affairs. Arthur Pidgeon, who was head of sections during the fifties, describes the system as follows: 'We always made the head of each language section responsible for the final product. No one else could be. There are so many elements that go into the final product that no one else could control, even the intonation of the announcer's voice. After all, this is a spoken word service; it's not a written service, and the only man who really knows how this is sounding, what kind of impact it has, and what kind of message it is giving, is the man who can understand the language and be responsible for it.' (6)

The head of sections was in total control of what the language sections put on the air. He operated in that grey area between policy, which is the theory of what government would like to have said, and broadcasting - the reality of what is actually said. As broadcasters, the International Service had the final word. But government policy had to be considered. And policy coordination was one avenue to that goal. Again, Arthur Pidgeon:

> The reason for the policy coordination position stems from the fact that a multi-language service has an appetite for material. It must broadcast daily. And have points of view. It must try to choose material that is relevant to its target area, that relates to it. It must also, of course, reflect the Canadian point of view. But we did give the individual language section, a fair amount of freedom ... if we commented on the North Atlantic Alliance to Great Britain, we might agree with the head of the Czech section that such material was of little interest to his market in the form presented to the British audience, and a version tailored to the awareness of his listeners would be written. It was a matter of style. (7)

The government of the day was very careful to avoid any appearance of censoring either news or other programme material, and the relationship between the International Service and the Department of External Affairs was one of cordial wariness: the one asserting its right to put on the air whatever its professionals considered newsworthy, the other noting, with discretion, that certain Canadian points of view must be considered. Veterans of the service cannot remember any instance of the government ordering the International Service to do anything.

Internal policy was another matter, and the director general of the time had decided opinions about what his service should be doing. He had arrived on the scene when pressures far removed from the International Service were converging on it - the international climate of Cold War, the 'red' scare in the United States that was reflected in Canada, and Canadian reactions to its own major spy story 'the Gouzenko Affair'. One of the pressures was a small Montreal newspaper The Ensign, whose editor Robert Keyserlingk was a shortwave listener. Keyserlingk launched his initial campaign against the service while Ira Dilworth was still director; after his departure, The Ensign increased its attack. The charge was that broadcasters in the Eastern European sections were partial to communists. Mr Keyserlingk said:

> This is a question which deals more with sins of omission than sins of commission, but in the battle of ideas as bitter, as dangerous and as fatal as our present struggle against communism is, studied neutrality at taxpayers' expense can be as misleading to the people on the other side as sins of commission. When we consider that central Europeans behind the Iron Curtain today face severe punishment, including death, for listening to foreign broadcasts, and when they do, hear singular neutrality in the face of the depredations of communism, it not only angers them but actually leads to the impression that Canada is not particularly concerned. (8)

Attacks in similar vein aroused the interest of the leader of the opposition in the House of Commons, George Drew, who wanted to know how much supervision was exercised by the Department of External Affairs over the International Service. The Liberal Prime Minister, Lester Pearson, was not impressed by the charges against the broadcasting service, which he claimed was doing useful work for Canada and playing a valuable part in the psychological war against communism. If Mr Keyserlingk had evidence to offer, let him offer it.

Such attacks left their mark on morale, and staff changes followed. Specific objectives were set for the Service. First, to expound and develop the aims and policies of the western democratic powers and particularly of Canada; second, to combat communist ideology and Soviet imperialism; and third, to project as far as possible a picture of Canadian life with special reference to social, cultural, and political development. The objectives reflected the attitude of that era. At the same time Canadian policy on shortwave broadcasting, which prevails to this day, was also forged. In a sense, it was altruistic, in that it depended on a belief in the right of people everywhere to know what was going on in the world around them. This applied specially to those in what are euphemistically called 'closed societies' by diplomats. There is no tangible profit in this sort of broadcasting. It does not increase trade; indeed, it may increase hostility. But it was felt by many, in government and in the International Service, that there was a moral obligation to perform this task.

Carroll Chipman, a commentary writer at the time

of Désy's departure, put it this way: 'We were supposed to be honest, fair-minded, objective and to avoid contentiousness ... although this certainly did creep into some of the material used. It has to be remembered that we were creatures of our times; the cold war was at its height; NATO was a real necessity in the minds of all reasonable people, and Stalin and Stalinism were abhorrent. We sincerely believed that political democracy was a good thing, and that our listeners behind the iron curtain ought to be told about it.' (9)

In 1953, Jean Désy, who had been on loan to the CBC, resumed his career as a diplomat in Paris, and Charles Delafield took over. In an interview 19 years later, Mr Delafield, who was the longest-serving of the International Service directors, commented on the relationship between a shortwave service and government: 'You can put out government propaganda if you want to, but if no one listens to it or no one believes it, the whole thing is self defeating. And this was well understood by the Department of External Affairs in Ottawa. We simply said to them: "You want people to listen, you have to leave it to us; we are the broadcasting experts. And we can only promise you that we will do a responsible job".' Delafield conceded the government's right to state its preferences in the following areas:

> This applies mostly to target area selection, and is based on factors ... developing diplomatic relations, trade possibilities and a whole raft of other considerations ... that have nothing to do with programme content or censorship. Censorship doesn't even enter into it. External Affairs may say that we should be moving in a certain direction, because they themselves are looking in that direction ... such as closer ties with Latin America, for instance. They would like to see us concentrate more on that region, perhaps to the detriment of an already-established target area. We still have the right to decide what we are going to do. On the other hand, it would be stupid if we did something entirely different which they thought was of no particular significance, or rather low on the priority list. We've got the perfect right to do it, but on the other hand, we wouldn't be very responsible if we did. (10)

The 1950s and the intense hostility between east and west peaked with the Hungarian revolt in 1956.

Radio Canada International

The International Service reacted instantly. Within a matter of weeks, it had a Hungarian Section in operation. In Canada, according to an observer of that period, the feeling was that the back of Soviet rule in Eastern Europe had been broken, and that Marxism had not taken hold.

By 1960, it seemed almost as if both sides had grown weary of the cold war. In 1956, Poland had stopped jamming broadcasts from Canada, and there were tentative moves towards a less hostile climate. In that year, the Department of External Affairs and the Canadian Broadcasting Corporation studied the relative priorities for Western Europe, Eastern Europe, and Latin America, as well as the broadcasts in English and French. The first priority continued to be the Eastern European services. Their joint report put it this way:

> Radio is virtually the only means at Canada's disposal for reaching the public in Eastern Europe. Although jamming still persists, except in Poland, there have recently been certain changes in the political atmosphere behind the Iron Curtain which in spite of some difficulties hold out the possibility of a cessation of this activity. Moreover, in these countries there is a curiosity about the west, which is increasingly important to satisfy. Tourism and exchange visits are becoming familiar occurrences and are a Canadian policy objective since such exchanges can rebound to the benefit of Canada and the west. Trade relations, as evidenced by the recent Canadian-Soviet trade pact, are also being cultivated. In order that Canadian views may have their maximum possible influence on the citizens of the Soviet Union and its satellites, broadcasts to the area should continue. (11)

One problem that bedevilled the Eastern European service was broadcast times. Many programmes were hitting the target areas when most listeners were at work. The Joint Report proposed a change. It also directed that the projection of the Canadian scene should receive greater prominence in transmitted programmes. But money for shortwave broadcasting was tight, and to maintain the emphasis on Eastern Europe, it was necessary to reduce transmissions to Western Europe and Latin America. Broadcasts in Danish, Dutch, Italian, Norwegian, Swedish and Finnish were discontinued. The reason was that information about Canada and Canadian attitudes could be freely circulated in Western Europe, making direct broadcasting less essential than to Eastern Europe. There was no question of any change in foreign policy. It was simply a matter of money.

Just how disastrous that matter of money was to become, surfaced three years later. The cold war seemed over, Canada was moving into exchange programmes with communist countries, and the mild spring of détente seemed at hand. Late that year, word was circulated in Ottawa that the government was considering drastic curtailment, if not outright abolition, of the International Service. The amount involved was Cdn $1,800,000, the entire International Service budget. Top management, under Charles Delafield, mounted a campaign that with the help of the national press, swept the country. No one had considered that, once lost, international radio frequencies could not be regained. No one, if the country's editorial writers were to be believed, could seriously consider such a move. The International Service, like most shortwave services, was little known in its own land, and for a time, as one senior officer put it, 'we were fighting for our lives'.

Early in 1964, the secretary of state for external affairs, Paul Martin, issued a reprieve. The whole matter would be studied, with an eye to integrating the International Service into the Canadian Broadcasting Corporation's main structure. The move gave breathing space, but little satisfaction to the nation's newspapers. The Ottawa Journal, in an editorial wrote:

> In times of international uncertainty, and especially in times of crisis, we hope that people in distant lands seeking the truth can tune into Canada as confidently as occupied Europe tuned into the British service during the war. If Canada has built a reputation for telling the truth objectively and impartially in North American accents, then the International Service serves democracy well, and is worth being preserved and presented with the facilities to do its job properly. (12)

Eighteen months later, the Canadian Press, the national news-gathering agency, reported that, 'Buoyed by an upsurge in listener response, particularly from behind the Iron Curtain, Canada's voice in international broadcasting has steadily raised its operating budget. It now is hopefully embarking on a major modernization programme in the near future.' (13) There was time, at least, for a sigh of relief. But only a short time. In 1965, the government appointed a committee on broadcasting and named Robert Fowler to head it. A year later, the Fowler Commission commented as follows about the International Service:

> It is an indirect aid to Canadian foreign policy. It is also a direct means to other important ends: the projection abroad of a Canadian image that reflects the nature of the country and its people, their policies, beliefs and tastes; the development for potential immigrants and tourists of an interest in Canada as a good place to live or visit; the promotion of international trade for Canada, which is the fifth largest exporting country in the world; and the maintenance of a personal link between Canadians and their relatives and countrymen overseas. (14)

A sudden end to jamming furthered the cause of the International Service, since one of the objections to its continued operation was that it could not be heard in many parts of the world to which it transmitted. No complete explanation of this cessation of interference has been advanced. Detractors of the International Service said that the Soviet Union had suspended jamming because Canada's programmes were so innocuous that they posed no threat to totalitarian regimes, or to anyone else. Carroll Chipman, head of the Ukrainian and Russian sections, had a more plausible explanation:

> It was a common belief that we were spared jamming because we were becoming bland, and were moving away from detailed comment on Soviet domestic affairs, and more toward projecting a specific view of Canada. My own belief is that the special relationships we developed with Radio Moscow, Poland and Hungary in the field of radio and television exchanges, were extremely important in the Soviet decision to sustain freedom from jamming. We were active participants in détente ... we were placing their programme elements on our networks ... sports, culture, travel items ... and displaying good will. The International Service was unique among western broadcasters in this

matter. (15)

Technical considerations (atmospherics and distances) helped to ensure Canadian signals reached their goals. George Hills, training officer for the BBC External Service, who spent some time at the International Service, noted the high cost of jamming, which could require the use of hundreds of interference transmitters to blanket one area. It was also not always effective, as the allies discovered during the Second World War, when they alternated transmissions on various frequencies to beat German jamming.

Whatever the reason, the 1960s promised to be golden years for the International Service, especially with Expo '67 coming up in Montreal. Canada was in a festive mood. One hundred years had passed since Confederation, and the country commemorated the centennial from coast to coast. The emphasis was on Montreal and the exposition Man and His World. Robert Shaw, deputy director of Expo, explained that a world's fair was a commercial market place, while an international exhibition, such as Expo '67, dealt with ideas and values. The theme Man and His World sought to stress international goodwill; the 70 nations which provided 62 national pavilions gave the event what Mr Shaw described as an 'ambassadorial' rather than a 'commercial huckster' role.

As a part of this one thousand acre exhibition, the CBC built an International Broadcasting Centre, at a cost of Cdn $10 million, to house facilities for visiting broadcasters. The International Service broadcast regularly from this centre. The 1967-68 annual report of the CBC described the year as one of the most exciting periods in the history of the Service. A year previously, International Service had received, from all listening areas, a total of 68,361 letters, cards and reception reports. In 1967, the total jumped to 74,379. Nearly 47,000 programme hours of recorded Canadian music were shipped to radio organisations all over the world, a four-fold increase over the previous year. It was exciting stuff indeed. But suddenly excitement turned to shock. On Thursday, 30th November, 1967, the government announced that for reasons of economy it intended to abolish the International Service.

That gave the International Service management exactly four days in which to lobby support in Ottawa and across the country. Within hours, a position paper had been prepared. It made several points which the Treasury Board, author of the abolition order, had apparently overlooked. The importance of international shortwave broadcasting is recognised by the government of every modern nation, the paper stated. It is the most effective way of transcending geographical, political and ideological boundaries. In the 20 years since 1945 the number of shortwave broadcasters in Canada had risen from 12 to 150. The CBC-IS provided, at minimal cost, a daily transmitter service in eleven languages to four continents, supplemented by related sound and television transcriptions to a potential audience of more than one billion people. This service cost the individual Canadian taxpayer 16 cents a year. The paper made one other point, that was a telling one to a government which had always stressed its belief that closed societies should be provided with the truth. Russian language mail to the International Service, it noted, consistently exceeded that received by the Russian language section of the British Broadcasting Corporation. Another point was that Canadian newspapers and magazines are not circulated internationally. Those who wanted to know anything about Canada tuned in to the International Service of the CBC. The International Service technical facilities were used by both the CBC Northern Service and the Armed Forces Service.

Two days after the abolition announcement, it was reported from Ottawa that the cabinet was split. The Department of Trade and Commerce, for instance, would lose its voice abroad and had strong objections. Individual members of parliament also took up the fight on behalf of the shortwave service, and so did the press. Dennis Braithwaite, columnist on the influential Toronto Globe & Mail, was scathing in his attack on the government. He wrote:

> I cannot believe that the government's proposal to scrap the CBC's International Service is based, as stated, on considerations of economy. The sum of money involved is less than Cdn $4 million, a mere trifle. Think of what would be lost. The 207 men and women who work for the International Service are the prime fashioners of Canada's image abroad. There has never been any suggestion that they are not doing this job well.
>
> Are they perhaps doing it too well? Six of the foreign language broadcasts emanating from the service's Montreal headquarters are directed to listeners behind the Iron Curtain.

Have the communist countries objected to these transmissions? If they have, then the Canadian authorities should say so, instead of trying to convince the public that the modest budget of the International Service constitutes an unbearable drain on the federal treasury. Are we really going to let a penny-pinching bureaucrat decide this vital matter of external relations, (assuming we are willing to swallow as I am not) that austerity is the prime factor? (16)

The director of the Service, Charles Delafield, was less harsh. He attributed the Treasury Board's decision to a lack of knowledge and understanding about the service itself and the importance of its operations. Following a press campaign overwhelmingly in favour of an operation which few Canadians knew about or listened to, the government reversed its position. The crisis had one happy result: integration into the corporate structure of the CBC, which became effective on 7th March, 1968. This did not mean that the Service severed its links with the Department of External Affairs. It was clear that the department was to play an important role in International Service's operations, defining priorities and providing information which helps the shortwave organisation to tailor its operations to Canadian policy needs.

Beginning in 1968, the International Service rented BBC transmitters to rebroadcast Eastern European services beamed to the target area. The result was an excellent signal which penetrated the Iron Curtain with ease. By 1970, broadcasts in Czech had reached seven hours a week, Slovak one hour 45 minutes, Polish five hours 15 minutes, transmissions to Russia five hours 15 minutes, Ukrainian three hours 30 minutes, and Hungarian one hour 45 minutes. The total weekly transmission time to Iron Curtain countries was 24-and-a-half hours, a figure which excluded transmissions in English and French to Europe which could be heard by listeners in communist countries. Including German-language broadcasts, the total to Western Europe on a weekly basis was 34 hours 30 minutes.

The programmes were similar in format, consisting of news bulletins, commentaries, news reports, features, actualities, interviews, music and replies to audience mail. They included contributions by Canadians in many walks of life who reported on or interpreted the Canadian scene, or who provided an informed Canadian reaction to international events. The transcription service provided a vast array of material, which in turn helped to improve relations between Canada and target area countries, including the Eastern Bloc. In 1969, for instance, the International Service distributed more than 49,000 programme hours of music to 130 countries around the world.

By 1970, it was possible for International Service management to breathe a collective sigh of relief. Stability had been achieved. The problems that remained were mostly of a technical nature. The original transmitter equipment was wearing out, and the cost of replacement was high. But integration of the International Service into the CBC helped there too, and expanded and improved facilities were approved.

In the 1970s, the service changed its name to Radio Canada International and Alan Brown took over from Charles Delafield as director, after 19 years. Brown had a varied background in communications. His most recent posting had been as second-in-command of Information Canada; and upon joining Radio Canada International, he served as head of the English section for some months, to familiarise himself with the style and problems of shortwave broadcasting. On his arrival, there were two major sections, English and French, running one-hour transmissions to various target areas. Other sections, including those broadcasting to Eastern Europe, drew the bulk of their material from these two sources, translated the material, and included it in their own programmes. Brown's changes retained the central news desk but, instead of a separate department handling newscasts for communist countries, one specialised editor attached to the main desk provided news items which would be of special interest to communist listeners. The entire output of both English and French newsrooms was also available for all sections.

Brown served on a task force, on whose report Bernard Hibbitts, in his analysis of the Canadian International Broadcasting Service as an Instrument of Foreign Policy (1949-79) commented:

> This was undoubtedly the most significant document produced in the 1970s dealing (at least in part) with the relationship of the Canadian international broadcasting policy to Canadian foreign policy. Indeed, the report, to a significant extent, grew out of confusion that certainly existed in Radio Canada International

and, one may assume, in External Affairs, over the exact meaning of the phrase 'in consultation with' which according to the 1968 Order in Council which integrated International Service with the CBC proper, was to continue to guide RCI in its operational relationship with the government department.

While the report reaffirmed the CBC's journalistic rights in terms of broadcast programmes and editorial policy, it did however consider that consultation on matters 'outside the area of broadcast competence' was an acceptable activity for the international service of the corporation. This applied especially to the choice of target areas. The CBC itself acknowledged 'that the choosing of target areas and broadcast languages is probably the most crucial and far-reaching decision that the external broadcaster has to face, and welcomed the expertise of the department. (17)

In 1973, a strict priority listing of External Affairs concerns would have read as follows: the United States, European Community countries, Japan, the Soviet Union, Mexico, China, Australia, Venezuela, North Africa, South Africa, Nigeria, Eastern Europe and India. Broadcasting needed a different priority order: shortwave had to consider the effectiveness of this type of broadcasting in a given area; other means of distribution had to take into account the acceptance by a foreign broadcaster of Canadian programming for use on his own station. Radio Canada International (RCI) did not have the money, the equipment or the staff to fulfil new priorities, and little hope of convincing the government of the day to provide them. Throughout the history of the service, there had always been difficulty in persuading governments that the service was actually heard in its target regions - even the BBC, with its vast resources, concedes that this is a problem. Audience surveys are expensive; in countries in the Eastern bloc, surveys would be all but impossible.

The Task Force report concluded, that the two priorities that governed broadcasting should be merged, to ensure that RCI provide a service that reflected as much as possible the priorities expressed by External Affairs, while recognising the broadcast realities dictated by financial constraints. Many department officials were unclear about their own priorities; and, within RCI, there was a strong, and natural, resistance to setting up language sections at great expense and with much difficulty, and then disposing of them just when an audience had been attracted.

Some members of parliament sensed the possibility of censorship over an organisation which had always operated on the principles of journalistic independence. In 1976, the Cossitt affair brought this to a head. Tom Cossitt, a progressive Conservative member, raised the question in the House of Commons, alleging that officials of the Department of External Affairs had been informally approached by the Soviet ambassador to Canada on RCI Russian-language transmissions. Cossitt claimed that this complaint had been passed to RCI, and that RCI had tightened its internal organisation to eliminate the possibility of future offence. Both the CBC and the Department of External Affairs denied this. It was quite true that an internal review had been going on within the shortwave service, but it had been started in 1975, before the incident alleged by Cossitt. Al Johnson, president of the CBC, appeared on national television and declared 'There is no censorship policy and never has been.' The statement left some doubt. It was pointed out that in September of 1975, one month after the signing of the Helsinki Accord with its Soviet-inspired provisions regarding non-interference in the internal affairs of other nations, a Central Talks department had been set up in RCI to coordinate commentary and similar material.

The reasoning behind the establishment of a central commentary department was, however, less sinister than alleged by RCI's critics. Under the previous system, section heads ordered their own scripts, and the result was confusion and duplication. Alan Brown, who sponsored a 'one-voice' policy on the grounds that there must be coordination of broadcast material, split responsibility for Central Talks between an English-speaking and a French-speaking head. Both experienced journalists with a background in current affairs, they determined the major stories of the day, assigned the writing of commentaries, backgrounders and press reviews, made events intelligible to a foreign audience, and generally presented the Canadian point of view. Of more concern to the director than controlling broadcasts to Eastern Europe was the need to present a single Voice of Canada in both official languages to ensure, during the difficult years of the emerging independence movement in Quebec, that there was a careful balance in programming.

Brown made many changes during his tenure in office. He organised a system of target area heads, whose task was to be responsible for all material, except news, beamed to their part of the world. This did away with the English section, French section concept as major fashioners of what was used. Programme times were shortened to half-hour transmissions, which could be slotted into a wider range of times and frequencies.

As Bernard Hibbitts pointed out in another section of his study on Radio Canada International, the question of governmental interference in shortwave broadcasting arises only during periods of high international tension. Otherwise, the External Affairs Department appears content to allow the service to use its own judgement. This does not mean that liaison has lapsed, only that Radio Canada International remains, despite problems, what it started out to be, a small-to-medium sized shortwave broadcaster whose chief mandate is to inform interested listeners abroad about Canada and what Canadians think and do.

The Present
The board of directors of the Canadian Broadcasting Corporation reflected in its minutes of May, 1980 the present day mandate of Radio Canada International, including the relationships and responsibilities of the CBC and the Department of External Affairs, 'which has taken account of RCI's technical and budgetary resources and Canadian foreign policy objectives...' (letter of 1st December, 1980 from Under Secretary of State for External Affairs to President, CBC).

> Consistent with the instruction contained in the 1968 Order in Council, Radio Canada International is directed by the CBC to provide a programme service designed to attract an international audience with the purpose of further developing international awareness of Canada and the Canadian identity by distributing, through shortwave and other means, programmes which reflect the realities and quality of Canadian life and culture, ... Canada's national interests and policies and the spectrum of Canadian viewpoints on national and international affairs.
>
> RCI also broadcasts programmes to the

growing number of Canadians abroad, in recognition of their need for more Canadian news and information, in those areas already served under the primary objective of broadcasting to foreign audiences. The policies of External Affairs form the basis for decisions on RCI target and language priorities, but programming and editorial policies are wholly the responsibility of the CBC.

When the Canadian Department of External Affairs press office holds a briefing, Radio Canada International journalists are shown no special consideration, but are treated as regular members of Canada's news gathering media.

Underlying all RCI programming is the awareness that Canada is not as well known as it should be; that its image abroad has not kept pace with realities; and that Canada is not represented on foreign newsstands by a Canadian daily or weekly press, nor by any but the most superficial coverage in foreign media. As one of the radio's former directors said, 'RCI has a world monopoly on Canadian news and information. If we want to make ourselves known to the world, shortwave radio is the only daily mass medium at our disposal.' This applies to the USSR and Eastern Europe more than any other part of the world. Our main duty is to fill this void, this lack of even remotely comprehensive information in Eastern Europe and the Soviet Union of our country, its view of the world and its everyday life.

How do we go about reaching our objective? RCI programme policy is based on a journalistic approach, attempting by a flow of information and balanced comment to reflect an attitude that allows freedom of opinion. RCI is not an image-maker, but an effective and clear reflector of Canada as it is. The Eastern European programmes start with a mixture of international and Canadian news bulletins. Canadian content is more evident in the rest of the programme, where discussions centre on Canadian events or on international and Eastern European stories with a Canadian angle. For example, an event such as the death of Soviet president Yuri Andropov would be reported in the news bulletin, based on reports from the major international news agencies. It would probably be followed by a report from the Canadian broadcasting Corporation Moscow correspondent, describing the mood in the Soviet capital and the reaction of Western diplomats, followed by an interview with a former Soviet journalist, now living and working in Canada. We would discuss with him the repercussions of the event, making use of his inside knowledge of the Soviet system, and examine possible chances of a new course in Soviet-Canadian relations. In addition, we would ask our Ottawa team of reporters to get some reaction to the death from government officials. We might commission a well-known Canadian journalist to write a commentary. Finally a press review or even a series of press reviews would be broadcast. All of this could not be used in one broadcast lasting 30 minutes, but we are talking about the variety of Canadian reactions to an event that could fill several broadcasts.

Broadcast Languages and Times. RCI's Eastern European department has five sections, which broadcast in eight languages. The five sections are: Russian, Ukrainian, Polish, Hungarian and Czechoslovak. The Czechoslovak section broadcasts in two languages - Czech and Slovak. There are also daily, 15-minute newscasts in English and French to the USSR. It is hard to estimate in how many countries RCI is heard. We have had letters from every Eastern European country (with the exception of Albania) from the Far East (Japan, China, India), Middle East (Israel, Egypt), Western Europe and North America.

We have four Russian broadcasts a day - three of 30 minutes and one of 15 minutes, a weekly total of $12\frac{1}{4}$ hours. Ukrainian broadcasts of 30 and 15 minutes total $5\frac{1}{4}$ hours weekly. Polish broadcasts of 45 minutes daily total $5\frac{1}{4}$ hours weekly. The Hungarian and Czechoslovak sections broadcast one half-hour each for a weekly total of $3\frac{1}{2}$ hours in each case. As mentioned earlier, the Czechoslovak section combines both official languages of Czechoslovakia in each broadcast. We alternate Czech and Slovak translations of news items, and use, for example, a press review in Czech and a report on some cultural event in Slovak, in a ratio of two to one, based on the actual ratio of population in that country. Adding in English and French newscasts, another $1\frac{3}{4}$ hours weekly, RCI broadcasts a total of $31\frac{1}{2}$ hours of programming directly to Eastern Europe.

Our Russian language broadcasts are heard in Moscow early in the morning - at 6.15 a.m. standard time, at 5.30 p.m, then at 7.45 and 8 p.m. Moscow standard time. Further east, they are heard later, of course. The Ukrainian language broadcasts are heard twice daily: at 6 p.m. and 7.30 p.m. Kiev standard time. The Polish language broadcast goes out from

4.45 to 5.30 p.m. Warsaw time; the Hungarian language at 7 p.m. Budapest time; the Czech and Slovak at 7.30 p.m. Prague and Bratislava time.

History of the Eastern European Department. RCI policy in the early days was closely connected with Canadian foreign policy goals during the Second World War: the United Kingdom, France, Germany and Czechoslovakia were the first priorities as target areas, hence the languages of the first broadcasts were English, French, German and Czech. The end of the war in Europe meant changes in RCI objectives, and a broadening of both target areas and languages. Western Europe remained the major interest, and broadcasts in Swedish, Norwegian, Danish, Dutch, and Italian were added. Priority was also given to Latin America (Spanish and Portuguese), the Caribbean and Australasia, bringing the number of broadcast languages to twelve.

The cold war period between 1949-63 was for RCI a time of both expansion and redirection. New language sections, mainly Eastern European were inaugurated: Russian in 1951, Ukrainian in 1952, Polish in 1953 and Hungarian in 1956. Eastern Europe became the International Service's major target. This priority has been maintained, but the rationale has changed radically from the days of the cold war. Nowadays, it is 'free flow' concerns that motivate shortwave broadcasting decisions.

Staffing. Drastic CBC budget cuts in 1978 made it essential for RCI to re-examine its activities. It was decided that programming should remain as unaffected as possible, but that reorganisation would be needed to bring serious reductions in administrative and support staff. After productivity studies, budget analysis and staff transfers, a lean RCI emerged. Minimum staff for any daily half-hour foreign-language broadcast was set at about four, plus a generous freelance budget. The Ukrainian and Polish sections, both with 45 minutes of daily programmes, have five announcer-producers each. The Russian section with one hour and 45 minutes daily has nine employees. The Czechoslovak section, with 30 minutes a day, has five employees, which is the basic four plus one because of the second language.

RCI continues to concentrate its limited resources on programming, with little support staff. The production staff consists of announcer-producers, who do everything required to put a programme on the air, including translating and adapting news and scripts, originating scripts, researching and retrieving information, interviewing, reporting, editing, announcing, producing. One assistant is assigned to the Eastern European department, consisting of over 30 production people, who orders office supplies, photocopies, requisitions studios, etc. The Eastern European department is headed by a manager, who is responsible for implementing RCI policy and for general planning. There are three supervisors of section personnel - one for the Hungarian and Polish sections, one for the Ukrainian and Czechoslovak, and one for the Russian.

In the past, each language section had a supervisor fluent in the language of the broadcast, but budget limitations forced choices on us. Rather than make further cuts at the production level, or close down entire sections, we opted for the thinning out of supervisory ranks. It is difficult to find qualified people fluent in both Polish and Hungarian, or Ukrainian as well as Czech and Slovak. However, the requirement holds, that the supervisors should have sufficient language skill to judge the content of their programmes, if not the quality of language. The specialised production staff monitors this too, which can bring about lively discussion. When programme evaluations are carried out with outside language specialists, we find that the self-monitoring has been successful.

Eastern European Programming. A typical 30-minute broadcast in Russian, Ukrainian, Czech/Slovak or Hungarian contains a news bulletin, a backgrounder, a press review on an important topic of international significance, and the magazine item, or spectrum of topical events 'reflecting the realities and quality of Canadian life and culture'. The RCI Polish broadcast, which is an uninterrupted 45 minutes, comprises more extended backgrounders, extra analysis of political or economic situations or events, a slightly longer magazine section, and ends with news headlines. Broadcasts fall into three distinct parts, served by different sources, and given different treatment and different presentation.

News bulletins originate in RCI's French and English newsrooms. Because RCI's Eastern European sections tend to have more staff with English as second language, they follow the English news, including line-up. (The Latin American target area uses the French line-up). The sections supplement their English news bulletins with news items taken from the French bulletin, especially items of specific target area interest. The normal length of the newscasts is 10 minutes, but in language sections this varies, according to translation and programme demands.

The second part of the broadcast consists of news reports, backgrounders and commentaries on major political and economic stories, for which a variety of sources is used. Every morning an editorial meeting is held with all target area managers and newsroom supervisors, and a conference call is placed to the Ottawa office, which is the nerve centre of the news gathering function. They are our link with parliament, government departments, foreign missions and visitors, and with the Canadian journalist community. The Ottawa team supplies first-hand reports on anything of importance happening in parliament and in Ottawa in general and, because they are in a position to inform us in Montreal about foreseeable events, this helps us plan suitable coverage.

Plans for the future include placing one Russian and Ukrainian speaking reporter in the Ottawa office, so as to report directly in both these languages. In addition to the Ottawa bureau, RCI maintains small offices in Toronto and Vancouver which gather regional information, suggest topics and deal with freelancers. Some reports from national and foreign correspondents are taken from CBC's national networks, again in both French and English. Commentaries, which are never written by staff reporters, are commissioned from specialists in a given field, such as recognised journalists and university professors. The Canadian newspapers provide a rich choice of editorials, stories by foreign correspondents and backgrounders by staff writers. We get newspapers from all parts of the country - from as far west as British Columbia, and as far east as Newfoundland.

The content of this second part of the broadcast, which is usually determined at the section level, varies from one section to the next. A major policy speech by the prime minister, or the opening of a new session of the UN General Assembly will be chosen by most sections as the main topic of the day, based on target area considerations. The majority of the material used in this segment of the programme is either translated or adapted by section translators. Often an English and a French report from Ottawa are combined in order to provide fuller coverage. When outside commentators speak one of the Eastern European languages they provide two versions of their commentary: English or French for translation plus the voiced version in the Eastern European language. This is very convenient and we plan to extend the service. Press reviews are done by the Ottawa journalists or in the newsrooms in Montreal, and then translated by the language sections. In the Polish and the Russian sections, where the demand for news-related material is the highest, some press reviews are done directly in each language.

The selection of topical events in the third part of broadcasts is left to the production team of each section. Teams either divide the days of the week among them, and each person prepares his or her own show in advance, or the content of the day's broadcast is determined at a meeting of the section's personnel and each person sits down to write or produce his component of the broadcast. Supervisors are not necessarily present, because the announcer-producers are well aware of the RCI mandate and close supervision is seldom needed.

This part of the programme covers social and cultural life, economy, science news, technology, agriculture, history and sports. Because most of the topics describe Canada to foreigners, it is called the 'Canadiana' portion, and differs from one language section to another. The Ukrainian community, for example, is particularly active, so the Ukrainian section often carries special coverage of Ukrainian events in Canada. Canadians of Ukrainian origin try to maintain their language and culture through the third and fourth generation of immigrants. They have dozens of cultural societies, youth organisations, folk ensembles, social clubs, church groups, historical and professional associations and political organisations.

The Polish community in Canada is also well organised - as demonstrated in the past few years, when the Polish organisations in Canada sent thousands of food parcels to church parishes in Poland. They also have held demonstrations, hunger strikes and mass prayers, and written petitions to arouse world public opinion to help overcome the oppressions in Poland. RCI reflects this in its Polish transmissions. It also broadcasts interviews with political scientists, journalists and spokesmen of different organisations and community groups, and reviews of items in the Polish-Canadian press, since there are a good number of Polish-language newspapers published in Canada.

Canadians of Russian origin are not so fortunate: there is practically no Russian-Canadian press and few political organisations or cultural bodies. Nonetheless, we have made several features about the Doukhobors in British Columbia, the Old Believers communities in the west of Canada, and the life of different generations of emigrants from pre- and post-revolutionary Russia. In an on-going series of interviews with Russian-Canadians every week, people from all walks of life tell their story, describe how they got to Canada, their everyday life, their interests, hobbies, convictions and activities. Some belong to the newest wave of Jewish emigrants, who discuss their difficulties and successes in settling in Canada, their efforts to get their families to join them and so on. At the other extreme there are the elderly former officers of the Russian Imperial Guards, aristocrats and other witnesses of the First World War and the Russian revolution, who recollect people and battles little known in present-day Soviet Russia. And in between there are hundreds of people with interesting life stories. We have few refusals to grant interviews, though we offer no remuneration.

In the Czechoslovak and Hungarian sections, interviews are also widely used, but with less ethnic emphasis, as both the Hungarians and the Czechs and Slovaks, while maintaining their language and cultural traditions, are well assimilated into the mainstream of Canadian society. They seem to have penetrated all professions and excelled in them, so that our announcer-producers have no trouble in getting an interview with a Hungarian or Czech-speaking scientist, sportsman, teacher, physician, or indeed, a hairdresser.

Each Eastern European section has a freelance budget, which provides variety, access to distant events and in many cases expert treatment of specialised subjects. Freelance contributors provide the essential regional coverage of this vast country. Under the guidance of the supervisor, the section personnel brief the freelancers and edit their reports.

To summarise the format: ten minutes of news bulletins from the RCI newsrooms, translated in the sections; about ten minutes of news background, commentaries and press reviews, which are also translated but come from the newsroom, RCI Ottawa reporters, CBC network correspondents (national and foreign), and outside commentators and newspapers; the final ten minutes may contain elements from any of the above, plus features from in-house writers and freelancers, on the spot reports and interviews.

Technical Facilities. RCI's shortwave transmitter plant is located in Sackville, New Brunswick, on the Atlantic coast. The site was chosen to avoid proximity to the magnetic field of the north auroral zone.

Radio Canada International has five 250 kilowatt shortwave transmitters, which can operate on any one of the international shortwave bands between 3.95 and 26.5. The additional three 50 kilowatt transmitters were recently due to be replaced by 100 Kw's. The transmitters receive radio signals from any of four distinct programme lines originating in Montreal. These carry RCI programme material for rebroadcast over a distance of some 600 miles to Sackville, via microwave. Eastern European broadcasts are transmitted to Europe, where they are boosted by two 100 kilowatt transmitters belonging to the BBC and located at Daventry, England, as well as two 250 kilowatt transmitters belonging to Deutsche Welle and located at Sines, Portugal. Because the existing British transmitters were built about 40 years ago and require constant maintenance, the BBC will soon install and maintain two new 300 kilowatt transmitters at the same site at Daventry. Work should be completed some time in 1986. These various improvements will guarantee a stronger, clearer signal in Eastern Europe and the Soviet Union for some years.

Listenership. How do we know whether enough people are listening to us? We have to rely on letters from listeners, contacts with visitors and emigrants from target countries, and on experiences of Canadians visiting them.

None of these sources is completely reliable: few people who listen, write, especially in Eastern Europe; and those who do write don't necessarily represent the average listener. Visitors and officials from closed societies do not always feel free to talk openly about foreign broadcasts, unless it is to criticise them. Emigrants, on the other hand, tend to feel negative about the country they left and cannot be regarded as objective. As for

Canadian travellers, their evidence depends on whom they meet. Though each of these sources individually can be considered doubtful, together they provide some means of measuring our effectiveness. In the past several years, responses from all these sources have decreased in number, and official contacts between Canada and Eastern European countries have fluctuated as a result of Afghanistan, Poland and the Korean airliner tragedy.

Private visits from the area have become rarer than ever, and emigration has dwindled almost to a halt. Even our last resort - letters from the listeners - are far from abundant. Every change in the political and economic situation in our target area tends to affect adversely the flow of audience mail. In 1967, the year before the invasion of Czechoslovakia, when many believed a certain relaxation was taking place in Eastern Europe, we received over twenty thousand letters. In 1983, this figure fell to just under three thousand eight hundred, $18\frac{1}{2}$ per cent of the 1967 total.

One reason for the decline is political: the fear to acknowledge mail contact with the west. Another is the high cost of mailing. We acknowledge and answer all letters, either directly or over the air in our letterbox programmes. All shortwave broadcasters know how hard it is to estimate the number of listeners. However, an informal survey conducted by Deutsche Welle some years ago, based on interviews with travellers from the Soviet Union, gave some information.

The late Mark Gayn, who was one of the most distinguished journalists and foreign affairs writers in Canada, not long before his death visited the Soviet Union. To his surprise, his contacts all knew him, because they had heard his commentaries on RCI. While there, he listened to the broadcast from Canada on a small portable radio. He admitted later that he had expected Soviets to listen to VOA, BBC, and Radio Liberty, but not Radio Canada International.

Our main business is to have our audiences discover Canada, to know the context in which we live and express ourselves, not only about our own country, but about theirs, and their neighbours. When it comes to reflecting Canada, we try to be as frank and open as possible, covering Canadian points of view and preoccupations. It may well be this quality, a particularly Canadian quality - the willingness to admit imperfections - that attracts, and disarms, our listeners in the East.

Notes

1. Peter Aylen, General Supervisor, CBC-IS, in The Voice of Canada, published in house organ, November 1946.
2. Politics of the Atlantic Alliance, Cottrell & Dougherty (1964).
3. Interview with Ira Dilworth, general Supervisor, CBC-IS, 1949.
4. Quoted from Sir Ian Jacobs, 'The Place of Broadcasting in International Relations', International Journal, 1949-50.
5. Royal Commission on Broadcasting, chaired by Robert Fowler, 1965.
6. Interview with Arthur Pidgeon, Head, Ottawa Bureau, Radio Canada International, 1978.
7. Pidgeon, RCI, 1978.
8. Radio address in Montreal by Robert Keyserlingk, Editor, The Ensign, January, 1951.
9. Interview with Carroll Chipman, Target Area Head, Latin America, Montreal, 1984.
10. Interview with Charles Delafield, retired Director, CBC-RCI, Montreal, 1971.
11. Joint Report, from the Department of External Affairs, Ottawa, and the Canadian Broadcasting Corporation, 1956.
12. Editorial from the Ottawa Journal, 1964.
13. Report released by the Canadian Press, 1965.
14. Fowler (1965), op.cit.
15. Chipman (1984) op.cit.
16. Dennis Braithwaite, columnist, Toronto Globe & Mail, December, 1967.
17. Hibbitts' analysis, quoted from the Canadian Broadcasting Corporation's International Service as an Instrument for Foreign Policy, (1949-79).

Addendum:

1. Radio Canada International's Eastern European Service (we have done away with target areas as too military) includes now a German section (previously in Western European Service);
2. On 30 March 1986, our Russian, Ukrainian and Polish broadcasts have been extended by 15 minutes each and we have now four half hour programs in Russian, two half hours in Ukrainian and Polish. This was done within the existing means, i.e. without any increase in staff.
3. On March 30, we started also following the clock in Eastern Europe: our local broadcast times are now constant throughout the year.

Chapter Three

INTERNATIONAL BROADCASTING AND US POLITICAL REALITIES

Frank Shakespeare* United States Ambassador to Portugal and former chairman of the Board for International Broadcasting, Washington, DC and Vice-chairman, RKO General

I am going to speak with several biases. My experience in Radios has been really as a publisher, not an editor, so my perspective of the international radios has been a broad overview. When I speak as a publisher it is because that is what I know. I have certain experiences I want to share with you and I have convictions, but I well recognise that what makes radios go, both in the private sector as well as in the public sector, are editors and writers and thinkers. So if I focus on the structural aspects to a larger degree, and from a policy point of view, it is not because I am unaware of reality. Reality is that editors and writers and broadcasters make programming.

My second bias is that I speak entirely from United States experience. While I have a general awareness of the German radios, Kol Israel, Radio Vatican, BBC, and Radio Canada International, as an observer through the years of international radio, I have no real functional knowledge.

Thirdly, I am going to speak almost exclusively of international broadcasting as it relates to the Soviet Union and Eastern Europe.

When someone with a lifetime in the private sector of American radio comes into government radio, as I did in 1969 for four years as director of the United States Information Agency (which operates the Voice of America), a natural and immediate focus on the Voice of America as being the single most important function by far of the USIA is understandable. And then, after returning to the

*Mr Shakespeare addressed the conference extemporaneously as is his custom. These edited remarks have been left essentially as they were delivered as best representing their author's views.

private world of broadcasting and coming back in this present incarnation as the chairman of Radio Free Europe/Radio Liberty, the other international broadcasting arm of the United States, my reaction is to be astonished - stunned would be the better word - at the lack of resources that a free society, the richest in the world, involved at a time of struggle of ideas, devotes to this enormous instrumentality of international broadcasting. We starve it; we run it in a third-rate way. So I want to address myself to why I think that has happened in the United States.

International radio in our country has no powerful constituency; the only people who have direct knowledge of the Radios are emigré groups. And while they can be very noisy, and they can in isolated situations have a little muscle and be helpful, on a national basis they have no continuing strength. The Baltic organisations, or the Polish organisations or the Hungarian, care. They can stir up difficulty; they can cause a few questions to be asked in the Senate Foreign Relations Committee; and that's all they can do. Politically one can over-emphasise their importance because they do make noise. When I say noise, I mean it in a very positive sense. But they have no strength to get anything done within our competence. Beyond the ethnic groups, the mass of the people have no knowledge of the Radios at all and could not care less. They never hear them, and there is no way to make them aware. You cannot take the people of Iowa and give them a sophisticated, useable knowledge of our broadcasts into Eastern Europe and the Soviet Union. To try with a public relations campaign to build some mass constituency is, I think, disfunctional.

Finally there are the committees in the continuing part of our government, the Senate and the House. The Presidency is not a continuing part of our government. Presidents come in to serve for four years or eight years and are gone. So does the apparatus which comes in with them - the White House staff, cabinet officers, and that sort of thing. Basically the Administration changes constantly in our structure. The permanent government is the Senate and the House. Some of the chairmen of the committees have been there for 30 years. So if you think of the United States government, you must think of leadership on a passing basis and the legislature on a permanent basis. That is an oversimplification, but if you don't understand that you will misjudge the United States.

The committees in each House which really know

International Broadcasting and US Political Realities

about the Radios and tend to be supportive are the Foreign Committees, that is to say, the Senate Foreign Relations Committee and the House Foreign Affairs Committee. Unfortunately, these committees have very little muscle in the House or Senate. In the Senate, the committees that carry great strength are the Appropriations Committee, the Armed Services Committee, the Finance Committee, the Labour Committee, the Education Committee - because they have huge constituencies. Under our Constitution the President makes foreign policy, and while the Senate has certain powers of confirmation and ratification, in point of fact foreign policy is basically a function of the Executive Branch. Young, aggressive, bright, able, tough-minded Senators don't want to go on the Foreign Committees because it doesn't help them. If you're from Kansas, or Illinois or California, you want to get on the Agriculture Committee, the Finance Committee, the Labour Committee, the Education Committee, the Appropriations Committee or the Defence Committee. Defence has huge installations all over the country and you can get something or other for your home state. On the Foreign Committees, members enjoy nice intellectual exercise, but really all this does basically back home is cause them trouble. Why are you spending so much time worrying about what's going on in Africa when I can't sell my wheat? So that while the Foreign Committees are interested, and like to be supportive, and can authorise appropriations, they really can't secure the funds to enable strong, functioning international radios. That is probably also true of the British Foreign Office - you had better have support at 10 Downing Street or in Parliament or you starve.

I made a tremendous misjudgment when I came into international radio. I spent my whole life in media in the United States, with CBS, Westinghouse, RKO - the best of the media in the United States. They are tough-minded, able and powerful. When I came into government under Nixon and now under Reagan, in these areas of communications - and I told you that I was simply stunned by the third-rate operations they were - I thought the media would have a natural interest in this. It was a dreadful mistake. The media in our country are negative, insofar as international radios are concerned. The reason is that in our country the media are inherently, irredeemably and correctly suspicious and antagonistic of a government 'propaganda operation'. They don't trust it. They mouth an occasional editorial about the importance of international broadcasting, but on a functional basis, and particularly at the reportorial level, they are suspicious.

Let me give an example. The Senate is the senior legislative body of the United States and it is an open organisation. It has requests from everybody who has a journalistic credential to be formally accredited to cover the Senate - that is to say, to have a pass to go into the press gallery and to use the technical and electronic facilities. The Senate didn't want to handle that, so the Senate in its wisdom took key elements of the United States media and said, you form yourselves into a committee and you determine who should be accredited to cover the Senate. These were such media as US News and World Report, AP, UP, CBS, NBC, Time, Newsweek - the first team. They accredited, because they felt they had to, TASS, Pravda, Izvestia, Radio Moscow, Janjuq and others. No accreditation at all for the Voice of America. No accreditation to Radio Free Europe and Radio Liberty. Why? They said, we cannot do anything about the state media of a foreign country because we understand that they would make a diplomatic demarche to the State Department, and therefore we must accredit them to cover the Congress. But we don't have to accredit our own government's 'propaganda' organisation to cover our own Senate. And there was no accreditation for 25 years for the VOA to cover the Senate. Later this prohibition was extended to RFE/RL.

A few of us, two years ago, raised a fuss about this and we got to the chairman of the Rules Committee, Senator Mathias, to hold hearings. Ed Fuelner (chairman of the commission advising the United States Information Agency), Ken Tomlinson (the VOA's former director) and myself (of Radio Free Europe and Radio Liberty), all testified. Who do you suppose testified against us? CBS, US News & World Report, AP - all saying that under no circumstances must we even sit in the gallery with representatives of these organisations. We had more muscle than they did, because we went to individual Senators and said, you continue to accredit TASS and Izvestia and Pravda and Tanjuq, and don't accredit the Voice of America, and we are going to blow you out of the water in your own constituency. That's the only way that we got accredited to the United States Senate.

I have spent my whole life in the media. For four years I was USIA director, responsible for the VOA, and for three years I have been chairman of Radio Free Europe/Radio Liberty. No citizen of the

United States except myself has run both these institutions. Never once in those seven years, by any reporter, at any time, for any reason, have I ever been asked: are the radios properly funded? They go into the studios, and they see things that ought to be in our Smithsonian Institution, they see decrepit installations, and they never inquire: are these things properly funded? They ask one question, and one question only: are they propaganda stations? It is the only question that is ever asked. Have we politicised the radios? Did the Nixon Administration - or the Carter Administration or the Reagan Administration - politicise the radios? This is the only question. It is generally a reporter who is 27 years old, very bright, right out of Harvard, highly suspicious of government propaganda, and he naturally sees this as a propaganda organisation. So he is going to be very courageous. He says: don't you politicise these radios. When you come into government radio, you find no domestic constituency apart from some ethnic groups. Certainly not the mass of the people. The Foreign Committees in Congress are helpful, but not really relevant. The media are a real negative. So what do you do about getting radios properly funded? I bring this up as a structural matter and you're not going to like the answer.

President Carter decided to appoint as director and deputy director of the United States Information Agency, which subsumes the VOA, two of the best foreign services officers this country had: Johnny Reinhardt and a man from the State Department. Johnny Reinhardt was a man I had promoted three times in my short period as USIA director. He was as good a foreign service officer as you could find - dispassionate, able, qualified, skilled, subtle - all the qualities of a foreign policy winner. The fellow from State was very good. They were appointed director and deputy director of USIA by Jimmy Carter in 1976, and neither they nor the Agency was heard from for the next four years. The Agency disappeared as if it had been dropped into the ocean. Splash, it was gone. Why? Because there is no constituency for that Agency. The only constituency you have at that Agency is the muscle, prominence, articulation, strength and contacts of the people at the top. They have to establish the strength of the agency. What that means is - and this is why your're not going to like this - in order to get radios properly funded in the United States, you must have at the very top of the organisation, that is, the director of USIA and the chairman of RFE/RL, people who have tight political connections with the administration. If you don't have them there, the radios will become weak.

I want to draw a distinction here. The operating executive of the radios need not be of that genre. We could put in as president of Radio Free Europe/Radio Liberty a first-class journalist, because the president is the chief operating officer. But the head of USIA, and the chairman of the RFE/RL board have got to be people who have the specific assets I have talked about.

When I was USIA director under Nixon, he was viewed by the press as getting his hands into everything, particularly ideas. In those four years, never once, directly or indirectly did anybody at the White House, even in the middle of Vietnam, with all those stresses, with academe and the media in open attack against the government over the role of the United States vis-a-vis South East Asia, the European alliance, Israel and the Middle East, with all of those incredible pressures, not one time in four years did I get any advice, pressure, orders, suggestions, nuances from the White House at all about what to do about VOA. Leonard Marks, who was my predecessor, had that job under Lyndon Johnson, who had a reputation, if it's possible to have a reputation tougher than Nixon, of being manipulative. Johnson had been the leader in the Senate, he was a consummate politician, he had been there for 30 to 40 years, he was known to be a vengeful man - you did it his way or bango. I said to Leonard Marks after I had been at USIA two or three years, 'Leonard, do you know nobody will believe it, but we don't get a scintilla, not a scintilla, of pressure on VOA.' He said, 'Frank, under Lyndon Johnson I never once had a conversation with him or anybody on his staff about VOA matters.'

Now in three years under Reagan, not once have I been pressured about RFE/RL. Presidents do not in my experience politicise international radio. Why they don't I have no idea. Is it because they are men of great vision, or too busy, or because they don't care, or because they are afraid there would be a scandal? I don't know what their reasons are, but I know the bottom line. The bottom line is they keep their hands, not partially off, not a little bit off, but totally off. If anything happens within the American radios that has strong philosophical nuances or political overtones, don't look to the White House. Look to the people in charge.

I got pressures from ambassadors and from the bureaucracy. Ambassadors may find that a particular report of the Voice of America is awkward for them in the country of assignment. They may have been called in by the president or the foreign minister because a particular broadcast has created disharmony in that country. In some situations juniors within the bureaucracy, looking for things to do, like to dabble. You have to say no early on, unequivocally, because if you give one inch in that area you are doomed. Remember what I said about not having career officers at the top. Career officers cannot say no in precisely the same way to another very senior officer or foreign leader in the way that political appointees can.

There is, not bias, but real philosophical ferment in the radios. Let me give some illustrations. There is in the world of Kremlinology immense concern about the post-communist Soviet world. Obviously communism is coming to the end of its string. It is disfunctional. Mankind has learned this after nearly 70 years of experience. Whether it goes on for 50 or 100 years, it no longer has anything to offer mankind. It is simply a curse. How one gets through the transition from the enormous oppressive power that exists to some measure of freedom is the only question left.

Those who are more profound than I in these matters are focussing their attention on the post-communist world. That takes the form of analysing such things as nationalism - the Solzhenitsyn approach - whether or not the Soviet Union will need to have some sort of a government with a high degree of central authority and strong democratic safeguards as a transition. The nationalists believe Russia cannot move directly to European parliamentary democracy. Then there are those who call themselves the democratic pluralists who believe just the opposite - that the only way for Russia to go is an immediate jump into democratic pluralism. That discussion is intense, astonishingly bitter, and far from dispassionate; they leak to the press; and they accuse one another of loading programmes on one side or the other of the argument. It's not a problem of politics - it's a problem of philosophy. But the media, often junior reporters who are not familiar with the problem and not very skilled at analysing it, deal with it in a sensational way.

Now let me talk a little about organisation. In our society there have been reasonable efforts to build in correctives. Let me address what I think some of those are. First, in Radio Free Europe/Radio Liberty, the board is made up of nine people, and is by structure bi-partisan. Under the present government, we typically have on our board five Republicans and four Democrats. The Democrats are not tabby cats. The Democrats on our board are Lane Kirkland, who is probably one of the single greatest forces behind activist Democratic politics in the United States; James Michener, who has said publicly, that while he doesn't advocate it for the United States, he thinks that any country other than the United States ought to move rapidly to a form of socialism; Michael Novak, who is a brilliant theologian; Ben Wattenberg, who is the founder and co-chairman of the Committee for a Democratic Majority. We've now been a board of this corporation for about a year. When we have our discussions we never talk about the bi-partisan structure. We talk about how best to operate the radios, how we can strengthen them, who are the best management people, how we can support the management, what we need to do about transmitters and signal strength. Each person has one vote, including the chairman. It's like the Supreme Court. If you are the Chief Justice of the Supreme Court, you have a lot of honour, but when a case is decided 5-4 you've got one vote. So that's one thing built into RFE/RL board structure, which in the very true sense of the word is bi-partisan. The media doesn't know that or understand it. Neither does academia.

A second structure is the West European advisory committee, which is an instrument of our own creation. We have tried to recruit for this committee one or two able, knowledgeable people from each of the major West European countries as advisors to the Radios in intellectual and substantive matters. Without going through all 15 of the membership, to give you an idea of the calibre of these people, I'll tell you about the two newest ones: Allan Chalfont from London, chairman of the defence committee of the House of Lords, who chaired a recent terrorism conference in Washington, a key voice at the terrorism conference in Israel, and who was for years the chief military analyst for <u>The Times</u> in London; and Luchinger, editor-in-chief of <u>Neue Zürcher Zeitung</u>, one of the most prestigious papers in Europe. We meet regularly.

A third approach is to try to keep the personnel on these radios mindful of diversity and ferment. The basic burden of broadcasting is on the staff and the management, the people in the US and the people in

Munich, but I'm talking about inputs from other elements of society. We make a conscious effort to keep our broadcasters aware of intellectual ferment. For example, at the beginning of a typical week Murray Feshbach, a foremost Soviet demographer and one of the best statisticians and demographers in the US, lectured to the editors of Radio Free Europe and Radio Liberty in Munich on the health situation in the Soviet Union. The next day, Michael Bordeaux, a distinguished cleric who is the head of Keston College in England, which does continuing research on the state of religion in the Soviet Union and Eastern Europe, gave a lecture on the ferment in religion in that area. The day after, Kremlinologists discussed nationalism: Solzhenitsyn and democratic pluralism, and whether fascism is rising, and all of the change within the Soviet Union. Adam Ulam, director of the Russian Research Center at Harvard; Peter Reddaway, London School of Economics; Andre Sinyavsky from Paris; John Dunlop from Hoover, Nicholas Riazanovsky from the University of California at Berkeley - some of the best Soviet experts in the world were there talking about those matters with our editors. At the end of this week in Munich, Colonel von Stauffenberg, whose father attempted to assassinate Hitler on 20th July, gave the Radios an historical perspective on the events of that day as his family records and his judgments showed them to be.

To recap: at the top of the organisation there must be someone who has the political contacts to make things happen. There must be political protection, which arises from a bi-partisan, balanced board, with only one vote for each member. Secondly, we have the West European Advisory Committee, made up of first class people. Add the inputs of the best intellectuals - such as Ulam of Harvard or Peter Reddaway, people whose integrity is beyond reproach. They may be right or wrong or have differing opinions but they are independent. The talk about our credibility in academe and the media is all utter nonsense and asburd.

Now I'll move into an area of judgment, one outside my experience. It seems to me that in the present situation, particularly in the Soviet Union, to a lesser extent in Eastern Europe, exclusive emphasis on news, which is the basic meat and potatoes of broadcast operations, is no longer an option. I am talking about emphasis and focus. One can make a case that after 60 or 70 years the people, particularly in the Soviet Union, are at the point of becoming intellectual cripples, except for the dissidents and the elites. They have had nearly 70 years of distorted history and distorted culture with no travel, no proper education, and very little outside media except Western radio broadcasts. They have been cut off for 70 years from fundamental thinking about religion, the nature of man, the nature of man's relationship to the state - all of the things that have been thought out in the west for hundreds of years. I think we must start to put more emphasis on history and culture, particularly as western man has experienced it. It is absolutely vital, and is a very different matter than just news. You know that an awful lot of news, while useful, can clog up your mind. You can get saturated with twenty items of news which are important this week and not important next Tuesday. But the nature of man is forever. The nature of the State is forever. One's cultural history is very important. The factual history of one's own state and society is very important. And it seems to me that we must think very carefully of an increased emphasis on history and culture in broadcasting to a people who, almost by definition now, are becoming intellectually crippled.

That's one place where I make a suggestion. In the Soviet Union, 50 per cent of the people speak Russian. This percentage is declining, with the people who speak a minority language increasing. The Turkic Muslim people, in the belly of the Soviet Union, where Tashkent, Samarkand, and Bukhara are located, constitute 17 per cent of the population now. By the year 2000 they will grow to 25 per cent. Al Haig, when he was Secretary of State, has said, 'By the year 2000 - that's tomorrow - between 33 and 40 per cent of all the draftable 18-year-olds in the Soviet Union will be Turkic Muslims, because they will be young and the Slavs will be old.'

Are they affected by events in Iran, or the ferment in the Islamic religious community? Of course. Are they affected by events in Afghanistan, right across their border? Of course. Are they affected by the fact that they are thousands of miles, not from places called Paris or London or Bonn or Rome, but from places called Odessa or Kiev or Moscow or Leningrad? That they are people from a totally different cultural background? They don't take Russian until the fifth grade. Now, how on earth can the Western international broadcasters not broadcast to those people in their own indigenous languages?

Take the Ukrainians 40 to 50 million people in

the Soviet Union. When the German forces marched in in 1941, at first they were greeted with flowers by the Ukrainians. The Ukrainians consider themselves in many ways separate. How can you broadcast to the Ukrainian people in Russian and insult them? How can you broadcast to the Turkic Muslim people in Russian? Take the tiny Baltic States. If you talk to Lithuanians in Russian, you are insulting them. It seems to me that other international radios, if they are serious about it, must add eight or nine language services to broadcast into the Soviet Union. It is tragic that the BBC - in my opinion the best international broadcaster of all - should broadcast into the Soviet Union in just Russian and English in 1984. For West Germany to broadcast simply in German and Russian, for Kol Israel to broadcast simply in Yiddish, Hebrew and Russian, is a tragedy*. Baltic languages, the Ukrainian language, Georgian, Armenian, Azerbaijani, and the Turkic Muslim languages are probably the single most important thing we do at RFE/RL. It's a matter for foreign offices to decide. It would cost $20 million or so to gear this up. Which would have more effect on the Soviet Union, three more destroyers or the establishment of minority language broadcasting to the 50 per cent of the people in the Soviet Union who are not Russian?

Lastly, audiences. Our broadcasts, at least at Radio Liberty, tend to be elitist. Now if you are a broadcaster the first thing you have to know is who your audience is. Your're trying to create a broadcast programme. Who is your audience? We are broadcasting to elites, to upper echelon people. We know this from feedback from Moscow, Leningrad, and other metropolitan centres.

Who are we not broadcasting to? The peasant? The farmer? An army private? Someone who lives in a small town 300 miles from Moscow and ain't ever gonna go anywhere? A blue collar worker? A man on the line in the factory? We pick such people up in our audience, but we are not geared to them. As Solzehnitsyn has said, that is the tragic effort of Western broadcasters. Is he right? I have no idea. Rostropovich says the same thing. It has been brought into focus for all of us by Poland. Czechoslovakia was a revolt of the intellectuals. Poland was a revolt of ten million people, blue collar workers. They were steelworkers and coal miners, the people

* Kol Israel's English Service is also heard in the USSR. Ed.

who built ships in Gdansk - and what did they say? They said this damned system doesn't work - it's rotten. It doesn't provide us food or freedom or support to the family. It was an intellectual revolt in the ultimate sense, but not in the immediate sense. Is Poland, rather than Czechoslovakia, rather than the intellectual dissidents in Moscow, to suggest the right focus for our broadcasting over the next 20 years? Is Poland to be the model for a transition from a system that has to be junked eventually? The approach must be careful because we have nuclear weapons and we can blow ourselves up. In this sensitive ferment, the Radios will necessarily be a catalyst. Radio Free Europe is an implement of almost staggering proportions for Poland. Should we be thinking consciously of the worker, of the peasant, of the private, and not of the intellectual? And if so, does that change the design of our programmes?

The United States is undertaking a build up of broadcast operations, building up both VOA and RFE/RL. President Reagan has made the strongest pronouncements about increasing the strength of the Radios. This is not because of any new cold war. It is a recognition that the struggle for ideas is becoming central. It is the responsibility of western man, which we have shamefully failed by having weak radios during the last 15 years.

Everything that I have talked about is from the point of view of the publisher - structure, money, and external influences. That is absolutely necessary to a vital organisation but it isn't its essence - the essence is editing, writing, producing, putting the programmes on the air. In the final analysis you people _are_ international radio.

Chapter Four

RADIO FREE EUROPE/RADIO LIBERTY IN THE MID 1980s

William A. Buell, vice president, US Operations, Radio Free Europe/Radio Liberty

Radio Free Europe and Radio Liberty have been broadcasting uncensored news and information to the people of Eastern Europe and the Soviet Union for more than 30 years. The purpose of this paper is to examine the radios' turbulent history during the past ten, since the passage of the Act for the Board for International Broadcasting (BIB) of 1973, and to take a look at the choices and directions facing the now-merged radios in the mid-1980s. I must emphasise at the outset that the views expressed here, either directly or by inference, are my own and in some cases may not reflect those of all of my colleagues.

The BIB Act, which became law in October 1973, brought to an end two years of controversy during which the continued existence of these valuable assets in the struggle for the right to know was constantly under threat. Powerful adversaries in the United States Congress, especially in the Senate Committee on Foreign Relations, who regarded them as 'relics of the Cold War', had come within a hair's breadth of eliminating RFE and RL from the airwaves. Since the passage of the BIB Act, however, no-one in a position of authority or influence in Washington has seriously questioned their worth. One may well consider the two stations a permanent feature of the electro-magnetic spectrum.

This does not mean, however that RFE and RL embarked upon a decade of smooth and uncontroversial existence. The headquarters of RFE and RL was moved first from New York to Washington and thence, after little more than two years, to Munich. The two stations, with widely differing traditions, philosophical convictions, personnel systems, benefits and pay scales, were merged into one. RL was bundled into an RFE building enlarged, but insufficiently, for the purpose. RFE and RL continue to maintain their separate identities as broadcast divisions, within a single corporation. The economies of scale were obvious, but to this day, eight years after the merger, not all of the resulting traumas have healed.

Managing an international broadcasting organisation such as Radio Free Europe/Radio Liberty presents all of the problems of running any technically complex operation with over 1,700 employees, plus a number of additional specialised headaches. Most of the working environment is overseas. Only about 100 of RFE/RL's 1,750 employees are based in the United States, 1,000 are in Munich, the balance at transmitter sites elsewhere in Germany, in Portugal and in Spain, with a further scattering to news bureaus in half a dozen other locations. A budget largely in three fluctuating European currencies and personnel systems operating under differing labour codes requires nimble footwork. The predominant nationality among Munich employees is German - the technicians, the administrative and maintenance staff. Bulletin board notices go up in English and German, with English laying a fragile claim to the company's <u>lingua franca</u>. Radio Liberty staff meetings are in Russian, German, English, Turkish or a mixture of all four.

The backbone of the entire operation is the emigré staff: writers, editors, announcers and producers from 21 nations of Eastern Europe and the Soviet Union. They are a stimulating, fascinating lot, a mixture of the very talented and the marginally so, the industrious and the time-serving, the physically fit and the chronically ill, the flexible and the obstinate. Most of them have in common a dedication to their work and a contemptuous loathing for the systems of government from which they fled. They are tough and headstrong. Many have been in prison for their principles.

They regard Radio Free Europe and Radio Liberty as their stations. Many have worked in Munich for 30 years. They look upon the thin layer of American management with attitudes ranging from loyalty and respect to a brooding contempt. Somewhere in between lies a pervasive amused tolerance. ('These, too, shall pass, like the others. We shall remain and persevere. We know our job. The Americans come and go, organise and reorganise, call things by different names. We have the job to do, day in and day out, and we get on with it, pretty much as always.')

The fractious among them bring from their homelands internal quarrels they could not leave behind. Successive waves of emigres arrive with differing values. Personal feuds persist, sometimes for decades. In the Czechoslovak Service, frictions persist between Czechs and Slovaks, '48-ers' and '68-ers' and even, as one director wearily put it, Slovaks and Slovaks. Among RL's Russians there are hostile feelings between those with strong Russian nationalist views and more recently employed emigrants of Jewish origin, reflecting divisions within the Soviet emigration throughout the west. All the racial and national passions of turbulent Mitteleuropa survive in microcosm at RFE/RL.

In their dealings with American management they are represented by four trade unions and one works council.

Continuity in management would seem desirable. However, since the passage of the Act for the Board for International Broadcasting this sprawling, heterogeneous, fractious undertaking has been presided over by six presidents, four board chairmen, and five Radio Free Europe directors. In the same period Radio Liberty has had two directors, one acting director, and a two-year stretch with no director at all. The Russian Service of RL has had five directors. In just the past two years, there have been changes at the helm of four of the five RFE language services. Three of the replacements have been brought in from outside the organisation.

Budget Worries
The revolving management of the stations during most of this period has had to cope with maintaining a broadcast schedule of over 1,000 hours a week with steadily decreasing financial resources. On paper the annual budgets always appeared to be growing from year to year. In real terms, they were shrinking drastically, not only because of the robust inflation rate of the 1970s but thanks to the dollar falling in four years to little more than half its previous value against the Deutschemark, the currency in which 80 per cent of the stations' expenditures are made. A transmitter modernisation programme begun in the Nixon-Ford years was continued under the Carter Administration. With the completion of the installation of eleven new 250-KW transmitters in Portugal and Germany in 1980, transmitter power was nearly doubled over that of the early 1970s. However, programme and operating funds remained insufficient.

The annual budget cycle was relentlessly

discouraging. Typically, the president's office of management and budget would set a budget limit well below the amount considered necessary by the radios merely to maintain current operations. Then _after_ submission of a budget at this figure, the OMB would reduce it still further. On occasion Congress took an additional bite, although Congress has been wholeheartedly in support of international broadcasting in recent years. Budget requests in the $100 million range were cut in this manner by between $2 and $8 million, prompting a move to eliminate entire language services.

Somehow the radios muddled through, by postponing maintenance schedules, making do with antiquated equipment, starving the freelance and travel accounts, withholding payments to the pension fund, and - most significantly - cutting back on personnel strength, making do with a cumulative reduction of nearly 600 employees.

The last few years of the current Administration in Washington have seen a radical improvement in RFE/RL's financial underpinning, a welcome trend unknown at the stations since the days of generous covert financing in the early 1960s. The upturn came in 1981 when the new administration supported a supplemental appropriation of $4 million. This was not immediately translated into programme funding, since most of it had to be spent on unanticipated reconstruction, equipment replacement, and new physical security measures following the bombing of the Munich headquarters in February of that year. (The bomb explosion, which effectively destroyed one wing of the building and severely injured several employees, remains an unsolved crime.)

Subsequent budget increases have enabled the forthcoming modernisation of the antiquated Munich studio complex, improved programme circuits, four more replacement transmitters in West Germany, and many other technical improvements essential to shortwave broadcasts beamed into a heavily jammed environment. There has been catching up with long overdue maintenance. From the standpoint of staff morale, perhaps the most important improvement was the interior painting and carpeting of the Munich building, which had deteriorated over many years to a gloomy, cracked and peeling slum.

Programming functions have been strengthened in several areas with the restoration of 75 positions, increased travel and freelance funds and the opening of bureaus in Hong Kong and Pakistan. Rejuvenation of the language staff has been accelerated, an important undertaking as 200 emigre programmers are due for retirement by the end of the 1980s. RFE/RL is now able to enter the modern world of word processing and data processing, in which the central newsroom has been a pioneer.

Broadcast Effectiveness

The budget request submitted to the office of management and budget for the fiscal year beginning in October 1985 called for a still more ambitious leap. It would increase the staff by over 200 positions and add over $100 million in modernised technical plant.

This paper has so far dealt largely with nuts and bolts, avoiding more fundamental questions such as these: is RFE/RL broadcasting today in the interests of the western alliance? Is it relevant to the process of change in Eastern Europe and the Soviet Union? Does it meet the needs of an audience starved for uncensored information? Is it effective?

First of all, what is RFE/RL broadcasting? What distinguishes it from VOA broadcasting or the broadcasting of other nationally sponsored radios? Significantly, the supporters of the establishment of Radio Marti, due to go on the air soon with broadcasts to Cuba, called for an 'RFE-type station' to convey to Washington decision-makers just what they had in mind.

RFE-type broadcasting ia narrowly focussed geographically. VOA Spanish covers all of Latin America; Radio Marti will be for Cuba alone. RFE-type broadcasting means more hours to a given country: 18 and a half hours daily to Hungary, for example, compared to two and a half by the VOA and BBC. RFE-type broadcasting is not just to the audience but about the audience, whereas VOA broadcasting is primarily about the United States. RFE and RL function, to the extent possible, as surrogate home services in competition with domestic media in the target country. RFE's Polish Service seeks a reputation not as a foreign broadcaster but as a Polish station abroad. The morning programmes of some services include the daily weather forecast and other useful bits of information to be absorbed while shaving and brushing teeth.

This kind of broadcasting can only be made possible with substantial investment in the information and research base. The RFE/RL central news division subscribes to five wire services and combs the daily western European and American press for reporting pertinent to the broadcast area. The research departments, numbering nearly 100 employees, subscribe to literally thousands of Eastern European and Soviet publications. (The research output, published in English for cross-reporting purposes, has a wide circulation in Europe and the United States and is highly regarded by academic specialists in the field.) A monitoring station in a Munich suburb follows Eastern European and Soviet radio broadcasting around the clock. From this mountain of information is produced the analyses upon which much of RFE/RL broadcasting is based. Programmers are in a position to know not only what their audiences are being told by their official media but also what the audiences are not being told. Gaps can be filled and distortions corrected.

Relevance to the political dynamics of the area is demonstrable. Probably the most significant example is to be found in Poland. RFE's essential role in such movements as Solidarity is to challenge a communist regime's inevitable attempt to isolate the movement's adherents - from the rest of the population and from one another. Broadcasting on Solidarity's tempestuous beginnings in the summer of 1980, based on reports by western journalists in touch with the committee for the defence of the workers (KOR), gave strikers in Lublin, Krakow and Gdansk the sense of community essential to the achievement of their objectives.

Some Solidarity members believe that RFE's influence, while important, was not as significant in the tactical struggle of that summer as it was in the year-in-year-out educating of a whole generation of Poles. One Solidarity leader, Andrzej Gwiazda, in a touching testimonial to RFE smuggled out of prison wrote, 'I do believe the events of 1980 would have taken place, independently of whether or not RFE had been on the air. I am not certain, however, that one would have found the people who would have started such a strike.'

Testimonials to RFE's impact have also come from representatives of the Polish communist government. In a recent Wall Street Journal interview, the government spokesman, Jerzy Urban said, 'If you would close your Radio Free Europe, the underground (Solidarity) would cease to exist.' Two years earlier Mieczyslaw Rakowski, the deputy prime minister, told the Sejm (parliament), 'The main role among (western centres) is played by Radio Free Europe. Solidarity activists underground avail themselves of its help on a big scale.'

The KAL 007 disaster is another example of direct impact on an issue of vital importance in East-West relations. While Soviet media were still denying that the passenger aircraft had been shot down, the Russian service was broadcasting the tape of the Soviet fighter pilot's report that he had accomplished just that. It is unlikely that Soviet citizens would ever have had access to any version of the event, even a skewed one, without western radio, which inexorably forced Soviet authorities to admit to the shooting.

While anecdotal support of the effectiveness of RFE-type broadcasting is reassuring, a more reliable yardstick is to be found in the audience research conducted by RFE and RL based on responses obtained from travellers from the audience area by independent western European public opinion institutes. The most recent surveys show audience ratings of 60 per cent and over of the adult population in Poland, Hungary and Romania, and 38 to 40 per cent in Czechoslovakia and Bulgaria. In some cases these figures exceed those of all other western broadcasters combined.

Radio Liberty's 17 million listeners in the Soviet Union do not represent as large a share of the western radio audience. This is in part due to the heavy jamming of RL transmissions which has existed since the station's infancy but also to other debatable factors beyond the scope of this paper.

Unresolved Issues

One constant in Radio Free Europe/Radio Liberty management, as noted above, has been frequent change. Some regard this as healthy for the institution. Others give wistful vent to wishes that the Radios could be granted a few years of managerial continuity, free of further tampering with the organisational chart.

Those who drafted the BIB Act of 1973 doubtless thought they had produced the definitive answer to the question of structure. The Radios had then been in business for two years in limbo as unwanted foster children of the Department of State after the severing of CIA sponsorship in 1972. During this period considerable thought was devoted in Congress and the Executive Branch to legislation which would preserve the independent character of the Radios, which had been so efficacious during the years of covert financing, and at the same time would institute a system of audit and management appropriate to open funding by Congress. A commission headed by Milton Eisenhower, named by President Nixon to make recommendations for the Radios' future, chose from among several options the establishment of a new government agency, the Board for International Broadcasting, to serve as a nexus between the independent corporation and the government.

The Act for the Board for International Broadcasting was a deceptively simple piece of legislation. The act declared that the continuation of RFE and RL as 'an independent broadcast media operating in a manner not inconsistent with the broad foreign policy objectives of the United States and in accordance with high professional standards, is in the national interest.' The Board for International Broadcasting, whose members were to be appointed by the President under the terms of the act, had limited functions. It was authorised to make grants to the Corporation; review mission and operations and evaluate effectiveness; encourage efficient utilisation of resources; keep audits; make and apply evaluation procedures to assess that there was no inconsistency with US broad foreign policy objectives; and report annually to the President and Congress.

The act didn't work. The reasons it didn't work will be variously described by the players in the drama. The Eisenhower commission report had hinted at potential conflicts in the new organisation but dismissed them with the statement that, 'We realise that able men of good will can make about any organisational arrangement work; and, conversely, that even the finest organisational arrangements do not guarantee efficient and effective operations.'

Able men were not lacking but good will certainly was. Friction between the BIB and its ten-person staff (half of it secretarial) and the RFE/RL board of directors and its senior executives existed just about ab initio. There was little or no dispute on broadcast policy but a considerable amount over managerial practices. Trench warfare over turf was unrelenting. Specific sources of dispute, such as the number of staff to be reassigned from Munich to the United States and who should conduct a relationship with members of Congress, and even who should be named to key executive positions, became unresolvable as each side dug in its heels in defence of its own estimate of its authority. Fundamental to this difficult relationship was the difference of opinion over the meaning of 'oversight', a term appearing only by implication in the BIB Act. The RFE/RL Board and staff insisted - or attempted to insist - that BIB's sole authority was to audit expenditures and to determine that broadcasting was 'not inconsistent with the broad foreign policy interests of the United States'. Beyond that it should keep its hands off the Radios' business. The BIB took the position that its responsibility to Congress gave it the authority not only to make operational recommendations but to see to it that they were enforced. A lamentable amount of staff time and energy was wasted in quarrelling over differing perceptions of authority.

Members of Congress and staff, notably in the Senate Foreign Relations Committee, ultimately decided that the two-board structure was unsound. They took action to restore peace and put the Radios' house in order with yet another piece of reorganisational legislation. The Pell Amendment, first introduced by the now-ranking Democrat on the Committee in 1977, raised its head as a hardy perennial in annual budget and authorisation hearings. It was finally passed - not without controversy - in the summer of 1982. It, too, was deceptively simple. It effectively eliminated the separate private corporate board by requiring that, by date certain, no funds would be granted the Radios unless the corporate board consisted of the members of the Board for International Broadcasting and no other members. Henceforth two boards, one private, one appointed by the President of the United States, would continue to exist in parallel but with identical membership.

Senator Pell was evidently concerned that something of value might be lost with the effective elimination of separate private board membership because at one stage in the proceedings he introduced an additional amendment determining that compliance, 'Shall not be construed to make RFE/RL Incorporated, a Federal agency or instrumentality'.

This language would appear to be largely hortatory. Board members are expected to make decisions requiring an extraordinary dichotomy of mind. As the BIB, they request from Congress the appropriations from which they make quarterly grants to the corporation, RFE/RL Inc. As the board of RFE/RL Inc, they hire, fire and set policy. Then as the BIB they must certify to the Congress that the monies have been wisely spent and that policies are 'not inconsistent with the broad foreign policy objectives of the United States'. As an oversight board, the BIB is in effect called upon to oversee itself. A conference committee of Senate and House members evidently thought the oversight function could be assumed by the BIB staff: 'It is the expectation of the committee of conference that this indispensable function (oversight) of the BIB still - totally separate from RFE/RL operations management - will continue to be exercised effectively under the new arrangement.'

Most of the members of the board who will have to meet the challenge of the new arrangement have been in office for only nine months. It is as exceptional a group of private citizens as ever assembled on a board of this nature, including in its ranks the nation's best-selling historical novelist, its foremost trade unionist, the chief executive officer of its largest advertising firm and others of similar distinction. It is by law a bi-partisan board: under the BIB Act no more than five of its nine voting members (the RFE/RL president being an ex officio tenth member) shall be of the same political party. Appointments are for three years, with terms of one third of the members expiring each year.

However, despite the efforts of Congress to ensure that the Pell Amendment would not 'politicise' the Radios, RFE/RL has arguably become more vulnerable to the political process, for good or ill, as a result of it. True, regardless of a change in the White House, BIB members are entitled to serve out their three-year terms. But would they all wish to do so? The President of the United States designates the BIB chairman and can be expected to do so from members of its own party on the board. Change in key management positions would also be likely if, against all present odds, the White House should change hands. Only time will tell if the amended BIB Act has created a structure more effectively administered than the original. It may eventually be recognised that the untidiness, overlapping and internal squabbling which marked the previous arrangement were not perhaps too high a price to pay to insulate the Radios from domestic American politics.

One of the most sensitive issues with which the new Board must deal will be broadcast content, style and tone. Western practitioners of the act of public diplomacy have been divided for decades over the most effective type of broadcasting and practically all the words used in the argument are loaded. They can be grouped generally in two categories: soft-sell and hard-sell. Soft-sell advocates believe that it is the business of international broadcasting to provide news and information in an objective, professional, accurate, balanced 'warts-and-all' manner, leaving listeners to make their own judgments. The hard-sell people believe that broadcasting is an instrument of political and social change which must be used aggressively, persuading the listeners by force of argument of the virtues of western values and the evils of Marxism-Leninism in theory and in practice. They see no value in dwelling at all upon the failures of western society, preferring only to extol its virtues.

Soft-sellers believe that the listeners are fully aware of the corruption, inefficiency and human degradation of the communist system under which they must live and should not be patronised by having lectures on how badly off they are. Hard-sellers hold that decades of indoctrination have taken root and the evils of communism must be addressed polemically.

Soft-sellers see hard-sellers as propagandistic, self-righteous, chauvinistic, boastful, sometimes dangerously inflammatory and politically partisan. Hard-sellers call soft-sellers naive, détentist (a bad word), immorally neutral, wimpish and woefully uninformed of the nature and purposes of the Soviet system. They claim that anything less than aggressive and partisan broadcasting is abuse of the taxpayers' money.

These are caricature extremes, of course. Most of those with a stake in the international broadcasting business hold views somewhere in between - few of them admitting to be in support of either soft or hard-sell. Furthermore it would be wrong to equate soft-sell with dove and hard-sell with hawk. Many who would describe themselves as hard-nosed and hawkish believe that soft-sell gets the best results.

The Radio Free Europe and Radio Liberty of the 1950s leaned towards hard. The early 1960s, when strict professionalism was introduced in newscasting, saw the beginning of a softer-sell approach which was enshrined a decade later in the RFE/RL Mission Statement and Program Policy Guidelines which are still, on paper at least, the definitive standard. (It would of course be hard to find a Soviet bloc leader who would have described RFE/RL broadcasts as soft-sell at any time. All a question of perspective.)

Proponents of the hard-sell and the soft-sell do not find common ground easily but a balance should be struck. Neutral, disinterested broadcasting may leave the listener wondering whose side the station is on. Bombastic, partisan sermonising - or anything that sounds tediously like 'government radio' – will lead him to exercise one of the few freedoms still available everywhere: the freedom to switch off.

Finally, another controversial issue which will draw the new board's attention: the degree to which broadcast content should be controlled by American management. At RFE/RL, the news wire material for use in the ten-minute newscasts at the beginning of each hour is prepared in English by the central news division. Individual language service editors may select from among a broad range of stories and determine their order. They are encouraged to avoid clumsy, literal translations but may not change the content or write their own copy. The selection and editing of programming for the other 50 minutes of the hour is left to the discretion of the chiefs – 21 of them – of the language services. Content monitoring and analysis for the use of American management is performed post-broadcast. This has been a tradition for decades at RFE, but was only recently introduced in the Radio Liberty Division.

The principles behind this exercise of independent editorial decision-making are easily defended: a broadcast service chief born and educated in Poland is the best judge of which programmes will be most relevant to a Polish audience. A Romanian director knows best what Romanians want to hear and the style in which they want it broadcast. Central scripting, whether by the news division or the research departments, plays its role, but much of the 'non-news' programming, including commentary, originates at the level of the language services. Broadcasts of one service may vary markedly in style and content from another. It is sometimes said that RFE/RL is not one station but 21. The differentiation among Eastern European countries is widely recognised in the Radio Free Europe Division. The challenge of broadcasting to a relatively open society in Hungary is different from that of broadcasting to Romania, a maverick in foreign policy but internally frozen in the Stalinist mode.

The granting of editorial independence to emigré programmers is an act of faith by American management which requires steady nerves. It is uncomfortable to be held responsible for this kind of highly differentiated broadcasting, even when emigré service chiefs and their principal deputies, who approve programmes for broadcast, are old and trusted hands. With a thousand hours a week going on the air from Munich there are bound to be glitches, some of them painful, particularly when they become the source of public controversy. Risks can be reduced through training and a strengthening of the functions performed by the Radios' broadcast analysis department. Solutions favouring increased central scripting and pre-broadcast clearance will produce dull radio, which can be switched off.

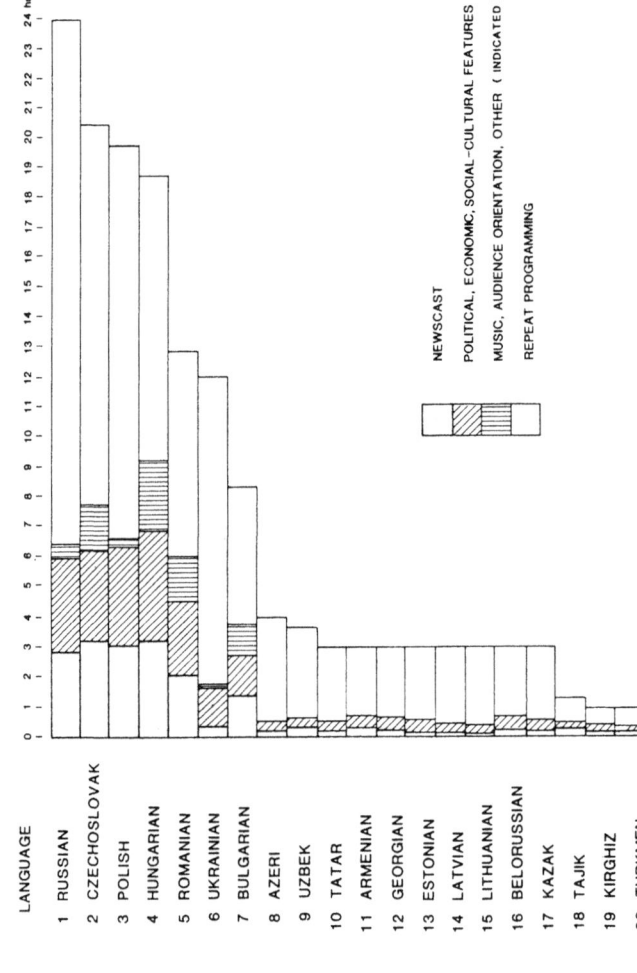

Figure 4.1: Daily First-run and repeat programmes by Language, FY 1984

Source: Based on Summer 1984 schedules and programming statistics for three quarters of FY 1984

Figure 4.2: First-run broadcast Hours per day, FY 1984

SERVICE / CATEGORY	RUSSIAN hours	RUSSIAN percent	POLISH hours	POLISH percent	ROMANIAN hours	ROMANIAN percent	CZECHO-SLOVAK hours	CZECHO-SLOVAK percent	HUNGARIAN hours	HUNGARIAN percent	BULGARIAN hours	BULGARIAN percent	UKRAINIAN hours	UKRAINIAN percent
NEWSCASTS	2:48	43.9	3:04	44.7	2:05	31.2	3:13	40.9	3:14	33.9	1:40	37.6	0:19	17.3
CORRESPONDENTS' REPORTS	0:19	4.9	0:26	6.3	0:16	4.0	0:04	0.8	0:26	4.5	0:04	1.5	0:05	4.5
NEWS ANALYSES	0:08	2.1	0:40	9.7	0:45	11.2	0:25	5.3	0:34	5.9	0:27	10.1	0:04	3.6
PRESS REVIEWS	0:03	0.8	0:07	1.7	0:20	5.0	0:10	2.1	0:15	2.6	0:07	2.6	0:01	0.9
OTHER FEATURES	2:23	37.3	1:25	20.6	1:28	21.9	2:18	29.3	2:37	27.5	1:09	25.9	0:55	50.0
READINGS	0:17	4.4	0:44	10.7	0:05	1.2	0:04	0.8					0:16	14.5
MUSIC & VARIETY SHOWS	0:01	0.3			1:05	16.2	0:50	10.6	1:31	15.9	0:34	12.8	0:01	0.9
AUDIENCE ORIENTATION	0:14	3.7	0:10	2.4	0:05	1.2	0:11	2.3	0:05	0.9	0:02	0.8	0:02	1.8
OTHER *	0:10	2.6	0:16	3.9	0:32	8.0	0:37	7.8	0:50	8.7	0:23	8.6	0:07	6.4
TOTAL	6:23		6:52		6:41		7:52		9:32		4:26		1:50	

* INCLUDES SPORTCASTS AND RELIGIOUS SERVICES

Source: Data are Based on Programming Statistics for Three Quarters of FY 1984

Figure 4.3: Geographic Focus of Feature Programmes, FY 1984

SERVICE	RUSSIAN		POLISH		ROMANIAN		CZECHO-SLOVAK		HUNGARIAN		BULGARIAN		UKRAINIAN	
CATEGORY	hours	percent	hours	percent	hours	percent	hours	percent	hours	percent	hours	percent	hours	percent
NATIONAL AFFAIRS DOMESTIC	1:38	49.5	2:14	62.0	0:50	26.0	0:30	13.8	0:59	20.8	0:21	15.9	1:10	78.6
NATIONAL AFFAIRS EXTERNAL	0:23	11.6	0:11	5.1	0:04	2.1	0:28	12.8	0:16	5.6	0:05	3.8	0:05	5.6
TOTAL NATIONAL AFFAIRS	2:01	61.1	2:25	67.1	0:54	28.1	0:58	26.6	1:15	26.4	0:26	19.7	1:15	84.2
CROSS REPORTING	0:17	8.6	0:12	5.6	0:24	12.5	0:24	11.0	0:28	9.9	0:17	12.9	0:05	5.6
EAST – WEST RELATIONS	0:16	8.1	0:14	6.5	0:23	12.0	0:21	9.6	0:27	9.5	0:19	14.4	0:01	1.1
TOTAL COMM. AFFS. & EAST – WEST	2:34	77.8	2:51	79.2	1:41	52.6	1:43	47.2	2:10	45.8	1:02	47.0	1:21	91.0
US DOMESTIC	0:08	4.0	0:02	0.9	0:14	7.3	0:08	3.7	0:16	5.6	0:06	4.5	0:01	1.1
US FOREIGN POLICY	0:06	3.0	0:04	1.9	0:06	3.1	0:07	3.2	0:07	2.5	0:08	6.1	0:02	2.2
WESTERN EUROPE	0:08	4.0	0:10	4.6	0:16	8.3	0:24	11.0	0:46	16.2	0:05	3.8	0:01	1.1
OTHER*	0:22	11.1	0:29	13.4	0:55	28.6	1:16	34.9	1:25		0:51	38.6	0:04	4.5
TOTAL	3:18		3:36		3:12		3:38		4:44		2:12		1:29	

* INDICATES INTERNATIONAL ORGANIZATIONS (UN), MIDDLE EAST, AFRICA, etc.

Source: Data are Based on Programming Statistics for Three Quarters of FY 1984

Radio Free Europe/Radio Liberty

Appendix 3.1*

The Mission of Radio Free Europe and Radio Liberty Broadcasts

The mission of Radio Free Europe and Radio Liberty is to encourage a constructive dialogue with the peoples of Eastern Europe and the Soviet Union by enhancing their knowledge of developments in the world at large and in their own countries. In openly communicating information and ideas to peoples restricted by censorship, RFE and RL help to maintain an informed public opinion in the USSR and Eastern Europe.

As media of news and news analysis RFE and RL observe high professional standards of accuracy, objectivity, timeliness and relevance to the interest of their audiences. RFE and RL are required by law to operate in a manner not inconsistent with the broad foreign policy objectives of the United States. Traditionally the United States has used its influence to promote basic principles of human dignity, individual freedom and the rule of law. The United States considers that the open communication of information and ideas can assist an orderly process of evolution in the USSR and Eastern Europe toward domestic and international policies more conducive to international understanding.

While the Voice of America concentrates on presenting US Government policy and projecting American society and institutions, RFE and RL reflect and project a diverse international awareness. Under American management and the statutory oversight of the Presidentially-appointed Board for International Broadcasting, the RFE/RL staff is composed of citizens of the United States, citizens of friendly European and other nations, and former citizens of the USSR and Eastern European nations. Together, they seek to create neither 'American radio', in the narrow national sense, nor 'exile radio', in the sense of organised political opposition, but international radio. It is international in the breadth of its coverage, its freedom from national or sectarian bias, its dedication to the open communication of accurate information and a broad range of democratic ideas. At the same time, it is 'local' in the sense that broadcast content is focused on the interests of the audiences.

*Reproduced from the Board for International Broadcasting, *Eighth Annual Report*, 1982

In pursuit of this mission, RFE/RL provide listeners, as accurately and quickly as possible, with knowledge of, and balanced perspective on, both the outside world and developments within their own societies. Specifically, RFE/RL programmes:
1   Report basic world news;
2   Provide comprehensive news and careful analysis of international affairs involving and affecting the peoples of the USSR and Eastern Europe, including all significant efforts to reduce East-West tensions and promote security and cooperation in Europe;
3   Communicate a broad range of world press reportage, analysis and opinion – as well as analyses based on their own expert research – on developments within the listeners' own countries;
4   Inform their specific audiences, through news and analysis based on expert research, of the particularities which distinguish various Communist-ruled societies and Communist parties from one another;
5   Broadcast and critically analyse documents and works of political significance and/or cultural merit which have been produced by citizens of the USSR or the Eastern European nations but have been denied official publication by censorship;
6   Provide timely, comprehensive coverage of political, economic social and cultural developments in the democratic societies of Europe as well as of North America.

In broadcasting about Eastern Europe and the USSR, RFE/RL programmes seek to make available to their listeners a more balanced perspective on events and trends than any single, official version can provide. RFE and RL do not identify themselves with any opposition group or groups, political party or organisation, located inside or outside the broadcast area. They espouse no single specific political, economic or religious creed. They are, however, committed to respect for human rights and to the principles of democracy, including freedom of opinion, the rule of law, and non-discrimination on the basis of race, sex, religion, or nationality. They are likewise committed to the free movement of people, goods and ideas between nations, and to the peaceful negotiation of international conflicts. By maintaining these values and observing high standards of accuracy, objectivity and timeliness, RFE and RL programmes should seek to earn the respect, if not necessarily the agreement, of present and potential listeners from all social and political groups.

In broadcasting about the United States and other free societies, RFE and RL should objectively report problems and setbacks as well as achievements, and maintain the critical distance from officials and official policies that is characteristic of responsible, independent international news media. They can do so by carefully reporting the open political, social and constitutional process through which problems are identified and approached, and proposed solutions are formulated, criticised, debated and reviewed in democratic societies. The view of the United States which RFE/RL listeners are enabled to form should be accurate and comprehensive, free of prejudice or exaggerated expectations.

Detailed programme-policy guidelines, including appropriate restraints, should assure the fulfilment of these objectives. Radio management is fully responsible for the day-to-day supervision of programme content in accordance with such guidelines. The Board for International Broadcasting is obliged by law to maintain a continuous review of the quality and effectiveness of RFE/RL broadcasts in order to fulfill its responsibility under the law that RFE/RL operate in a manner not inconsistent with broad US foreign policy objectives while maintaining professional independence and integrity. The Department of State assists the Board in carrying out its function by providing it with information regarding the foreign policy of the United States.

In broadcasting by shortwave to nations and regions with an aggregate population of more than 335 million people, RFE/RL observe demographic, historical and political priorities. At this time, an examination of those priorities, by language of broadcast, suggests the following broad groupings and relative degrees of importance:
I - Russian.
II - Polish, Romanian, Czech/Slovak, Hungarian, Ukrainian, Bulgarian.
III - Uzbek, Armenian, Georgian, Azeri, Belorussian, Tatar-Bashkir, Kazak, Lithuanian, Latvian, Estonian.
IV - Tajik, Turkmen, Kirghiz.

Insofar as practical, RFE/RL should avoid broadcasting in languages of III and IV simultaneously with the Voice of America.

Within this framework of priorities - which will be subject to continuing review - RFE/RL should concentrate its technical resources and personnel to fulfil its distinctive mission most effectively as part of a comprehensive US international broadcast policy.

Appendix 2*

RFE/RL Programme Policy Guidelines

Basic Framework. Radio Free Europe/Radio Liberty is an independent radio service to Eastern Europe and the Soviet Union authorised by the Congress of the United States and conducted under private American management as a team effort with men and women from East Europe and the Soviet Union, as well as West Europeans and others, RFE broadcasts to Bulgaria, Czechoslovakia, Hungary, Poland and Romania; RL broadcasts to the USSR and the Baltic States.

The purposes of RFE/RL are set forth in the Board for International Broadcasting Act of 1973, in which the US Congress finds and declares:

> That it is the policy of the United States to promote the right of freedom of opinion and expression, including the freedom "to seek, receive, and impart information and ideas through any media and regardless of frontiers", in accordance with article 19 of the Universal Declaration of Human Rights;
>
> That open communication of information and ideas among the peoples of the world contributes to international peace and stability, and that the promotion of such communication is in the interest of the United States;
>
> That Radio Free Europe and Radio Liberty have demonstrated their effectiveness in furthering the open communication of information and ideas in Eastern Europe and the USSR;
>
> That the continuation of Radio Free Europe and Radio Liberty as independent broadcast media, operating in a manner not inconsistent with the broad foreign policy objectives of the United States and in accordance with high professional standards, is in the national interest.

In order 'to encourage a constructive dialogue with the peoples of the Union of Soviet Socialist Republics and Eastern Europe,' the Act established the Board for International Broadcasting, which is authorised 'to review and evaluate the mission and operation of RFE/RL, and to assess the quality, effectiveness, and professional integrity of their broadcasting. ...' In conformity with the Act, the

*Reproduced from: the Board for International Broadcasting, Eighth Annual Report. 1982.

Radio Free Europe/Radio Liberty

Board issued on September 27, 1976, a statement on 'The Mission of Radio Free Europe and Radio Liberty Broadcasts' defining the objectives and priorities of RFE/RL programming.

These guidelines are designed to assure the fulfilment of those objectives, and the Board considers Radio management fully responsible for the day-to-day supervision of programme content in accordance with these guidelines.

The essence of RFE/RL's programme policy continues to be the practice of independent, professionally competent, and responsible broadcast journalism. RFE and RL provide uncensored news and information on domestic and relevant world affairs and convey a broad spectrum of ideas to audiences whose governments attempt to exercise a monopoly of information.

RFE and RL espouse no single specific political, economic or religious creed. They have no relationship to any political party or exile organisation; nor do they identify themselves with any opposition group or groups, political party or organisation, located inside or outside the broadcast area. RFE and RL are, however, committed to respect for human rights and to the principles of democracy, including freedom of opinion, the rule of law, and nondiscrimination on the basis of race, religion, sex, class, or nationality. They are non-sectarian, defending freedom of religious faith and observance for all creeds. They are committed to the free movement of people and ideas among nations; to cultural, scientific and economic exchange; and to the peaceful negotiation of international conflicts. They subscribe to the principle of equal rights and self-determination of peoples as expressed in the United Nations Charter and most recently affirmed by the Final Act of the Conference on European Security and Cooperation, which states that:

> By virtue of the principle of equal rights and self-determination of peoples, all peoples always have the right, in full freedom, to determine, when and as they wish, their internal and external political status, without external interference, and to pursue as they wish, their political, economic, social and cultural development.

In contrast to the Voice of America, whose primary mission is to present US policy and to project US society and institutions, RFE and RL seek to identify with the interests of their listeners, devoting particular attention to developments in and directly affecting the peoples of Eastern Europe and the USSR. In focussing on the special concerns of their audiences, they perform some of the functions of a 'home service' as well as a surrogate free press.

Editorial Policy. Assumptions and Techniques. In broadcasting to peoples lacking free access to information, RFE and RL proceed from the assumption that informed societies can make more responsible judgments about their own and world affairs, while misinformed societies may more easily be manipulated in directions threatening peace. RFE and RL further assume that the growth of an informed public opinion contributes towards moderating repressive or adventurous official policies. As information media and as a forum for many-sided analysis of public affairs, RFE and RL seek to encourage among their listeners a more balanced perspective on events and trends than any single official version can provide. They seek to draw their audiences into the climate of a more open world, in which their own problems as well as those common to many nations are discussed freely, objectively and without ideological or other prejudice.

The principal criterion for selection of broadcast materials is the relevance of the information to the needs and interests of the audience - i.e., whether such news, analysis, or other information will contribute to the listener's knowledge of significant developments and trends in and affecting his own area.

Accuracy and objectivity are essential to maintain listener respect. Inaccurate, biased or carelessly prepared material damages the reputation of RFE/RL. Objectivity requires that information neither be omitted nor slighted in broadcasting because it may seem favourable to the East or unfavourable to the West. Nor should information be broadcast only because it may seem unfavourable to the East or favourable to the West. The ability of RFE/RL to deliver information in balanced as well as timely fashion encourages domestic media to report faster, more objectively, and in a more comprehensive context.

RFE and RL seek to approach both the world scene and internal developments from the point of view of thoughtful individuals in the audience who wish to know, understand and form independent personal judgments on what is going on inside and outside their own countries. This approach requires constant attention to the most up-to-date knowledge of audience concerns, as well as awareness of the gaps and distortions in local media. The use of a variety of programme formats - news, interpretive analysis, surveys of world press comments, roundtable discussions, the verbatim reading of important documents - broadens the listeners' perspective.

The objective of 'filling the information gap' should not be understood in an exclusively political or narrowly local sense. The task of RFE/RL includes a comprehensive coverage of the many issues of concern to all humanity, such as technological and scientific advance, population growth, environmental pollution, urbanisation, the distribution and depletion of world resources, and the changing patterns of family life. With their full access to Western information and thought on these subjects, as well as their knowledge of conditions in the audience area, RFE and RL have a unique opportunity to provide a continuing flow of information, and a broad spectrum of analysis and ideas, on such complex issues of common concern.

In reporting on open societies, RFE and RL programmes should reflect their problems and setbacks as well as achievements. It is particularly important to reflect the open political, economic and social processes through which problems are identified and approached, and through which proposed solutions are formulated, criticised, debated and reviewed - by executive, legislative, and judicial branches of government at national, provincial and local levels; by the independent media of public opinion; and by private individuals, civic groups and political parties. Discussion of such economic issues as planning, management, agricultural productivity and foreign trade is most effectively related to the welfare of individual citizens and consumers. Comparisons between one or another society and the listener's own area may be drawn when required for context or perspective. However, invidious comparisons or criticism for criticism's sake should be avoided, and judgments should not be imposed on listeners.

Programming on the domestic affairs of the broadcast countries concentrates on keeping listeners informed of important developments in their country which are unpublicised, distorted or inadequately discussed by official media. Such information includes, when appropriate, the views of citizens who, denied access to the public media of their country, seek expression through foreign correspondents or by means of uncensored (<u>samizdat</u>) writings. The content of <u>samizdat</u> or other documents originating in Eastern Europe or the USSR should be carefully scrutinised prior to broadcast use; the same applies to the content of exile press material and organisational statements. Comment on domestic affairs should be constructive, calm and reasoned and deal with important issues, directed toward clarification of specific problems. Critical comment on governmental policies or practices in the area should be based on solid knowledge of the facts involved and expressed in responsible fashion. If possible, such critical comments include constructive elements, such as explanations of how similar problems are handled elsewhere. Overall, the purpose of RFE/RL in discussing domestic affairs is to provide full and honest information, broader perspective, and a responsible forum for a diversity of views. RFE/RL do not prescribe programmatic solutions nor offer final conclusions.

Since official ideology often fosters distortion of the historical past, RFE/RL also offer listeners basic historical and cultural materials on the heritage of their own areas. Historical events should be approached in a critical as well as tolerant spirit, avoiding chauvinistic or sectarian bias. Historical and cultural programmes should be chosen for their relevance to the present concerns of the audience. Discourse and description, rather than lecturing, offer the appropriate format for such programmes.

'Cross-reporting', a very important technique, conveys to RFE/RL audiences objective information on developments in Communist countries other than their own and in the case of RL, in different parts of the USSR as well. This is a vital function because conditions vary considerably, and because official media coverage is often inadequate or distorted. Programmes also pay special attention to developments in nonruling Communist parties, especially those in which lively debate is currently occurring on basic ideological and political terms. Cross-report programmes make extensive use of RFE/RL research analyses as well as of Western and Communist-published materials.

RFE's and RL's newscasts are among the most important components of their broadcasting. The quality of newscasts helps set the tone for the credibility of the entire programme output. The news must be accurate, objective, timely, interesting and relevant to the concerns of the listeners. Materials made available for newscasts must be thoroughly verified by news personnel as to facts and sources, as well as to avoid any suggestion of bias or sensationalism in news presentation. Confirmation by two independent sources is required when facts appear to be in doubt; clear attribution to the source is required when the information content clearly constitutes opinion or can be considered partial or self-serving.

Newscasts are supplemented by news analysis, correspondents' reports, and press review programmes which reflect a broad variety of American, European and, if possible, world opinion on major international developments and questions of significance to the audience. Interviews and roundtable discussions, preferably with the participation of outside experts, provide a useful means of airing the clash of opinions on controversial issues. Although decisions on day-to-day programme content to the largest extent possible reflect the outstanding issues of the day, programming on longer-term problems and trends should not be neglected. Advance programme planning is essential to assure greater depth and attention to broad, less immediate issues.

RFE/RL programmes must recognise the special aural problems of absorbing information, as well as those of broadcasting in conditions of jamming. Preoccupation with programme content should not be at the expense of attractive format. Individual programmes, as well as the overall format of broadcast schedules, should be presented at the highest possible level of modern broadcasting practices. RFE and RL will continue to study and adapt new radio techniques. Analyses of radio listening patterns among the audience, research on the changing patterns of populations in the broadcast area, and careful attention to new trends in domestic radio and television services should form the basis for a continuous re-evaluation and updating of programme formats and schedules.

<u>Restraints</u>. Tone, language, and manner of presentation are as important in adhering to RFE/RL policy as broadcast content. Therefore, the following restraints will continue to be observed:
1   Avoidance   of   emotionalism,   vituperation,

vindictiveness, stridency, belligerency, arrogance, pomposity, pretentiousness or condescension.

2   Avoidance of sweeping generalisation, propagandistic argumentation, gratuitous value judgments, unsupported criticism of the Communist system or its representatives, as well as the use of obsolete or inaccurate terminology such as 'the Communist bloc', 'Communist satellite countries', and 'capitalism vs communism'. While RFE and RL are concerned with correcting the gaps and distortions in the official media, they do so by presenting the facts, avoiding polemical treatment of the kind the audiences are known to resent.

3   Avoidance of any programming, the content of which could be legitimately construed as inflammatory or conducive to irredentism. Judgment must be exercised as to the potentially inflammatory nature of any programme.

4   Avoidance of any comment or broadcast of any material which could be reasonably construed as incitement to revolt or support for illegal and violent actions. Programmers may, however, remind listeners of standards governing basic civil rights as outlined in domestic legislation, international agreements which Soviet or East European states have obligated themselves to observe, and such internationally accepted documents as the Universal Declaration of Human Rights.

5   Avoidance of tactical advice, by which is meant recommendations for specific action in particular cases, except in unusual circumstances, and then only to calm moods in tense situations. The peoples of East Europe and the USSR, provided they know the relevant facts, are better qualified to judge the efficacy and consequences of their actions than anyone outside the countries. Such advice is likely to be resented and, if acted upon, could cause harm to the people involved.

6   No programmes will be broadcast which are based upon or use rumours or unsubstantiated information. If, under unusual circumstances, a constructive purpose will be served by calling attention to a prevalent rumour, it will clearly be identified as such.

7   Editorial opinions, whether by RFE/RL staff, in press reviews, or originating in <u>samizdat</u> documents or exile organisational statements, shall be clearly distinguished from news and news analysis and the source of the opinion identified.

8   Avoidance of any programming that could be construed as encouraging defections. No information

on 'how to defect' will be broadcast, and programmes on defectors living in the West will carefully avoid any suggestion that others should follow their example.
9   Avoidance of any suggestion that might lead audiences to believe that, in the event of international crisis or civil disorder, the West might intervene militarily in any part of the broadcast area.
10 Avoidance of any material which could be characterised as petty gossip, slander, spiteful reference to or attack on the personal lives or families of government or party leaders, or on individuals as such. The discussion of public acts of public officials should be conducted in a dignified, dispassionate, responsible manner.
11 With regard to attacks on RFE and RL themselves in East European and Soviet media, no comment or response shall be made without prior consultation on its form and content with the directors of the appropriate radio.
12 In the event of emergency conditions affecting the broadcast area, the directors of RFE and RL will consult with the Chief Executive Officer or his designated alternate. No programmes referring to these conditions will be broadcast by any RFE or RL language service prior to such consultation.

East European and Soviet Audiences. While the above principles of RFE/RL editorial policy are binding on all language services, they should be implemented with due regard for the fact that their audiences are not homogeneous. Unique circumstances distinguish country from country and region from region. Nuances in approach are essential to address differing audiences effectively. While adherence to the principles above is essential to assure that RFE/RL programming is consistent, due regard for the specificity of differing audiences is essential.

The five nations of Eastern Europe to which RFE broadcasts and the three Baltic States have been and are more exposed than is the USSR to Western information, ideas, economic and cultural influences. Although under Soviet domination, these nations in varying degree regard themselves as part of the West or of the European family of nations. Western thought and cultural values are broadly accepted by large elements of the population, which aspire to participation in the economic, cultural, and political life of Europe.

In broadcasting to areas which have suffered greatly from nationalistic excesses, it is essential that RFE avoid any programming that could be construed by East European listeners as reinforcing cultural or national prejudices toward other East European nations, toward the Russian people or toward other nationalities of the USSR. Cross-reporting to Eastern Europe regarding Soviet developments, in particular the discussion of dissenting Soviet opinion, contributes to the awareness that unofficial thought in the Soviet Union shares much in common with that in Eastern Europe.

Radio Liberty's audience ranges from the highly Westernised Baltic nations to the Islamic peoples of Central Asia whose contact is mostly with other Islamic countries. Official ideology, Soviet censorship, and rigid restrictions on freedom of movement have for many years impeded the peoples of the USSR from coming into closer contact with non-Communist countries and tended to reinforce the sense of belonging to a sui generis culture and society.

In view of the prolonged isolation and continuing insulation of Soviet society from the diversity of the contemporary world, RL faces the continuing challenge of contributing to the growth of sophistication among its various audiences. However, this cannot be achieved by indiscriminate exaltation of purely Western values, or by criticism of the Soviet system in purely Western terms. Listeners should be presented with examples of the process of free discussion, with a variety of opinions and evaluations of both national and international problems.

RL and RFE make available to audiences a broad spectrum of thought concerning issues of political, social and economic organisation. This spectrum should encompass unorthodox Soviet and East European as well as non-Soviet, non-East European, Marxist thought; information on the practice of socialism in other countries; and current non-Marxist political and economic theory.

RL and RFE serve Soviet and East European citizens by airing and discussing their own views which are denied an opportunity for expression in public media by censorship. They act as a forum for indigenous political, social, religious and philosophical thought, without permitting their programmes to become the vehicles for any single point of view.

RL's broadcasting in the major languages of the USSR reflects its commitment to the right of nationalities to be informed and to communicate in their own languages. RL neither supports nor encourages any separatist or secessionist movement, and does not raise territorial issues.

While broadly committed to basic principles of human rights, the rule of law and nondiscrimination among peoples, RFE/RL have no mandate to advocate the establishment or disestablishment of any particular system, form of state organisation, or ideology in the areas to which they broadcast.

RL scrupulously avoids stimulating any antagonism among the peoples of the Soviet Union. It sympathises, however, with the right of all national groups to thrive, to be able to display pride in their historical and cultural achievements, and to express themselves in their own language. RL also supports the right of individuals freely to assert their national origins as well as their religious and political convictions and to be secure against discrimination on these accounts.

RFE and RL programmes express respect for all peoples, religions, and culture and should under no circumstances fan or fuel chauvinism. They should contribute to better understanding of one another among national groups; to recognition of shared concerns among the peoples of the USSR, as well as the nations of Eastern Europe, for the right of unfettered development and progress; and to a broader perception of the interdependence of nations and peoples in the modern world.

If necessary, supplementary programme policy guidelines may be issued for the use of individual RFE or RL language services. These will develop the general principles set forth in the present document with specific reference to the needs of a particular audience.

Chapter Five

THE VOICE PAST: VOA, THE USSR AND COMMUNIST EUROPE

Alan Heil, director VOA Broadcast Operations, and Barbara Schiele, research analyst, VOA Broadcast Operations

On 24th February 1942, during its first moments on the air the Voice of America promised its listeners:

> Here in America we receive news from all over the world. The news may be favourable or unfavourable. Every day we shall bring you this news - the truth. (1)

Those critical sentences were not simply a newswriter's dramatic opening, but policy based on conviction. Robert Sherwood, the successful playwright who had persuaded President Roosevelt to establish the Foreign Information Service (FIS), VOA's first organisational home, believed that 'The truth coming from America, with unmistakable American sincerity, is by far the most effective form of propaganda.' (2) Sherwood's theory of the power and potential of truthful information became the Voice of America's commitment and the cornerstone on which the station was built.

VOA's first broadcasts originated in three tiny studios at 270 Madison Avenue in New York. In the summer of 1942, the rapidly-expanding broadcast service moved to new and larger quarters at the corner of Broadway and 57th Street, and to a new organisational home - the Office of War Information (OWI). By July 1944, VOA broadcast operations reached their wartime peak. Some 119 hours of programming in 50 languages and dialects were transmitted daily. (3) A year later, the war was finally over. OWI was demobilised on 31st August, 1945 but its Overseas Branch, continued to operate as the Interim International Information Service (IIIS) until 31st December, 1945, when it became the Department of State's Office of Information and Cultural Affairs (OIC).

During those first post-war years, maintenance of the foreign broadcast and information services in peacetime was hardly a popular cause in either branch of government, and the weakened OIC services struggled to operate without adequate authorisation or resources. VOA had begun peacetime broadcasts as a significantly smaller service. In the last months of 1945, its personnel ranks were slashed by half and programming reduced to less than 65 hours daily in 24 languages. By 1947, minds in Washington were changing. A year later, the Smith-Mundt bill provided legislative recognition that international broadcasting and other overseas information programmes were a requirement of post-war diplomacy.

In the words of veteran diplomat and VOA director Charles Thayer 'The efforts of Radio Moscow, combined with the more brutal persuasions of the Soviet armies in Eastern Europe,' proved convincing evidence of the need for continuing, and indeed expanding, VOA broadcasts.' (4) Thayer's first assignment at VOA was to begin Russian language broadcasts. This initiative had been urgently advocated by diplomats familiar with the Soviet Union, including Averell Harriman. Resources for the new broadcasts, launched on 17th February, 1947, were so scarce, Thayer recalled, that volunteers, including Harriman's daughter Kathleen, were recruited to help in the studios.

In addition to the initiation of Russian broadcasts, changes in other VOA programming were also begun. VOA broadcasts, Thayer wrote, had continued to reflect the 'friendly relations' which had existed betwen the Soviet Union and the United States during the war and a reorientation was necessary. Thus, two years after the war, the VOA broadcasts turn its listeners' attention from what the Nazis had done in Europe to Soviet actions. The programming reflected the realities of the times - the Berlin blockade in 1948, President Harry S. Truman's 'Campaign of Truth' in April 1950 and the outbreak of the Korean War in June of that year. Existing broadcast services were expanded, new services were inaugurated in the Baltic and non-Russian languages of the Soviet Union, and in October 1951, VOA opened its European outpost - the Munich Program Centre.

In his 1959 book <u>Diplomat</u>, Thayer reviewed those years in VOA's history. Although some experienced diplomats at that time advised the Voice to adopt a cool, dispassionate, almost impartial attitude in addressing its Soviet audience, he recalled, VOA was anxious to prove its worth to the Congress and the public and, 'We frequently fell to the temptation of broadcasting bitterly sarcastic, almost vitriolic, anti-Stalinist attacks ... The result was that the programmes lost much of their credibility.' Thayer also predicted the future of the foreign information programme: 'That it is essential to our defence against totalitarian diplomacy is indisputable. That it will develop into a powerful auxiliary arm of American diplomacy depends on whether its leaders and Congress understand its proper role, its limitations, and its need not for numbers but for qualified personnel.'

The cold war in Europe and the hot war in Korea led to increased VOA broadcasts as well as changes in the programme content and tone in the early 1950s. In June 1950, VOA was broadcasting fewer than 30 hours daily in 23 languages; but a year later, it was transmitting nearly 50 hours daily in 45 languages. Among the new or restored broadcasts to Eastern Europe and the USSR were Albanian, Estonian, Latvian, Lithuanian, Slovene, Armenian, Azerbaijani, Georgian, Tatar and Turkestani. The expansions peaked in 1952 and reductions began in 1953 - partly because of the end of the Korean War, partly as a result of the McCarthy hearings, and partly because of the recommendations of a Presidential commission.

As is widely known, the VOA and its parent organisation were for a time the object of Senator Joseph McCarthy's search for Communist influence in the US Government. Although none of the allegations raised were proven, there were disastrous results from the hearings including a delay in the construction of a transmitter network that was to ring the Soviet bloc. After the McCarthy hearings, the core of the plan - two large domestic relay stations - were abandoned. It wasn't until ten years later that the replacement for the originally-scheduled east coast station went on the air from Greenville, North Carolina. (5) The hearings may also have contributed to the severe reduction in VOA's 1954 budget, which was slashed from $22 to $16 million. (6) Funds earmarked for VOA's move to Washington were, however, untouched. Thus VOA moved into its present headquarters in Washington, equipped then with 14 studios and a 'master control' panel. Much of the same complex is still in service today.

Concurrently in 1953, President Eisenhower's committee on international information activities, chaired by William H. Jackson, a former deputy

The Voice Past

director of the CIA, was looking intently at the information programmes. The committee's appraisal, submitted to the President on 30th June, 1953, led to the separation of information activities from the State Department and the formation of US Information Agency (USIA). The Jackson committee also recommended that USIA broadcasts and publications 'concentrate on objective, factual news reporting', avoid 'a propagandist note', but make 'forceful and factual refutations of false Soviet accusations'. Responding to the committee's critiques on broadcasting, VOA director Leonard Erkison maintained that there should be a distinction between 'broadcasts to Iron Curtain listeners, who have a strong emotional need for a hard-hitting anti-Communist message and broadcasts to free world listeners, who tend to be hypersensitive to a propagandistic approach.' The Jackson committee also questioned spending a third of the budget on broadcasts to the Soviet Union since little was known about the audience or the effectiveness of jamming. Despite the Jackson committee's appraisal, most VOA broadcasts to the USSR were continued, but the Tatar, Turkestani and Azerbaijani language services were eliminated. (7)

Between 1954 and 1957, VOA programming become considerably less strident notes Professor Donald Browne of the University of Minnesota. (8) Certainly, the charges raised after the Hungarian revolution in 1956 that VOA broadcasts had helped incite the rebellion were refuted by subsequent reviews. USIA research director Oren Stephens' detailed study of programme content before, during, and after the rebellion, for example, noted that VOA broadcasts during the crisis were almost exclusively newcasts and coverage of special events such as the UN debates. 'There was,' Stephens concluded, 'No hint whatsoever of any possibility of American aid in arms or men,' except for American assistance through the Red Cross or to the refugees who had fled the country. (9)

The Stephens review did, however, criticize other aspects of VOA programming in 1956, including the output of the Munich Programme Centre (MPC), which had been originating entire broadcasts for Eastern Europe and the Soviet Union since 1951. The circumstances which led to establishment of the centre, he felt, no longer existed. If broadcasts were to continue to originate in Munich, there would have to be closer VOA-MPC coordination to 'prevent a cleavage in tone and approach and news duplication

The Voice Past

which now prevail'. His view was shared by Henry Loomis, who became VOA's director in July, 1958. Loomis felt that the 'MPC had been set up to do what Radio Free Europe was now doing' (10) and one of his first actions at VOA was to transform MPC from an originating station into an overseas news bureau of VOA Washington covering Eastern as well as Western Europe. It should be noted that other 'programme centres' met similar fates, including the African programme centre which operated in Monrovia, and the Arabic programme centre on the Isle of Rhodes. On the other hand, VOA overseas correspondent bureaus with no direct broadcast responsibilities have flourished and continue to multiply. Today, there are 21 Voice news bureaus outside the United States, including those in London, Paris, Munich, Vienna, Geneva and Rome.

Henry Loomis was to serve at VOA from July, 1958, until March, 1965, and during his tenure - which spanned the Eisenhower, Kennedy and Johnson administrations - there were two significant developments concerning Voice broadcasting to the Soviet Union and Eastern Europe. One was the VOA Charter, which outlined the programming content principles which still govern the organisation. The other was the development of VOA's worldwide transmitter system. The Greenville, Marathon, Liberia, and Rhodes relay stations all went on the air during the Loomis years. The Rhodes project laid the basis for later transmitter construction in northern Greece, which was of immense importance in strengthening VOA's reach into the Soviet Union and Eastern Europe.

VOA programming changed significantly during the 1960s. More live broadcasts (in English and the major foreign languages such as Russian and Spanish) imparted a new sense of presence to VOA broadcasts. Listeners were transported to the scene during some of the nation's most tragic moments and some of its greatest. They could hear live accounts of the John F. Kennedy funeral in Arlington in 1963 and the words of Neil Armstrong as he set foot on the moon in 1969.

John Chancellor, VOA's director from 1965-67, stressed a new style of international broadcasting: brief, fresh and timely news and features. Chancellor understood the significance of that special relationship between broadcaster and listener that is so important to effective radio communication. He described it on VOA's 25th anniversary in 1967:

There is something magic about these studios,

something that leads one to a deeper understanding of the basic significance of the Voice of America. Every day, almost every hour, from the second floor at 330 Independence Avenue, SW, there exists a link to someone in another country. When the Russian service goes on the air late every morning, radios are switched on throughout wide parts of the Soviet Union. And that broadcaster sitting in front of a VOA microphone is suddenly speaking into the ears of people in dachas, barracks, farmhouses, offices and apartments. The United States is on the air. The broadcasters at the Voice understand this magic link, because the reality they perceive is the reality of the listener. For the VOA Russian broadcasters, it is no longer noon on a bright sunny day near the Capitol in Washington, but early evening in Leningrad, Moscow, Kiev. They realise the basic fact which makes the VOA important: that the studios in Washington are really foreign posts. They understand that micro seconds after they speak, what they say is communicated to people in bedrooms, living rooms, tents, cars, caravans, as they enter the world of the listener. The official corridors of Washington fade, and the broadcasters are with the listeners. It is essential that this connection be understood, for without this knowledge, no understanding is possible of what I unashamedly call the magic of the Voice.

During the 1960s, this magic reached listeners in the Soviet Union and Eastern Europe to a greater extent than in any previous decade. One reason was the first prolonged cessation of jamming of VOA by the Soviet Union since Joseph Stalin initiated it in February, 1948. For the Voice of America, there have been two protracted periods free of Soviet jamming: 1963-68 and 1973-80. Dr Maury Lisann, a specialist on international broadcasting, who studied the Soviet decision to lift jamming in 1963, concluded that the Soviet leadership then hoped that the spread of domestic television, coupled with improved news reporting on domestic radio, would draw the Russian public away from foreign broadcasts.

Because the Soviet system and processing information was so cumbersome, self censorship among Soviet journalists was so ingrained, the Soviet listeners were so curious about world and domestic events, the experiment failed. (11) The influence of foreign broadcasts increased, and the Soviet invasion of Czechoslovakia in August, 1968 was accompanied by a resumption of jamming.

Five years later, Soviet jamming of VOA was once again lifted - from September 1973 until August 1980. The second cessation preceded the 35-nation Helsinki accords under which the United States, the Soviet Union and the other signatories agreed to permit a free flow of ideas across national borders consistent with the United Nations Charter and Article 48 of the Montreux International Telecommunications Convention. However, events in Eastern Europe and an extension of Soviet military power in Afghanistan provided the background for a resumption of Soviet jamming of VOA broadcasts in 1980. The action was taken as the Solidarity labour movement was extending its influence in an unprecedented fashion in Poland, and less than eight months after the Soviet invasion of Afghanistan.

Three times in its history, VOA has engaged in 'saturation broadcasts' to the Soviet Union aimed at overriding jamming. The first (nicknamed VOA's Sunday Punch) was on 5th November, 1961 and carried news accounts of world reaction to the Soviet government's secret, protracted high-megaton nuclear testing. A year later, on 24th October, VOA used 52 transmitters with a total power of 4,331,000 watts to report on the US quarantine of Cuba. The third occasion was in September, 1973, when VOA added Russian broadcast hours and grouped transmitters to intensify coverage of global reaction to the Soviet downing of the Korean airliner. Jamming is prohibitively expensive. Studies of current jamming in Eastern Europe and the Soviet Union indicate that operations require the services of from 7,500 to 10,000 technicians. Estimates of annual costs range from $150,000,000 to $300,000,000. (12)

Currently, VOA broadcasts in the following languages are jammed: Armenian, Azerbaijani, Dari, Estonian, Georgian, Latvian, Lithuanian, Pashto, Polish, Russian, Ukrainian and Uzbek. VOA Bulgarian was jammed from 1981 to 1983, resumed briefly during the summer of 1984, but has now ceased again.

A few months after jamming was lifted in September, 1973, there was a debate on Voice of America content with significant implications for broadcasts to the Soviet Union and Eastern Europe. The discussion centred on the extent to which Voice current affairs and language service programmes might treat Alexander Solzhenitsyn's <u>Gulag Archipelago</u>. Comprehensive VOA news coverage of

The Voice Past

Gulag's publication and global reaction was never in doubt. Between 29th December, 1973, when the book was released, and the first week of March, 1974, VOA's Russian service broadcast 387 reports and features on the subject, including comments by President Nixon and other world leaders, and analyses by reviewers in the United States and elsewhere. Questions arose, however, about whether or not the Voice should depart from programming practice of the preceding years and broadcast substantial excerpts of the text of Gulag Archipelago. In the words of USIA director James Keogh:

> VOA has covered this developing story just as it traditionally covered other aspects of the dissident movement in the USSR. USIA's approach is exactly the same now as it was before the Soviet Union ceased jamming in September without our foreknowledge and without explanation. Soviet officials are criticising this policy. We are holding to it. What we do not do - as the official radio voice of the United States - is indulge in polemics aimed at changing the internal structure of the Soviet Union. To read from the book would be far outside the normal style of Voice of America programming and would tend to reinforce Soviet charges that the United States is utilising these events as a political weapon and is intervening in the domestic affairs of the USSR. USIA has not muted its Voice. At the same time, we have not acceded to suggestions that we turn backward to the old cold war style of broadcasting. (13)

The Keogh view prevailed as broadcast policy, but was questioned by several senior Voice officials and members of Congress. In the words of one draft guidance paper prepared at VOA, 'Broadcasting material about the book without extensive use of excerpts has the disadvantage of not adequately providing the flavour of the book. In effect, it tells the audience what others thought of the controversy without giving the substance of the book so that the listeners themselves would make up their minds and evaluate the facts against the stream of distortions delivered against the author by the domestic (Soviet) media.' (14)

In the words of Representative Bob Sikes of Florida, to forego broadcasting passages from Gulag, 'Would be a distinct disservice to people who listen

The Voice Past

to the VOA and it would bring about a loss of confidence in statements we've made so many times that we tell it like it is.' (15)

The controversy over handling of the widely-discussed Gulag Archipelago was one of several which affected VOA in the mid-1970s. In handling one of the most sensitive domestic stories of the post-war period, Watergate, the Voice was lauded by the Wall Street Journal and other newspapers for its accuracy and thoroughness. In the words of Professor Donald Browne 'VOA coverage of Watergate, which most reporters had described as comprehensive, balanced and carefully analytical, reminded critics and VOA staff alike that the Voice did win some credibility battles'. (16)

Debates over programme content are inherent in any broadcast organisation, but especially those which are funded by governments. In the words of Gerard Mansell, the former managing director of the BBC External Services:

> There is, of course, a contradiction in terms between a free press, on the one hand, and the sponsorship by government of a powerful means of disseminating information which it alone controls. The system is only tolerable if governments exercise restraint and if constitutional means are found to distance the broadcasters from their paymasters so that they may get on with the job without undue interference. (17)

For VOA, 'constitutional means' became available on 12th July 1976. That was the date President Ford signed the VOA Charter into law.

The development of a permanent framework to govern VOA broadcasts and provide a means for resolving disputes concerning broadcast output actually began in the late 1950s. Conflicts about programming had erupted periodically since 1943 and generally stemmed from divergent views of two basic issues: (1) the possible impact of VOA on US policy initiatives - the Solzhenitsyn - Gulag episode is a pertinent example; and (2) whether VOA broadcasts serve US interests best by simply informing, or by persuading, listeners. The VOA Charter, outlining principles which would govern the broadcasts, was first issued as a US Information Agency directive in 1959, and VOA authority to determine its own programme content was prescribed in an instruction issued by USIA director Frank Shakespeare on 9th

The Voice Past

June, 1970. By 1975, however, two privately-sponsored panels, the Commission on the Government for the Conduct of Foreign Policy (the Murphy Commission) and the Panel on International Information, Education, and Cultural Relations (the Stanton panel) still felt that VOA broadcasts would be more effective if the Voice became an autonomous government agency. The US Congress, however, chose another means to resolve the question of content integrity at VOA by changing the VOA Charter from a USIA directive into Public Law 94-350, signed by President Ford the week after the nation's bicentennial anniversary. The VOA Charter mandates that:

> The long-range interests of the United States are served by communicating directly with the people of the world by radio. To be effective, the Voice of America (the broadcasting service of the United States Information Agency) must win the attention and respect of listeners. These principles will therefore govern the Voice of America (VOA) broadcasts:
> 1. VOA will serve as a consistently reliable and authoritative source of news. VOA news will be accurate, objective and comprehensive.
> 2. VOA will represent America, not any single segment of American society, and will therefore present a balanced and comprehensive projection of significant American thought and institutions.
> 3. VOA will present the policies of the United States clearly and effectively and will also present responsible discussion and opinion on these policies.

Since 1977, every American President and every USIA director have endorsed Public Law 94-350. USIA and Voice directives based on the document have enhanced the Voice's ability to inform its listeners. In May, 1977, USIA director John Reinhardt issued a statement subscribing fully to the principles of the Charter and re-affirming that VOA is solely responsible for the content of its newscasts. Later that same year, former Washington Post national correspondent Chalmers Roberts headed a panel of broadcast and print media journalists which evaluated VOA's foreign correspondents and recommended that they operate under guidelines which clarified their status as bona fide news gatherers. Since 1978, VOA correspondents have been administratively separate from US embassies and missions, have travelled with regular rather than official passports, and leased office space overseas as commercial news organisations do.

Despite the changes, allegations persisted that Voice programming about the Soviet Union was equivocal. Alexander Solzhenitsyn himself charged in a <u>Foreign Affairs</u> article in May, 1980, that Voice directors, 'are constantly trying not to arouse the anger of the Soviet leadership. In their zeal to serve détente they remove everything from their programmes which might irritate the Communists in power'. (18) The Solzhenitsyn contention followed months of prominent coverage by the Voice of the Soviet invasion of Afghanistan, including live reportage in Russian from the United Nations of the General Assembly's 104-nation condemnation of the invasion. Moreover, unlike 1974 and the <u>Gulag</u> affair, VOA's Russian service carried substantial excerpts of Andrei Sakharov's writings when the Nobel prize-winning physicist was exiled to Gorky. Audience data indicated that the Voice was then, and remains today, far and away the most listened-to foreign broadcaster in the Soviet Union.

John H. Trattner, a former State Department spokesman and VOA broadcaster, assessed the criticisms of the Voice on the op-ed page of the <u>New York Times</u> in early 1982. It is important, he wrote, that purists on both sides of the 'news versus propaganda' argument be clear about three things:

> First, the integrity of its news is the key to the Voice of America's success. Second, each Administration has title to use the government's radio station to present and explain its foreign policy ideas and actions. Third, applying these truths cannot ignore what is most important of all: the overseas listeners .... Many correctly sense that the Voice's news is guided not by what serves policy goals of the moment, but by what quite simply, is news. (19)

The opinions of listeners are the ultimate test of the broadcaster's effectiveness. As Gerald Mansell wrote in March 1982:

> What matters is the view taken by the listener of the accuracy and dependability of what he is hearing and the picture he forms in his mind of motives of the broadcasters. There is no greater error than to think of the listener's mind as an

empty vessel, or as putty to be shaped at will by the broadcaster. It simply does not work. (20)

The VOA Charter expresses this thought in a single phrase - VOA 'must win the attention and respect of listeners'. Survey figures help to measure VOA's audience size and composition, and listeners write to the Voice or tell others about VOA broadcasts. Here are some comments from the Soviet Union and Eastern Europe:

*A defecting KGB agent, interviewed by The Times in May, 1980, said the penchant of Soviet journalists and intelligence operatives to report what they believe Moscow wants to hear cannot last because of the growing popularity of international broadcasts. 'Ninety-nine per cent of the Soviets who are interested in politics listen to BBC or VOA, as indeed do the Soviet leaders ... With the immense growth in the influence of BBC and VOA in recent years, Soviet authorities have reassessed their propaganda effort. Last year, a central committee directive called for a more persuasive approach and less "gray" attempts at window dressing.'

*A week after VOA's Russian service recounted the end of World War Two in Asia in a 1980 historical series, Pravda columnist Marshall Ustinov complained that the 'transoceanic falsifiers of history' distorted the glorious Soviet victory over Japan. Only three months later, however Alexander Solzhenitsyn wrote to the Voice: 'I am a constant and grateful listener to your historical broadcasts Thirty-five Years ago. I also received requests from the USSR to thank you for these broadcasts and to ask you to continue them in their present form ....'

*A Financial Times article by Paul Lendvai (in November 1980) quoted a leading Warsaw intellectual, who said that 'international broadcasting is more than the only source of full information for our people. It is also our most important ally in the battle against domestic or foreign oppression.'

*In early 1981, a Czech dissident and Charter 77 signatory who had recently been expelled and settled in Canada, telephoned VOA to say that dissidents in Czechoslovakia listen to VOA even in prison, where they use radios smuggled in by relatives or guards. The Charter 77 membership, the caller said, was grateful to the Czech-Slovak Service for its coverage of human rights.

*In early 1983, a prominent Czech dissident

The Voice Past

released from a Czech prison and allowed to emigrate to West Germany sent VOA the following recorded message: 'The Voice of America is the radio station most listened to in all of Czechoslovakia. Many people in the government, while they could not admit to it, listen eagerly to VOA, (which) is called Prague 3. I would personally like to thank our friends at the Voice of America for the important information they provide and for the encouragement they give to people trying to survive the terror that surrounds them everyday.'

*John Kifner, Warsaw correspondent for the <u>New York Times</u>, reported (in a despatch dated 30th March, <u>1984</u>) that there is not a single word about crucifixes in the Polish press ... people hunched over short-wave radios learn about this and other issues through despatches filed by western resident correspondents that are then broadcast back by Voice of America, Radio Free Europe, the BBC and the French radio. A Polish journalist told him that, 'I spend all evening dialling the radio. It is necesssary.'

These comments on the impact of VOA broadcasts in the Soviet Union and Eastern Europe coincide with extensive efforts by VOA's Russian service to make its programming more relevant. In May, 1984, VOA's director of Russian broadcasts, Mark Pomar, travelled to Vermont to interview Alexander Solzhenitsyn about his latest literary work, <u>August 1914</u> (Volumes 1 and 2). In the 25-minute conversation, Mr Solzhenitsyn spoke about the novel, his investigations of Russian history, and about his work in general. Mr Solzhenitsyn also recorded several hours of readings from Volume 2. VOA Russian is now in the process of broadcasting a 25-part series of programmes incorporating the readings. Mr Solzhenitsyn said he granted the interview as a token of his appreciation for what he called 'the many positive changes that have taken place in VOA Russian Service programming.'

Aside from improved programming, a significant thrust of the VOA strategy in the 1980s is desperately needed modernisation of its facilities. Technically, America's Voice is very weak. Years of neglect in capital improvements – an experience common to many international broadcasts – have taken an especially heavy toll at the Voice. More than 80 per cent of VOA's 108 transmitters are 15 years old or older; more than 35 per cent are 30 years or older. VOA has six 500 kilowatt superpower transmitters (actually combinations of aged 250

KWs), compared to 37 modern units used by the Soviet Union and its Eastern European allies.

Senior management, with the support of the Reagan Administration and the Congress, has launched a $1 billion modernisation programme, expected to extend over the next five years. Agreements have been reached in the past year with Sri Lanka, Morocco, Thailand and Costa Rica to build new relay stations or add to existing sites. New transmitters will be constructed to enhance the Voice signal in the Soviet Union, Eastern Europe and elsewhere. For 1985, the Congress has authorised the expenditure of $85 million for Voice modernisation. During the past year, news bureaus have been added in Geneva, Islamadad, Costa Rica, and one reopened in Rome.

A decade ago, VOA director Kenneth R. Giddens campaigned consistently for sufficient resources to strengthen VOA programming and engineering. His efforts did not yield results until just before he left the Voice, in April, 1977. Based on several studies conducted in 1976, the Carter Administration recommended to Congress that new transmitters be constructed by both VOA and RFE/RL. The Voice subsequently received authorisation for 12 new transmitters. Even with this expansion, Voice facilities were taxed to capacity. As director Giddens had pointed out, the Voice too frequently was reacting to, rather than anticipating, needs because of limited resources. The Soviet Union began expanding its Dari and Pashto broadcasts in 1978, a year ahead of the Afghanistan invasion. VOA broadcasts in Dari did not begin until 1980, and in Pashto in 1982. Following the resumption of Soviet jamming and in 1980, programmes in Russian, Armenian, Georgian and the Baltic languages were increased by the Voice in January, 1981. Polish broadcasts were expanded from two and a half to seven hours daily about a year later, several weeks after Warsaw's declaration of martial law.

A 1982 study of Voice of America programming and facilities recommended expansions in broadcast hours and languages (especially to Eastern Europe and the Soviet Union), and the necessity of acquiring new high-powered transmitters, especially those beamed on regions where there is jamming. The VOA modernisation of the 1980s is fully supported by the Reagan Adminstration.

At a signing ceremony in March, 1984 marking agreement with Morocco for construction of new VOA transmitters in that country, President Reagan summed up the past and present of Voice broadcasting to the Soviet Union, Eastern Europe and other areas of the world:

> The Voice of America has been a strong voice for truth. Despite problems of jamming, the Voice of America has been able to spread its message of truth around the world. Were it not for many years of neglect, the Voice of America could be heard more clearly by many more people around the globe. And that's why our Administration has made the same kind of commitment to modernising the Voice of America that President Eisenhower and President Kennedy brought to the space programme. It's our firm commitment to the Voice of America which brings us here today.

Notes

1. John Houseman, Front and Center (Simon & Schuster, New York, 1979), p.37.
2. Houseman, Front and Center, p.28.
3. Robert Pirsein, Voice of America (Arno Press, New York, 1979), pp.91-2.
4. Charles Thayer, Diplomat (Harper & Brothers, New York 1979), pp. 189,200.
5. Pirsein, Voice, pp.175-96. And Marcel C. Fodor, Voice of VOA USIA Library.
6. Donald R. Browne, International Radio Broadcasting (Prager Publishers, New York, 1982).
7. Thomas C. Sorenson, The World War (Harper & Row, New York, 1968), pp.42ff.
8. Browne, International Radio, p.101.
9. Oren Stephens report, 'USIA Meets the Test' (New York, June 1957).
10. Pirsein, Voice, p.389.
11. Maury Lisann, Broadcasting to the Soviet Union, (Prager Publishers, New York, 1975).
12. USIA Research Report R-4-83.
13. James Keogh's Response to Representative Robert L.F. Sikes (5th March, 1974).
14. Talking Paper, Office of Programs, VOA (26th February, 1974).
15. John D. Lofton's column, 'Détente Laryngitis', (27th February, 1974).
16. Browne, International Radio, loc. cit.
17. Gerald Mansell, 'Taking a Cue from the BBC', Washington Journalism Review (March, 1982).
18. Alexander Solzhenitsyn, Foreign Affairs (May 1980).
19. John H. Trattner, New York Times (February, 1982).
20. Mansell, 'Taking a Cue'.

Chapter Six

THE VOICE PRESENT AND FUTURE: VOA, THE USSR AND COMMUNIST EUROPE

Edward Mainland
chief VOA European division and
Mark Pomar
chief VOA USSR division and
Kurt Carlson
formerly staff, VOA European division

In 1984, the Voice of America broadcast 986 hours of programming weekly in 42 languages; 399 are broadcast each week to the Soviet Union and Eastern Europe, nearly twice the hours transmitted to any other world area. Of these, 63 hours are in English, the rest in 18 other languages: Albanian, Armenian, Azerbaijani, Bulgarian, Czech, Estonian, Georgian, Hungarian, Latvian, Lithuanian, Polish, Romanian, Russian, Serbo Croatian, Slovak, Slovene, Ukrainian and Uzbek. Broadcasts in these 18 languages constitute 44 per cent of VOA's non-English transmissions.

Fifty-two million people in Eastern Europe and the Soviet Union listen to the Voice of America, according to the most reliable estimates available. They account for nearly half of the 110 million people worldwide who tune to VOA each week. In their individual countries, they constitute measureable segments of the entire adult populations - 12% in the USSR, 40% in Poland, 30% in Czechoslovakia; and 20% in Bulgaria, Hungary and Romania (see appendix 1). VOA audiences in Eastern Europe have grown steadily since 1978, according to a recent report of the Board for International Broadcasting: in Poland, two out of five adults listen each week; in Romania, the VOA audience has nearly doubled to more than 3.5 million listeners; in Czechoslovakia, approximately one third of the adults listen to RFE and a similar proportion to VOA; in Bulgaria, VOA and BBC attract about 20 per cent of the adults who listen each week; and in Hungary, VOA has nearly two million listeners. (1)

Estimates of audience sizes in Eastern Europe and the Soviet Union are based on interviews with visitors or emigres from those areas who also provide information on audience composition and listener opinion on signal quality, schedule preferences, programme tastes and station credibility. They also reveal how listening habits are affected by jamming or international crises.

The Voice of America's first broadcast, on 24th February, 1942, was in German, and its Polish and Czech/Slovak Services were initiated just a month later. After World War Two, VOA and the other foreign information activities of the Office of War Information (OWI) might well have been dismantled or allowed to slowly fade away. As several historical accounts note, however, it was Joseph Stalin's actions in Eastern Europe which ultimately saved these broadcast services and led to an expanded effort. VOA introduced its Russian service on 17th February, 1947; Ukrainian programmes went on the air in 1949, and in 1951, services were introduced in the languages of Baltic countries and several of the non-Russian Republics. The language services for Eastern Europe and the Soviet Union are, therefore, among the oldest at VOA and with few exceptions, have enjoyed uninterrupted tenure on its airwaves. They are an important and essential part of VOA - its present and its past.

VOA CHARTER

The long range interests of the United States are served by communicating directly with the people of the world by radio. To be effective, the Voice of America (the Broadcasting Service of the United States Information Agency) must win the attention and respect of listeners. These principles will therefore govern Voice of America (VOA) broadcasts:

> VOA will serve as a consistently reliable and authoritative source of news. VOA news will be accurate, objective and comprehensive.
>
> VOA will represent America, not any single segment of American society, and will therefore present a balanced and comprehensive projection of significant American thought and institutions.
>
> VOA will present the policies of the United States clearly and effectively, and will also present responsible discussion and opinion on those policies.

Public Law 94-350   Gerald R. Ford
President of the United States
July 12, 1976

The Voice Present and Future

VOA will serve as a consistently reliable and authoritative source of news. VOA news will be accurate, objective and comprehensive. (VOA Charter, Public Law 94-350, United States Congress, 1976)

VOA's basic policy objective in broadcasting to the Soviet Union and Eastern Europe is to furnish listeners with truthful information. Listeners consistently tell VOA by mail or through audience sampling that they tune into VOA to get accurate, timely news that they can believe. According to Kenneth Tomlinson, VOA's former Director:

> People depend on the Voice of America and a handful of other western broadcasters for access to the truth, access to what basically is happening in the world. There is also the importance of reaching the people even in strict totalitarian societies. It's important to be able to broadcast the truth to the people of the world. Where there is truth, there is hope for a better tomorrow. (2)

The VOA Charter, in the broadest sense, serves as the basis for all programming. It establishes the parameters for VOA broadcasts, guiding them in the pursuit of truth and journalistic excellence. Though concise, the Charter contains the main underpinnings of VOA programming policy. For listeners behind the iron curtain, VOA is, at times, the only source of truthful information about America. In a ceremony marking the 40th anniversary of VOA, President Reagan stated:

> By giving an objective account of current world events, by communicating a clear picture of America and our policies at home and abroad, the Voice serves the interests not only of the US but of the world ... We are justifiably proud that, unlike Soviet broadcasts, the VOA is not only committed to telling its country's story, but also remains faithful to those standards of journalism that will not compromise the truth.

Implicit in President Reagan's remarks are two important points: (1) that VOA is above all a journalistic enterprise dedicated to the free flow of information and ideas; and (2) that by broadcasting the truth VOA serves the interests of the world and, in particular, the peoples living under totalitarian regimes which control and often distort information.

Much has been written about how best to define

and convey truth in newscasting. The current VOA consensus is approximately as follows in respect to the USSR and Eastern Europe (1) News (the day-to-day partial detailing of individual episodes in ongoing stories) must be rigorously checked, relevant to listener interests and clearly presented; (2) Information (establishing an overall framework, stimulating fresh listener perspectives, conveying meaning, imparting consistency, background and relevance, and moving the listener closer to reality) must be comprehensive, treat key aspects, provide general context and enrich factual content. VOA doctrine calls this the current affairs approach. As former VOA Director Tomlinson explained:

> If we take a current affairs look at the issues of unemployment in (the US), it should be in the context of the world economic situation. We should expect the full story to be covered - and that includes an indication of what economic system (i.e., the free market) has produced a measure of prosperity for the people and what economic system (i.e., socialism) has not achieved. But this can best be done by strict adherence to journalistic professionalism. (3)

The Voice of America received letters and postcards from 225,927 people in 1983 (5,372 from Eastern Europe and the USSR). Many more arrive through American embassies. In the first few months of 1984 audience mail from Eastern Europe surpassed the 1983 final total. This tells VOA what people think it is doing right, doing wrong, not doing enough of or over-doing. Audience needs are a key consideration in deciding what is broadcast. In August, 1982 VOA created the office of audience relations. The office publicises VOA programming and supports efforts to serve better those who listen. An improved system is being devised for handling listener mail - a system maintained by research specialists who, with the help of automation, bring the audience closer to programme planning and review.

VOA's information on VOA audiences is based also on listener comments gathered by United States Information Service posts abroad, informal contacts with recent refugees and emigrants, and surveys conducted by USIA, by Radio Free Europe-Radio Liberty or by independent contractors under the auspices of USIA's office of research. These surveys usually cover national or urban populations, measure the size, composition and programme interests of foreign radio audiences, and explore why individuals select VOA. Through the use of surveys, VOA can receive important information about the target audience, and especially suggestions to improve broadcasts, although this technique has severe limitations in Eastern Europe.

News for foreign language services is provided by a central news division. Drawing on VOA's network of correspondents around the world and the commercial wire services, VOA's central newsroom issues news items, headlines, summaries and advisories. Each language service draws exclusively from this output in assembling its own newscasts. The newsroom also transmits suggested lineups consisting of ten to 15 stories for each newscast. Although news items are occasionally designated 'must lead' or 'must use', VOA encourages the individual services to put together well-balanced newscasts.

VOA currently allots about one third of its airtime in languages of the Soviet Union and Eastern Europe to hard news and one third to current affairs. How then does VOA avoid falling into the pattern of Soviet propagandists, i.e. fairly factual but tendentiously chosen news (malenkaya pravda) within a general context of consistent but basically self-serving and often preposterous explanations (bolshaya pravda)? It does this by a variety of means. In addition to traditional correspondent reports from VOA reporters abroad, the Eastern European and Soviet services now draw on Focus, a series of five 20-minute documentaries each week which explore issues in the news by providing balanced background from several different outside experts; Close-up, adaptations of Focus programmes which condense the longer programmes into five minutes for use by services with small amounts of airtime; Viewpoint, dialogues in which regular pairs of commentators trade contrasting opinions on serious topics currently in the news; and Backgrounders, in-depth looks at such topics. Former director Tomlinson has argued:

> What is meant when (the US law governing VOA) speaks of balance? I submit that balance does not lie somewhere between Washington and Moscow. I submit that balance is within the American political spectrum – within the spectrum of Western values ... This principle is an extension of the philosophy on which (our) nation was founded. The founders believed that people, when exposed to a diversity of

information and opinion, could decide for themselves - and do it wisely. That is precisely what we propose to do in broadcasting facts and information and ideas to the people of the world. (4)

VOA believes that modern competitive broadcasting and reporting requires immediacy and intimacy. To take the listener to where it is happening, VOA's language services are increasingly taking live on-the-scene coverage from correspondents and stringers. Examples of this type of coverage include the Pope's 1983 visit to Poland, Lech Walesa's Nobel Prize ceremony, the Los Angeles and Sarajevo Olympic Games, and the US national Democratic and Republican conventions.

Research shows that Soviet and Eastern European listeners are interested mostly in news of their own region, Europe as a whole, East-West relations and America. News about other parts of the world rate much lower. The state of arms negotiations, trade, cultural exchanges, Soviet action in Europe and the third world, and illegal transfer of western technology to the Soviet bloc receive regular attention. Most critical is the war in Afghanistan. Although the Soviets have committed more than 100,000 troops in a war that has lasted longer than World War Two, the media in the USSR have avoided any mention of the true conditions in Afghanistan. Whenever the war is discussed, it is portrayed as a Soviet effort to help the Afghans repel invading imperialist troops. Information about Afghanistan, gleaned mostly from reports by western correspondents, Soviet defectors and Afghan refugees presents a different picture.

Of no less critical importance are western reports on specifically Soviet and East European topics. News about dissidents and ordinary citizens denied their rights form an important part of VOA broadcasts. Reports of the plight of Jewish refuseniks, the struggle of Andrei Sakharov and Yelena Bonner and the persecution of religious leaders (to cite but three examples) are not only part of comprehensive journalism but also are of personal interest to many listeners in the countries of the Soviet bloc. VOA and other major international radio broadcasters are usually the only source of such information. By reporting on these subjects, VOA informs its listeners about key dissidents and the world reaction to their struggle for human rights.

VOA's Soviet and East European services are

giving increased emphasis to their audience's need for news about neighbouring communist countries. For example, daily regional windows are used in most services for the cross-reporting of trends. There is fresh VOA emphasis also on current affairs reporting on the internal developments within target countries. The aim is topicality, comprehensiveness, relevance and audience building. This reporting draws not only from US journalistic and academic analyses and comments but also interviews and reflections of personalities and ideas within or from target countries. The point of view and tone is always American, not exile or domestic surrogate, and the volume and detail of such internal reporting necessarily are less compared to, for example, Radio Free Europe's, whose primary mission is domestic coverage. Within its central newsroom, VOA currently operates regional news desks, including one for Europe staffed with Soviet and East European experts. VOA encourages cooperation and flexibility between the central newsroom and language services.

VOA will represent America, not any single segment of American society, and will therefore present a balanced and comprehensive projection of significant American thought and institutions. (VOA Charter, Public Law 94-350, United States Congress, 1976)
In VOA's broadcasts the emphasis is on the many voices of America. VOA reflects significant American voices from all walks of life and points of view. The interview format is increasingly used in language broadcasts to take advantage of the hundreds of thousands of Americans who speak target languages well and who are authorities on subjects of interest to listeners. VOA uses a wide definition of 'American thought and institutions'. In practice, the US is a sounding board for world thought. The US was founded and structured on the basis of explicit assumptions about the nature of man and society, human rights, power, checks and balances, and the state and the individual. Since American thought is intertwined with global issues, VOA's intellectual mandate is broad.

A critical mission of VOA broadcasts is to represent American society, thought and institutions not from a simple point of view but in a broad, well-balanced context. This is not an easy task because VOA must reflect American political, geographic, cultural, ethnic, religious, and social diversity in a way that is meaningful, tasteful and true.

The Voice Present and Future

President John F. Kennedy sensed this difficulty when he stated:

> The VOA carries a heavy responsibility. Its burden of truth is not easy to bear. It must explain to a curious and suspicious world what we are. It must tell them of our basic beliefs. It must tell them of a country which is in some ways a rather old country, certainly old as republics go. And yet it must make our ideas alive and new and vital in the high competition which has gone on around the world since the end of World War Two.

A portion of what VOA projects about America will be its ethnic diversity and in particular, how Americans born in the target country contribute to American intellectual and economic life. For instance, a Romanian-speaking attorney who is a naturalised American would explain the American approach to justice or constitutional limits of power.

The difficulty of presenting American thought and institutions is compounded by the fact that American intellectual, scientific, religious and artistic life does not exist in a narrow cultural sphere; it is not, strictly speaking, sui generis. From its earliest times, America has been enriched by continuous waves of emigration, each bringing its own character. Since World War Two, moreover, America has become the crossroads of world thought. Prominent works of American writers, scientists, and artists are known in most countries. Important foreign cultural figures and scientists often play a key role in American life. The world is very much interrelated. To cite but one small example, New York has recently become the capital of contemporary dance. Innovations and experimentation in choreography have been fashioned by American artists drawing on American tradition, but a very prominent role has also been played by the Russians, English, Danes and others. Contemporary dance is thus both an American and world phenomenon.

To fulfil the mission of representing America, the VOA has to be judicious in its selection. To present everything in American life is impossible; the key is how and what to select. Two criteria generally govern this aspect of VOA programming. One is to broadcast the most significant stories of American life, the ones that receive the most serious attention in the country. The other is to tailor features to the target audiences from the flood of materials that are representative of some aspect of American life.

In VOA's Russian service, the largest foreign language broadcasting unit, these two goals are realised in two different types of programme. One is the current affairs programmes, which present up-to-date political and cultural material: Breakfast Show, Panorama, Events and Opinion, Nightowl, and Far East Shows. Generally these shows are not repeated, although individual items, deemed especially important for the Soviet audience, may appear in several programmes - conditions of jamming make this imperative. The other type of programme is the feature show which focuses on one subject; these are of varying length, and are repeated several times throughout the week. At present there are many feature programmes, for example: Religion in Our Life, The World of Jazz, Conover on Jazz, Youth Show, Science and Technology, Medicine, Books & People, Performing Arts, Cultural Life of New York, Agriculture, Labor Show, Jewish Show, Pop Music, Pages of History, Forum, Film, Art Today, Sports, Literary Readings, American Magazines, and Radio Magazine.

In general, the Russian service tries to maintain a balance between stories dealing strictly with American topics (although many, as in the case of dance in New York, have an international air) and those dealing with Soviet and Russian subjects in a broad East-West context. Some programmes, notably the science and music shows, rely mostly on American topics and use many centrally-produced English scripts. The jazz programmes, for instance, have been popular in the Soviet Union and helped educate several generations of jazz fans, even inspiring some to become musicians. Several shows, in particular those dealing with literature and art, have introduced more and more stories on prominent Russian emigres living in the West, notably Alexander Solzhenitsyn, Mstislav Rostropovich and Yuri Lyubimov. It is no exaggeration to say that the best Russian writers and artists are now living outside the Soviet Union.

This situation presents unique opportunities for VOA. On the one hand, programmes about Russian writers, artists and thinkers whose works have been recognised in the US help display the diversity of American thought and the rich contribution of people from around the world to the vitality of American artistic and intellectual life. On the other hand, by broadcasting works of Russian writers and conducting interviews with prominent artists and thinkers, VOA can help sustain Russian culture, thereby gaining the respect of many Russians and inevitably increasing the size of its listenership.

A number of examples illustrate these points. Approximately three years ago Vasily Aksyonov, for nearly two decades one of the most popular writers in the Soviet Union, began a weekly series on VOA entitled Capital Shift. After moving from Moscow to Washington, Askyonov began to note the differences between the two capitals and used these differences to explain American life to Russians. His ten-to-twelve-minute talks - according to all reports very popular in the Soviet Union - have ranged from literary and religious matters to popular culture. In each talk there is an authentic Russian voice, recognised by nearly all Russian listeners, explaining American life and making it relevant to people who have but a vague notion of its reality.

Maestro Rostropovich's contributions represent a somewhat different approach to VOA programming. In a series of lengthy conversations, Rostropovich discusses his understanding of music, thoughts on religion and art, and appreciation of American life and Western concepts of freedom. More free-ranging in style and content than Askyonov's scripts, these conversations have given VOA's Russian listeners the opportunity to experience the nature of freedom of expression. Rostropovich's frank opinions, wry observations of the musical world, and ability to place different aspects of American life in a context comprehensible to a Russian, communicate very successfully the spirit of America.

Alexander Solzhenitsyn's interview and reading from his latest novel, volume two of August 1914 (part of the historical series, The Red Wheel), represent another approach. Although ostensibly not about America, Solzhenitsyn's contributions to VOA programming embody one of America's most cherished values: the freedom to pursue truth and to create freely. Denied access to archival material in the Soviet Union, Solzhenitsyn was able to write his massive historical opus only in America, using Russian sources found in American libraries and archives. It is ironic (but fully in keeping with Western traditions of freedom) that Solzhenitsyn can pursue his artistic goals best in the pastoral hills of Vermont. Through his many books and public appearances, he has become a part of American life. His voice and presence on VOA, moreover, contribute greatly to the popularity and importance of Russian language broadcasts beamed to the Soviet Union.

The nationality services of the USSR divison - Ukrainian, Georgian, Armenian, Azerbaijani and Uzbek - also present the diversity of American life by drawing on notable native speakers living in the West. The Ukrainian service regularly interviews prominent artists and scholars. Recently Vakhtang Jordania, a former Soviet conductor, participated in several programmes for the Georgian Service, explaining the differences between musical and artistic life in the USSR and the United States. All the nationality services have invited prominent dissidents now living in America to communicate Western concepts of freedom and their own views to the target audiences.

The playwright Eugene Ionesco has given two interviews to VOA for Romanian-language listeners in which he talked about America and Eastern Europe within the context of his iconoclastic world view. The Polish-born writer and winner of the 1980 Nobel prize for literature, Czeslaw Milosz, works closely with VOA's Polish service. The Czech writer Milan Kundera, who resides in France, is published in the United States and thus is reported on by VOA's Czechoslovak service.

Religion occupies an important place. The Russian service, for example, has a 45-minute broadcast called Religion in Our Life (focusing primarily on Russian Orthodox Christianity) and a 45-minute Jewish Show. To a degree both shows talk about religious life in America, its spirit and tradition but also try to explain the spiritual basis of the two religions. This is a formidable task because the Soviet Union has practised militant atheism for more than 60 years. The Religion in Our Life programme consists of talks by important Russian Orthodox church leaders, and information about Christians of all denominations in the US and the Soviet Union. Feature material about American churches and religious life is presented in a broad context, understandable to a Christian. On Sundays and major holidays, the Russian service broadcasts an hour-long liturgy. The Jewish Show discusses how Jews celebrate their religion and customs in America. It marks the important religious holidays and includes talks by prominent religious figures. Although Religion in Our Life and Jewish Show are not intended strictly for religious listeners - they try to attract the sympathetic non-believers - they see their primary responsibility as one of spiritual sustenance of a people virtually denied their basic right of religious practice.

The East European and Soviet nationality services also have religious programming though because of limited airtime, they are generally not able to have programmes as lengthy and detailed as those of the Russian service. Broad questions of Christianity, Judaism and Islam (the emphasis changes depending upon the target area) are regularly addressed. The goal is to acquaint listeners in Eastern Europe and the Soviet Union with the religious traditions of America and to provide them with a better understanding of their own religions, in terms of both history and spiritual basis. Whenever possible, all the services present prominent clergymen living in the United States who speak the languages of the target areas and regularly review important books and publications on religious matters.

The emphasis in VOA feature programming is on America ideas rather than American things. VOA broadcasts are more likely to project how Americans think than the scenery. VOA broadcasting is currently seeking to correct past listener perceptions of triviality or cultural insensitivity in projecting America - and to keep at the forefront audience needs, sensibilities and conceptions of America.

VOA will present the policies of the United States clearly and effectively, and will also present responsible discussion and opinion on these policies. (VOA Charter, Public Law 94-350, United States Congress, 1976)

Since 1982, VOA has been broadcasting editorials: these are approximately four minutes long and give the administration in office a chance to speak out in the tradition of a newspaper's editorial page. The editorials have focused on East-West issues, human rights, and on the questions of why the West is prosperous and totalitarian nations are not. This format has the advantage of directly conveying the policy aims of the sitting administration while clearly separating such labelled editorialising from straight news and current affairs material. In Eastern Europe, reaction has been mixed. On the one hand, clarity about what the Administration believes has been welcomed even when listeners do not agree with the message. On the other hand, some uneasiness has been expressed over what some perceive as a hard-sell tone. Former director Tomlinson has clarified the intent of the VOA editorial:

> The Voice is certainly not going to become a propaganda arm ... These editorials replaced the typical commentaries that were mixed with editorials before. The editorials I've seen since I've been on board crisply but firmly reflect the positions of the US government on the major issues of the day, whether these issues be arms control or Afghanistan, or Poland ... those editorials are going to be forceful in advocating the values of the West. (5)

Unlike other English language scripts, the editorial is prepared in VOA's policy office and translated word-for-word by the language services. It is aired at least once a day, usually on a current affairs programme. Along with these editorials, the VOA regularly carries Presidential addresses live and covers the statements of other American officials. To explain how America views a particular international problem or how it will respond to a crisis is an important responsibility of VOA programming. This commitment often places VOA, in former director John Chancellor's words, 'At the crossroads of journalism and diplomacy'. The major emphasis is on journalistic work, as distinct from the policy advocacy functions which USIA serves. As noted above, editorials are separate and distinct from VOA news and news-related material. The news is solely the province of VOA editors and programme planners. VOA rejects interference that could be construed as violating Public Law 94-350 (VOA's Charter) which mandates that VOA be a consistently reliable and authoritative news source. VOA does cooperate, however, with policymakers from the Department of State and elsewhere, and with US embassies abroad, but does so mainly to draw on their expertise. The same professional standards of journalistic integrity and responsibility expected in the private sector apply to VOA's journalists as well.

As the Charter states, the VOA has a parallel responsibility to reflect the entire spectrum of American opinion on US government policies, including Congressional reaction and a cross-section of American editorial comment. The language services broadcasting to the countries behind the iron curtain present all policy statements relevant to their audience; and supplement them with critical reactions. In the words of former VOA director Henry

Loomis:

> If we want to make the world safe for diversity, if we believe that a good and strong society is based on free choice, we must by our very stance communicate to our audience the fact that diversity is preferable to uniformity. To acknowledge the existence of forces and views in disagreement with those of the policymakers, to take these especially into account in the formulation of our output, is a sign of strength ... We must show that the United States derives strength, not weakness, from diversity.

Another way listeners hear US policy is directly from US policymakers: it broadcasts not only taped interviews on particular Soviet and East European issues involving the United States, but direct feeds from Presidential press conferences and radio talks. For example, the President's radio talk to the people of the USSR in 1983 was aired live from a VOA studio, as a news-making event, with voiced-over translations by several of VOA's USSR and East European services.

Discussions of US policy have also come to be handled in structured dialogue between noted commentators from contrasting ends of the US political spectrum and in reviews of US press opinion and columnists.

Future Outlook

By 1990, resources permitting, the airtime of VOA's USSR and East European services is expected to increase (see Appendices 1 and 2 for a description of VOA's East Europe and USSR language services).

In the USSR Division, the Russian service is slated to expand from 17 to 18 hours of daily broadcast time. The extra hour is intended to strengthen overall programming. As new staff is brought on board, the Russian service will expand further, creating separate programming blocks for central USSR and the far east. The emphasis will be on more news-related broadcasts and special programmes of interest and relevance to the target areas. The Ukrainian Service recently introduced one hour of programming to the far east of the USSR, where there is a sizable Ukrainian community. In future years, the service will expand its programming both to the Ukraine proper and to the far east. Armenian, Georgian, Azerbaijani and Uzbek are also scheduled for expansion and there is general discussion about introducing more language services in the USSR division.

In the European division, the Polish Service's medium-wave transmissions have recently been expanded to seven hours daily from the original four, a considerable increase over the 1¾ hours alloted before December, 1981. An RFE-RL 1983 report, <u>Listening to Western Radio in East Europe</u>, stated that listenership to VOA in Poland has doubled since 1981. The report indicates that 11.5 million people now listen to VOA's Polish language broadcasts - a figure representing more than 40 per cent of Poland's adult population. VOA intends to consolidate or expand early morning news shows to one-half hour for several East European countries and to expand broadcasts to Czechoslovakia and Albania in 1985, resources permitting. New positions were filled in East European services by intensive recruiting.

According to the RFE-RL report, there has been audience growth in the early 1980s for nearly all VOA East European language services. This may reflect listeners' efforts to circumvent actions by East European regimes to stifle and control contacts with western ideas and information, as well as VOA moves to increase the quality and quantity of broadcasting into the region (for figures of VOA listeners in Eastern Europe and the Soviet Union, see Appendices 3 and 4).

The Soviet Union currently jams the Voice's shortwave broadcasts to the USSR and Poland. In the case of the Polish Service, medium-wave broadcasts are relatively unaffected by jamming. In September, 1983 Bulgaria ceased the jamming of VOA that it had begun with the Soviets in December, 1981, after martial law had been declared in Poland. In July, 1984 jamming of VOA Bulgarian broadcasts was resumed by both the Soviets and the Bulgarians, only to have the Bulgarians stop and the Soviets continue for a week in August, 1984, after which all jamming ceased.

The Soviet policy on jamming has varied with the ebb and flow of East-West tensions and crises, internal or external. The Soviet Union intermittently jammed western broadcasts from 1948 to 1973. After a seven year hiatus, jamming of VOA and the BBC resumed in August, 1980, as the Solidarity movement in Poland gained strength. At about the same time, Soviet involvement in Afghanistan was drawing a strong US reaction.

Although there is no easy technical way to overcome jamming, VOA programmes do penetrate it to

The Voice Present and Future

some extent. During morning and evening hours, when jamming is technically least effective, VOA has steadily increased its broadcast hours in Polish and in the languages of the Soviet Union and the Baltic states. English language programmes heard in Poland and the Soviet Union are not jammed at all. It is estimated that it costs the Soviets many times more to jam than it costs VOA, Radio Free Europe, and Radio Liberty to broadcast. It is beyond dispute that there is not, and very probably cannot be, a truly effective technical solution for overcoming the impact of persistent jamming on the audibility of broadcast signals. The only assured way of removing the problem would be to negotiate with the Soviets and their allies for a cessation of their jamming activities.

VOA broadcasts to Albania, Czechoslovakia, Hungary and Romania are not jammed. A major VOA concern, however, is the unsatisfactory and diminishing strength of the VOA radio signal into Eastern Europe from outside transmitters. Shortwave reception is below par, even without jamming, in many target areas. VOA has proposed to Congress a $1 billion six-year programme to modernise neglected capital equipment worldwide. East European broadcasts would benefit from VOA modernisation through a more effective and audible signal to their audiences.

Apace with technical modernisation, VOA's USSR and East European services aim at modernised sound. Modern radio requires pace, conciseness, colour, diversity, informality, humour and appeal. VOA has been experimenting with dialogues, roundtables, outside target language interviews and radio drama - for example, VOA's Romanian service's dramatic adaptation of George Orwell's <u>Animal Farm</u> and the Russian presentation of Beckett's works - to convey information about values more effectively.

VOA broadcasts also must keep up with the style, language and political orientation of competing media and monitors local broadcasts in the targeted area to make certain that the language use in VOA broadcasts is up-to-date. Information about the competition comes from friendly broadcasters with whom VOA maintains direct liaison, such as the BBC, Deutsche Welle, and RFE/RL.

VOA broadcasts to the Soviet Union and East Europe will continue to emphasise religious issues, youth shows and human rights. A study in 1957, <u>USIA Meets the Test: A Study of Fast Output During the Hungarian and Suez Crises</u>, alleged that VOA had used religion as propaganda incitement against communist regimes. In the 1980s, VOA has matured and now broadcasts a wide variety of news and analysis of religious problems in both East and West. Similarly, the world economy has forced VOA to become more competitive with coverage of trade, finance, most-favoured-nation legislation, and banking bail-outs in East Europe. The United States' differentiated policy toward individual regimes in the Soviet bloc and the diversity of these countries has increasingly led VOA to allow considerable language service autonomy in tailoring broadcasts to fit individual audiences.

VOA's general broadcasting policy is to practise honest journalism - that is, not to shield the Soviet and East European regimes from the consequences of their folly or to protect the status quo even when it might seen expedient to avoid diplomatic pressure from those regimes. In East Europe, facts themselves speak for change, and VOA reflects this reality. While VOA has been careful not to raise false expectations among listeners, its very existence challenges the monopoly of information the Soviet and East European regimes impose on their citizens. Broadcasts of VOA and other Western stations undermine the credibility of information dispensed by state-controlled media and thereby elicit official invective: 'slander', 'subversion', 'hostility', 'abuse of goodwill' and 'destabilisation'. It is fair to consider VOA's current broadcasting policy toward the USSR and Eastern Europe as activist in this sense: it is based on the notion that freedom (the opportunity to establish for oneself how reality is perceived, and to seek, receive, and impart information and ideas through any media regardless of frontiers) is a rare thing in human history and should be defended and advanced. This view received its most forceful endorsement from Seth Cropsey, former VOA director of policy:

> The United States is a force for political good in the modern world. We are therefore obliged to ourselves and to others who would live in freedom, not only to act according to our principles but to argue on behalf of, promote, support and in every decent way advance those principles. (6)

Notes

1. United States Information Agency Research,

The Voice Present and Future

VOA Audiences - 1984.
   2. Interview with Kenneth Tomlinson, <u>Human Events</u>, 4th February, 1984, p.10.
   3. Tomlinson, <u>Human Events</u>, p.10.
   4. Tomlinson, p.10.
   5. <u>USA Today</u>, 29th March, 1984, p.8a.
   6. <u>Roundtable</u> discussion, Institute for Contemporary Studies, 1983.

Appendix 6.1
VOA East European Language Services 1986. VOA East European language services broadcast $159\frac{1}{4}$ hours weekly in twelve languages: Albanian - $10\frac{1}{2}$ hours; Bulgarian - $10\frac{1}{2}$; Czech and Slovak - 21; Estonian - $8\frac{3}{4}$; Hungarian $17\frac{1}{2}$; Latvian - $8\frac{3}{4}$; Lithuanian - $8\frac{3}{4}$; Polish - 49; Romanian - $12\frac{1}{4}$; Serbo-Croatian - $8\frac{3}{4}$; and Slovene - $3\frac{1}{2}$. A programme in German is also produced for broadcast by RIAS in Berlin.

The Albanian Service broadcasts three half-hour programmes daily at 6 and 8.30 p.m. Albanian time and a new half hour morning programme at 6.30 a.m. local time. Since the United States does not have diplomatic relations with Albania, the VOA broadcast is the only medium available to explain US policies and emphasise the traditional friendship between the American and Albanian peoples. Moreover, as VOA Albania is the only regular language broadcast service from the West, it is the most important source of information regarding the outside world. VOA Albanian broadcasts were begun in May 1943, but were terminated in 1945. Albanian language broadcasts were resumed in May, 1951.

The Bulgarian Service, on the air since August, 1942, broadcasts a half-hour morning news programme and two 30-minute evening programmes (at 6 and 8.45 a.m., 7.30 and 10 p.m. Bulgarian time). There is little feedback: Bulgarian law prohibits foreign research on radio listenership in the country, and there is virtually no comment by mail from listeners.

The Czechoslovak Service, broadcasting continuously in the Czech and Slovak languages since March, 1942, transmits a half hour morning news programme (at 6 a.m. local time), a half-hour early evening show (6.30 p.m. locally), and a two-hour late evening

The Voice Present and Future

broadcast (9 p.m. in Czechslovakia). Feedback from a variety of sources indicates extensive VOA audience.

The Estonian, Latvian and Lithuanian Services were introduced in 1951. Each of these language services broadcasts a 15-minute morning programme and two half-hour evening programmes. These broadcasts have been jammed by the Soviet Union since 1980. In addition to news reports, backgrounders and features on world and US developments, an important programme element is coverage of Americans of Estonian, Latvian, and Lithuanian background and ethnic group activities.

The Hungarian Service, on the air since August, 1942, broadcasts $2\frac{1}{2}$ hours daily, beginning with a morning news programme (at 7.00 and 7.30 a.m. local time), then a 2 hour evening programme (7.00 p.m. Hungarian time). A significant finding of the latest available research surveys is that VOA Hungarian listeners are representative of a younger age group than the audiences of the BBC or RFE. There are also secondary audiences among the Hungarian speakers in Austria, Czechoslovakia, Romania, Yugoslavia and the Soviet Union.

The Polish Service's broadcasts were expanded from $1\frac{3}{4}$ to 7 hours daily with the imposition of martial law in December, 1981: a 2-hour morning programme, 6-8 a.m. in Poland; and a 5-hour evening broadcast from 8.00 p.m. to 1.00 a.m. local time. The broadcasts are jammed, but the jamming is not total since medium-wave transmissions ($5\frac{1}{2}$ hours daily) remain free of interference. VOA Polish has been on the air since May, 1942.

The Romanian Service, on the air since November, 1942, broadcasts a 15-minute morning programme and, in the evening, one-hour and half-hour shows, for a daily total $1\frac{3}{4}$ hours. Programming includes interviews with US foreign policy experts and personalities in the fields of business, science and the arts, especially those who have a Romanian connection. VOA's audience is estimated at 3.5 million in a country with a total population of 20 million.

The Voice Present and Future

The Yugoslav Service broadcasts in Serbo-Croatian (since 1942) and Slovene (which has had off-air periods, the most recent in 1975). At present, Slovene is broadcast only in the morning from 6.45 - 7.15 a.m. local Yugoslav time. In Serbo-Croatian, there is a 15-minute broadcast at 5.45 a.m. in Yugoslavia and a one-hour broadcast at 9.30 p.m. local time.

The German Service prepares reports or analyses daily for Radio in the American Sector (RIAS), Berlin, which deal primarily with US political and economic developments that are of interest to RIAS listeners in East Germany. The service also covers late-breaking stories for RIAS' prime morning and evening news programmes. Feeds are transmitted at 11.45-12.00 midday, Monday-Friday; and at 9.45-10.00 p.m. Sunday-Friday.

Appendix 6.2
VOA USSR Language Services 1986. The Azerbaijani Service was re-created recently at VOA after a 29-year absence. VOA broadcasts in Azerbaijani were first introduced on 14th June 1951, cancelled on 13th September, 1953, and reinstated on 4th July, 1982. A one-hour programme is broadcast daily from 11.00 p.m. to midnight, Baku time. Although news-oriented for the most part, the broadcasts frequently include features on scientific and political developments and cultural affairs. The primary audience are the people of the Azerbaijan Republic in the USSR, and there are potential listeners in Iran's Azerbaijan Province.

The Armenian and Georgian Services, introduced in 1951, broadcast morning and evening programmes to the Soviet Caucasus. Armenian programmes can be heard in Yerevan from 6 to 6.15 a.m. and 7 to 8 p.m.; while the daily Georgian broadcasts are transmitted from 6.15 to 6.30 a.m. and from 12.00 to 12.30 a.m. Tbilisi time. In addition to news and news-related backgrounders, the broadcasts carry features on scientific, cultural and religious topics and reportage on the Armenian and Georgian communities of America.

The Russian Service broadcasts 17 hours a day and is

The Voice Present and Future

heard in the Soviet Union from 5 to 8 a.m. and from 6 p.m. to 3 a.m. in Moscow; from 7 to 9 p.m. and from 6.00 to 7.00 a.m. in Novosibirsk; and from 6 to 9 p.m. in the Soviet far east. VOA Russian, introduced on 17th February, 1947, is today the Voice's largest foreign language service. News and news-related reporting account for more than half the daily broadcast schedule. Programmes include Events and Opinion, Panorama and The Breakfast Show.

The Ukrainian Service, on-the-air continuously since 12th December, 1949, broadcasts four hours daily to the Soviet Ukraine. The morning programme - transmitted from 5 to 7 a.m. Kiev time - is devoted almost entirely to news and news-related features and backgrounders. The evening show - broadcast from 7 to 9 p.m. Kiev time - carries a wide range of features and reportage on cultural, scientific, economic and religious topics, as well as news and news-related coverage. In July, 1984, VOA added a one-hour broadcast in Ukrainian to the far east from 6 to 7 a.m. local time.

The Uzbek Service broadcasts morning and evening programmes from 6 to 7 a.m. and 8 to 9 p.m. Tashkent time. The evening programme includes world news and features on current events, Islamic religious developments, music, cultural affairs and a broad range of other topics. The morning programme is more news-oriented, but does carry feature material - particularly on religious topics - when appropriate. Uzbek language broadcasts were first introduced on VOA in 1956, cancelled in 1968, and reinstated in September 1972.

Appendix 6.3
Listenership Radio Set Availability: Eastern Europe

Country	VOA audience* per cent			VOA listenership as a percentage of western radio audiences
Czechoslovakia	35	=	4,130,000	45
Hungary	25	=	2,130,000	33
Poland	43	=	11,910,000	51
Romania	24	=	3,980,000	32
Bulgaria	22	=	1,560,000	39

Country	Listeners to western broadcasts per cent	Radios (National)** per cent	Shortwave per cent
Czechoslovakia	77	98	85
Hungary	73	100	91
Poland	85	100	91
Romania	75	96	88
Bulgaria	56	98	87

VOA Audience Trends 1978-83*

Country	1978 - early 79 per cent	1979 - summer 80 per cent	1981 - early 82 per cent	1982 - early 83 per cent
Czechoslovakia	24	26	32	35
Hungary	20	20	22	25
Poland	20	22	37	43
Romania	15	14	21	24
Bulgaria	21	20	19	22

*Adult audience, 14 years and older.
** Per cent of national adult population with access to radio.

Sources: Listening to Western Radio in East Europe, RFE-RL, 1983; VOA Data Bank, Radio Set Availability; and Audience and Frequency Use: VOA Broadcast Options, USIA, 1984.

The Voice Present and Future

Appendix 6.4
Listenership and Radio Set Availability: USSR

	VOA Audience Listenership per cent
Overall Rating	15
Age	
16 - 29	17
30 - 49	16
50+	13
Education	
Less than secondary	10
Secondary or more	27
Sex	
Men	26
Women	7
Residence	
Rural	9
Urban	19
Geographic Region	
European RSFR**	15
Moscow and oblast	17
Leningrad and oblast	17
Siberian RSFSR	14
Baltic SSRs	17
Belorussian SSR	9
Caucasian SSRs	19
Central Asian SSRs	12
Moldavian SSR	7
Ukrainian SSR	18

Per cent of adults with access to radio sets

Any radio	Radio with shortwave bands
90	75

* Adult = 16 years and older.
** Does not include the cities and oblasts of Moscow and Leningrad.

Sources: Soviet Area Audience and Opinion Research Office, RFE-RL, Research Memorandum, April 1984; and VOA Data Bank, Radio Set Availability, USIA, 1984.

Appendix 6.5
VOA Broadcasts to Eastern Europe and the Soviet Union

Services and their inaugural dates	Hours per week						
	Dec 1955	Dec 1960	Dec 1965	Dec 1970	Dec 1975	Dec 1980	Dec 1984
Albanian – May 1943	15.45	10.30	7.00	3.30	7.00	7.00	7.00
Armenian – June 1951	15.45	7.00	7.00	7.00	7.00	7.00	7.00
Azerbaijani* – June 1951	*	*	*	*	*	*	7.00
Bulgarian – August 1942	35.00	12.15	8.45	10.30	10.30	10.30	10.30
Czech and Slovak – March 1942	15.45	14.00	10.30	14.00	14.00	14.00	14.00
Estonian – June 1951	26.15	10.30	8.45	7.00	7.00	7.00	8.45
Georgian – May 1951	14.00	7.00	7.00	7.00	7.00	7.00	8.45
Hungarian – August 1942	24.30	17.30	14.00	14.00	17.30	17.30	17.30
Latvian – June 1951	12.15	10.30	8.45	7.00	7.00	7.00	8.45
Lithuanian – February 1951	24.30	10.30	8.45	7.00	17.30	7.00	8.45
Polish – May 1942	42.00	14.00	14.00	14.00	10.30	14.00	49.00
Romanian – November 1942	21.00	8.45	12.15	10.30	17.30	12.15	12.15
Russian – February 1947	129.30	52.30	63.00	77.00	98.00	98.00	112.00
Serbo Croatian – March 1943	10.30	12.15	8.45	7.00	7.00	8.45	8.45
Slovene* – July 1944	7.00	3.30	3.30	3.30		3.30	3.30
Ukrainian – December 1949	24.30	14.00	3.30	7.00	28.00	28.00	35.00
Uzbek* – February 1956	*	*	*	*	7.00	7.00	14.00
Total Hours to E. Europe & the USSR	418.15	204.45	185.30	196.00	252.00	255.30	332.30
Per cent of VOA's non English broadcasts	62%	48%	33%	34%	44%	40%	44%

Note:* Azerbaijani programmes were broadcast from 1951 to 1953; a new service was begun on 4th July, 1982. Slovene broadcasts were off the air for a one year period for 1975 to 1976. Uzbek programmes were transmitted from 1956 until 1958; and re-introduced on 3rd September, 1972. VOA also broadcast to the USSR in Belorussian (1956-7), Tatar (1951-3) and Turkestani (1951-3).

Part Two

EUROPEAN BROADCASTING OVER THE IRON CURTAIN

Chapter Seven

THE BBC EXTERNAL SERVICES: BROADCASTING TO THE USSR AND EASTERN EUROPE

Peter Fraenkel, controller, European Services, BBC External Services

It is impossible to analyse the current policies of the BBC's Russian and other East European services in isolation, because they reflect very closely the policies of the BBC's External Services as a whole while these, in turn, are only an adaptation of the policies of the BBC's domestic services - both in radio and television. One could go further and say that these have their roots deep in the society from which we broadcast.

That might, however, suggest that the current practices were inevitable, given the society we operate from. This is, of course, not so. Other societies with similar deep democratic roots - like the United States - have developed very different media. Conscious choices were made; it is necessary to explain the choices made at the beginnings of the very first foreign language service of the BBC - because that set the pattern which effects how we broadcast today.

In 1937, the BBC was reluctant to take on foreign language broadcasting. It feared that it would introduce an element of propaganda - like the pioneers of foreign language broadcasting, the Russians, the Italians and the Germans; and propaganda was seen as a bad thing, the enemy of truthfulness.

Lord Reith, the first director general of the BBC, would only agree to take on the government's assignment of broadcasting in Arabic provided he was guaranteed that it would be as independent of government interference as BBC domestic transmissions. (1) The Foreign Office at the time thought him unreasonable. Rex Leeper - later Sir Rex Leeper, ambassador in Athens - said that these BBC reservations were 'sheer obstructionism. One would think from the BBC's attitude that there was no

BBC External Services

international crisis at all:' (the date was 1937). He wanted the BBC's Arabic service to concentrate on news of Italian atrocities in Libya to counteract Italian propaganda on alleged British misdeeds in Palestine. Since Lord Reith refused to play ball the Foreign Office was forced to explore other avenues. They considered a station to be set up in Jerusalem or in Cyprus under direct government control. Various British embassies and administrators were consulted. They advised against it. Ambassadors in Arab lands said that such a station would lack credibility. After seven months of back-and-forth argument, the Foreign Office came back to the BBC. But Leeper still argued, 'Straight news may be suitable for sophisticated audiences, but news in Arabic requires omission and selection.' Spanish and Portuguese for Latin America were also under consideration, but were regarded as less 'sensitive'. Lord Reith appeared to compromise: 'In the case of Arabic, the BBC might have to show more elasticity, and perhaps be more amenable to the Foreign Office view than in the case of other languages.' On the basis of this vague, apparent concession (Gerald Mansell calls it 'a fudged gentleman's agreement' in his book Let Truth Be Told the BBC was entrusted with a job of broadcasting in Arabia. (2)

The service was launched at the beginning of 1938. Alas, the very first news bulletin – on 3rd January, 1938 – gave prominence to an item about the execution of an Arab terrorist in Palestine that day. The telegraph wires hummed! The British embassy in Saudi Arabia protested that the broadcast had 'spread a painful tenseness in the atmosphere'. Leeper fumed that the BBC was 'augmenting Mussolini's station in Bari rather than countering it.' Another Foreign Office official minuted: 'The effect in numerous popular cafes can only be disastrous.' The BBC's answer was magisterial: 'The omission of unwelcome facts and the consequent suppression of truth runs counter to the Corporation's policy.' (1) It was, in fact, Reith's juniors who had insisted that the truth be told. I am not suggesting that the BBC has always succeeded in maintaining this policy absolutely pure these 50 or more years. In times of war, between 1939 and 1945, the policy was frequently compromised. Political and military considerations did influence the selection of news at the time. However, in times of peace, lost ground was reclaimed and many honest people have since striven to maintain it just as it was formulated in 1938: 'The omission of unwelcome facts and the consequent suppression of truth runs counter to the Corporation's policy.'

Recent reports of the United States Information Service refer to foreign broadcasting as part of 'public diplomacy'. This is a concept alien to the BBC - though not to the Foreign and Commonwealth Office (FCO). Their spending some £80 million of public money on external broadcasting this year is undoubtedly due to diplomatic considerations. We in the BBC, however, do not see ourselves as diplomats nor as adjuncts of diplomacy. Our criteria are those of journalists. Our roots are in the British domestic media - media almost as critical and irreverent as those of the United States of America. We employ hardly any person who has been a diplomat. This was not so in the war years. However, it has become so with the increasing professionalism of the BBC.

The BBC's brief - as laid down in the Charter - is to 'broadcast in the national interest' but the BBC has always argued - and this has been endorsed by Parliament and by numerous government commissions - that veracity, which brings credibility, is very much in the long-term national interest. To quote one Government White Paper: 'In the Government's view the impartiality and objectivity of the BBC is a national asset of great value and the independence which the Corporation now enjoys should be maintained.' (3) The FCO - being pragmatists - recognise that giving our journalistic approach free rein makes sense from their long-term point of view - though it can cause acute embarrassment temporarily.

Let me now turn to how all this affects the pattern of our broadcasting towards Eastern Europe. The backbone of our transmissions is, naturally, news and current affairs - as with most other western stations broadcasting to Eastern Europe. Unlike some others, news is, however, highly centralised. Very similar news bulletins go out in Hindi and in Hausa, in Serbo-Croat and in Russian. External Services news bulletins are, however, different from BBC domestic bulletins which concentrate far more on British local preoccupations. The External Service bulletins attempt an overview of the entire world, though it is patently impossible to achieve perfection in this. Is an ethnic clash in the Punjab worth more lines than one in Saudi Arabia or Nigeria? Are the rising living standards in the Arab world or Japan more important - in the long run - than an argument over crucifixes in Poland? Could economic debates in Brazil perhaps matter more than those in Hungary?

Since a really Olympian view of what matters in the light of history is patently beyond mere mortal news editors we add the rider that we report the news 'as seen from London', a modest excuse for having to make do with a vantage point at the bottom end of Fleet Street rather than the top of Olympus. It is, however, an attempt to explain to our listeners that, while we are trying to be honest and detached, our vantage point, our education and social class cannot fail to influence our work. Our Marxist critics would insist that it is our class position, most of all, that influences our perception. 'In the guise of dispassionate news, a class-orientated point of view is cleverly put over.' (4) I would argue that this is not part of a subtle plot. Society inevitably influences our thought processes. We can never achieve total detachment. But I would argue that what matters is that there is an honest striving towards it. Compare that with the honest striving, for example, of a leading Soviet media man. I am referring to the editor-in-chief of <u>Literaturnaya Gazeta</u>, Alexander Chakovskiy. When he was awarded the Order of Lenin on his 70th birthday in August, 1983 Pravda said that his political credo had always been: 'I see it as my task to strengthen still further certain individuals' beliefs in the correctness of the path to communism we have chosen, to draw others who are wavering to our side and to unmask yet others, our enemies.' (5) Obviously a striving different from our own.

To revert to our news policy. That our news bulletins should be centralised, with only very limited regionalisation, is a matter of debate within the BBC. There is a strong lobby for greater decentralisation. They argue: audiences are self-centred and want to know what is going on in their own country and its immediate neighbours. British domestic media give such parochial news to domestic audiences - why not the External Services of the BBC? So far the 'centralists' have always won: the reputation for detachment, they argue, depends upon this attempt at a world view with the rider 'as seen from London'. To pretend to, say, a Bulgarian listener that his country is the centre of the world, by emphasising its affairs, is to mislead him. It is a form of distortion, they argue. Besides, it is virtually impossible to report accurately on the affairs of a 'far away country of which we know little' - especially when we are actively prevented from knowing more.

In the usual pattern of BBC broadcasting, what follows the news bulletins is normally a current affairs sequence of despatches, commentaries, interviews, discussions and press reviews. These sequences are far more decentralised than the news bulletins. Decisions on what goes into the Bulgarian sequence, for example, are made by the staff of the Bulgarian section under light guidance from the head of the East European services. The sequences start, normally, with despatches or commentaries on the main international stories of the day. Thereafter they concentrate on a circle around the target area. In the case of Bulgaria, that would be the affairs of Turkey, Greece, Yugoslavia, the Soviet Union and other Warsaw Pact states. But the circle is not seen as purely geographic. Vietnam or Cuba might be seen as close to the concerns of Bulgaria. Finally the programme will broadcast such material as is available on Bulgaria itself. Of course, the order does not have any inevitability but depends on the importance of the items.

There are variations from service to service dictated by 'objective criteria': for example, it has been possible to run a press review on 'Poland in the British Press' almost every day for several years. It has not been possible to cull such material on Bulgaria from the British press. For these current affairs sequences our language services can draw on despatches from 31 staff correspondents abroad and nearly 100 stringers. These are people who are employed either by BBC television services or by domestic radio services or by the External Services. Virtually everything that any of these reporters files is transcribed and made accessible, through an electronic distribution system, to every language section of the External Services. In addition, various language services have – over the years – built up small, embryonic networks of stringers of their own who file to their special requirements, some in English, some in the language of the target country.

Within these current affairs sequences there will also be commentaries. These commentaries and analyses may come from a central department supplying some five or six such commentaries each day on the main world events, or they may come from specialists dealing with Central and East European affairs attached to the regional departments. In addition, these departments can request talks from, say the Latin American or Far Eastern departments' specialist writers on – for example, Cuba or Vietnam. They further commission talks or interviews from academics, journalists and so on. All these decisions are decentralised.

BBC External Services

In a typical transmission the ten-minute news bulletin is followed by a 20 to 25 minute current affairs sequence which, in turn, is likely to be followed by a feature - cultural or political or scientific. Here again decisions on what to include are decentralised. However, shortage of funds or staff often dictates that central material is used. There are various central departments - a group of five science writers, a book review unit, a feature writing unit and so on. These central units provide - as part of their output - material which 'projects Britain'.

Acquainting our audience with what is going on in Britain - our theatre, our industry, our politics - is seen as part of broadcasting 'in the national interest': the coal miners strike in Britain, discussions of Orwell's book <u>1984</u> (to what extent has it come true?), commercial <u>pirate</u> radio stations, the raising of the 16th century warship <u>Mary Rose</u>, the Marks and Spencer chain of retail shops, attempts to stimulate rural development in Scotland, British primary education policy, and so on. However, even these central departments do not confine themselves to the affairs of Britain but tend to look at world problems - liberation theology, drought in Africa, the long-term effects of the microchip, diseases of affluence, new trends in western philosophy, and so on.

The feature spots of the Russian Service will include such subjects of special regional interest as 19th century Russian philosophers, the anniversaries of the deaths of Bukharin and Trotsky, 18th century British travellers in Russia, the Nomenklatura, Chagal, Tarkovsky, and so on. Bulgarian transmissions will include programmes on the Traicho Kostov trials; the Czech and Slovak services might cover the Slansky trial; a Hungarian broadcast would feature Koestler's <u>Darkness at Noon</u>, in our own translation. Our features programmes strive to break down the cultural isolation of Eastern Europe by telling listeners what is going on in western theatre and philosophy, and in political and economic thought. Isolation from the west is acutely painful to the best of the East European intelligentsia and we see it as our task to help them overcome it.

To get a clearer view of the policies and practices of the BBC's Eastern European services it is useful to examine criticisms of these practices. I shall look at the views of three types of critic: (1) the spokesmen of the Soviet and other Eastern European regimes (2) various East European emigres, and (3) British politicans, academics and journalists who have occasionally, though comparatively rarely, found fault with our approach.

An attack in <u>Komsomolskaya Pravda</u> in 1957 is typical of the curious awkwardness of many of the East European official attacks since then:

> The foundation of the BBC propaganda is the latest news, broadcast with emphatic objectivity. It should be noted that in selecting material for broadcasting to the USSR, the BBC does not draw any conclusions of its own but leaves this to its listeners who sometimes, through lack of experience or lack of knowledge are hooked by those who for years have made it their practice to fish in troubled waters ... 'White' propaganda is waged by the enemies of communism under the mantle of 'impartiality' and 'objectivity', but this does not lessen its hostile nature. (7)

In other words: the BBC may seem objective to you, but only because <u>you</u> are naive and <u>they</u> are extremely cunning. I quote a more recent attack, vintage 1980:

> The BBC makes great play of its independent status, presenting itself as an impartial observer ... yet £20 million are assigned every year from the budget of the Foreign Office for the External Services of the Corporation alone. As far as private subsidies are concerned, also by no means inconsiderable, they are contributed by the big-wigs of monopolistic capitalism. (8)

That year the Foreign Office's grant-in-aid to the BBC's External Services was, in fact, not £20 million but £55 million. As for private subsidies there were none and never have been. The present grant-in-aid is £80 million and there is still no private subsidy, though we get a modest return from selling our English-by-Television programmes to foreign broadcasting stations, including Soviet, Polish, and Chinese ones.

The most elaborate of attacks have come from V. Artemov and V. Semonov in their book on the BBC (9) and more recently an article by the same Artemov which appears to have been syndicated in the Soviet press. (10). These writers similarly expound the theme that the BBC surrounds itself with a 'halo of objectivity and justice, yet (is) striving at the same time to achieve its reactionary aims'. Our stance over Czechoslovakia in 1968 had 'demonstrated once again that to regard the BBC as the most reliable source of information during crises ... costs people a lot'. (10) Many politically inexperienced young people had been misled. Our sympathetic tone when talking even about honest communists showed that 'London pretended that it is far from being against socialism, but on the contrary is concerned about how to improve it.' But the truly subversive nature of our intentions had been demonstrated. How? 'Making use of the introduction of Warsaw Treaty troops, the BBC attemped to drive a wedge between the Soviet Union and other socialist countries and set Czechoslovakia against them.'

Apparently it was BBC broadcasts rather than Soviet tanks that harmed harmonious relations between Czechoslovaks and Russians. The book by Artemov and Semonov reiterates the theme that our propaganda is particularly dangerous because 'the bias of the BBC is not, so to speak, visible to the naked eye'. We use 'factological propaganda' which is defined as 'the manipulation of individual, established facts in the name of a global lie ... It must always be remembered that never, in BBC programmes, is there a single shot fired at random.' (9)

Other East European media, with somewhat lesser frequency repeat the same theme. Thus a Polish paper speaks of 'The BBC - that station which is so independent, especially of the truth.' (11) Because their own media have published little but advertising copy for the party line, and acknowledge this as their proper task, they have to assume that others are similarly motivated. The class struggle demands it. When the evidence suggests that this is not happening - that facts unfavourable to British policy are frequently published by the BBC - they argue that this must be an example of 'the jesuitically refined methods of the English bourgeoisie, the oldest in the world.' (12) The purpose of broadcasting such news items must be intended to befuddle the listener into believing in our objectivity so that we may better infiltrate other items favourable to capitalism and subversive of the Soviet system, for the purpose of 'liquidating the revolutionary gains' of the Soviet people. (13) I would argue that every professional broadcaster knows that credibility cannot be achieved by the insertion of an occasional item of 'negative projection' of Britain, nor by offering the odd 'loss leader'. There has to be a day-in-day-out honesty over very long periods, particuarly during stressful crises for Britain like Suez, the Falklands, or Northern Ireland. Artemov and Semonov seem convinced that listeners can be deceived by the occasional 'negative' item, which shows the usual latter-day communist contempt for the intelligence of ordinary people.

However, in striving for credibility we face a real problem: nations brought up to believe that media invariably lie find it difficult to accept that some might strive to be truthful. One Soviet listener writing to the BBC put it this way: 'I know that all radio stations lie, but you seem to me to be lying less than others.' The same theme appeared repeatedly in a batch of letters sent from all over the Soviet Union to some Soviet citizens who had been subjected to persecution and whose predicament had been mentioned in one of our programmes. These letters eventually reached Britain. Several of them started roughly as follows: 'I do not know whether you really exist or whether the BBC invented you but if you do exist I want to know that ...' A deep alienation and cynicism underlies such letters.

Let me now turn to some criticism from Soviet emigres. I shall concentrate on the most prominent of these and probably the most critical, Alexander Solzhenitsyn. He came to the BBC's External Services in January, 1976 and spoke from carefully thought-out notes, to a small group of senior staff. A transcript was subsequently published in Kontinent (23) He said that the BBC's policy of broadcasting to the Soviet Union in one language only, in Russian, was wrong. The BBC should broadcast in numerous other Soviet languages. 'You are using Russian to address a number of very different nations.' His reason for objecting to this was interesting. If only we took on other languages, "the Russian section could then become more specifically Russian ..." deeper in contact with the Russian people, their religion and their history in particular. Solzhenitsyn pleaded for more broadcasting of Russian Orthodox services. As an example of our lack of sympathetic understanding of Russian attitudes he quoted our serialisation of Richard Pipes' book Russia Under The Old Regime. Pipes' thesis is that Soviet communist expansionism and authoritarianism are direct descendants of Russian Czarist expansionism and authoritarianism. This, argued Solzhenitsyn, implied that the antagonist faced by the West is Russia, rather than communist - an erroneous conclusion, in his view.

BBC External Services

Solzhenitsyn further complained of the excessive publicity of repression in post-Franco Spain, compared with repression in Eastern Europe. No such sympathy had been extended to the far greater numbers of Stalin's victims. He further argued that it was wrong and counter-productive to include, in BBC press reviews, quotations from the British communist party daily The Morning Star. He next complained of our wasting time on jazz and pop and sports. 'Russia has no time for dancing.' He attacked the commentaries of the BBC's chief commentator, the late Anatol Goldberg as 'lacking in substance'.

As regards broadcasting in Soviet languages other than Russian - as Solzhenitsyn himself realised - the decision on which languages we use and for how long is not the BBC's but that of the British Foreign and Commonwealth Office. In this field the BBC's function is purely advisory. However, our advice has been consistent: that, while we have limited funds, limited transmitter-capacity and a shortage of frequencies it is more cost-effective to concentrate on the Russian language. There is, however, an underlying philosophical conflict. We do not see it as our function to be the mouthpiece, or one of the mouthpieces, of Holy Russia. We use the Russian language to communicate, just as we use French to France, Belgium, Switzerland, Zaire, the Ivory Coast and any other place where French is understood. Our first priority is not to reflect back the soul of Russia, but to report world news, as seen from London.

However, it is true that in our non-news programmes we do broadcast Russian literature, both classical and modern, as part of our output. Until some years ago it was our policy to broadcast such readings only when, in translation, the work had made a stir in Britain and we could quote reviews from British journals by way of introduction. This policy became increasingly unrealistic. It was, in fact, largely Solzhenitsyn's own work which made it so. When we saw Russian texts of his books - well before English translators had tackled them - we knew we were faced with writings of extraordinary quality and power. We could predict that they would eventually make an impact in Britain. It seemed unrealistic to sit on our hands and wait for that to happen before we broadcast excerpts. We also suspected that our competitors would not wait! As for broadcasting the views of Pipes - we were quite unrepentant. We do not take sides between Pipes and Solzhenitsyn, nor between Solzhenitsyn and Sinyavsky, nor between

BBC External Services

Medvedyev and Shafarevich ... between Slavophiles and Westernisers. We see ourselves as publishers of ideas which we believe will interest our listeners. As representatives of a pluralist, democratic society we think that the presentation of ideas and the stimulation of thought are part of our function. That is why we also think it essential – as a demonstration of respect for ideas, including those we disagree with – to quote the communist <u>Morning Star</u> in our press reviews when the subject matter seems of interest to our audience. What could demonstrate more clearly the difference between an open, tolerant democracy and a closed, authoritarian regime?

Solzhenitsyn's complaint – you fuss about abuses of human rights in Spain and Chile but not in the Soviet Union – is, in our view, quite false. Soviet abuses of human rights have had very extensive publicity and continue to receive it. However, the complaint, 'you see other peoples' agony but not mine' is, alas, a familiar one to my colleagues broadcasting in 36 different languages. I happen to have been the BBC's Greek programme organiser at the time of Colonels' dictatorship. The left-wing composer Mikis Theodorakis – who was exiled to a remote mountain village – used to smuggle his compositions out to London and we broadcast first performances of several of his works. I recall one of his songs. The lyrics were his own. They said (I am quoting from memory), 'I am a European' – by which Greeks mean a Frenchman or German or British, but not a Greek – 'I am a European. I have two ears. With one I hear the cries of the people of Russia and Poland. The other is deaf. I do not hear the suffering of Greece. I do not hear the cries of her tortured daughters.' It does seem to me essential for the reputation of the BBC – and for the personal integrity of its staff – to speak with the same voice of torture in Spain or Greece or Latin America as in the Soviet Union, while not losing sight of the scale of repression.

In one way, however, our policy has altered somewhat: We do now put more effort into our Russian Orthodox religious programme. Audience feedback – Solzhenitsyn included – showed that greater thought for the religious searchings of our audience was needed.

I now turn briefly to the criticism of other Soviet exiles. A very common form of criticism is reflected by the writer Andrei Amalrik, who on a visit to the BBC, said that our output showed, 'A certain wishy-washyness - on the one hand, on the other ... I suppose that is how the British are.' In other words, we were not sufficiently forthright and polemical. Bukovsky, while agreeing, attributed this to pressure from the Foreign Office.

I would argue, that it is not that we do not recognise absolute values of right and wrong, but that we have considerable diffidence about pressing our values upon others. The attitude 'on the one hand, on the other' is a reflection both of a pluralistic society and of a respect for our listeners. 'Give them the facts,' we have always argued: 'Give them the arguments on either side. Let them make up their own minds.' To revert to Bukovsky: he claimed that he had been partly instrumental in changing BBC policy but that in part this change had been the result of the change of government from Labour to Conservative. I quote: 'substantial changes were made in the composition of the management, in the programming and also in the way the BBC was run. When the Conservatives came to power these changes became very substantial.' (14)

In so far as there is any detectable change at all, it is because a more confrontational East-West situation is reflected in parliamentary debates, which we report, and in the newspaper editorials, which we quote. As regards Conservative pressure on our policies, Margaret Thatcher did indeed call for 'a massive propaganda campaign of the kind we have never mounted' in the direction of Eastern Europe and the Soviet Union. (15) That was in 1980. The implication was 'BBC: pull up your socks.' The following day, the managing director of the BBC External Services, Gerry Mansell, reiterated the BBC's traditional view: 'To convert what we do now into propaganda, in reverse to what Radio Moscow carries out, in my view, would be utterly counter-productive.' (16) And this remains our view.

In a recent unpublished internal discussion paper, a Russian member of our staff criticised the BBC (as well as other western stations) for not 'answering back'. I quote with his permission:

> Soviet propaganda has one crucial weakness which renders it vulnerable to exposure ... its inherent need to lie and distort. Western radio stations have assumed that to argue with the Soviet propagandists would be counter-productive, that it is better not to repeat their inventions and distortions ... (However) the absence of a direct challenge merely

enhances the impact of Soviet propaganda. (The Soviet listener) can only conclude that the western broadcasters have been unable to prove that the Soviet press and radio are lying and have therefore dodged a direct confrontation.

If we did go in for polemics, our broadcasts might be more lively! However, the BBC decided against such a policy very early in the 1939-45 war. By giving up airtime to answer Goebbels' lies we would be leaving it to him to choose the subject for debate. The policy was reaffirmed early in the cold war by the controller of European Services, Sir Ian Jacob: 'Britain has to struggle against calumny ... Our part in counter-acting this is not by refuting it but by seizing and retaining the initiative.' (17) One further consideration: the polemical tone of 'hitting back' would make us some friends, but a greater number of enemies.

I turn now to criticism of the policies in the British press, focusing on the debate about the BBC Russian Services' policies in the weekly The Spectator in 1957. A number of academics and journalists - of whom Professor (as he became later) Peter Wiles was the most active - attacked the policies of the Russian service in 1957. The charge was that we 'very rarely uttered a word which could irritate even the touchiest of listeners' in the Soviet Union. We appeared to be speaking to the Soviet establishment - to government and official circles - in the language of diplomacy rather than in appealing to the masses who wanted hard hitting programmes discrediting the regime and the system. For example, we had not broadcast the full text of Krushchev's secret speech denouncing Stalin at the 20th party congress. This was an example of our 'moral compromise and appeasement'. The programme organiser of the time was accused of an 'esoteric, right-wing Marxism'. The man in quesion was Anatol Goldberg. (18) The late Professor Leonard Schapiro, who supported Wiles, wrote:

> For what audience is the service intended? One view is that the service should mainly be directed to government and official circles and their supporters. The other, that it should be mainly directed to the growing number of Russians who are aware that there is much wrong with communist rule and who are beginning to say so almost openly. If we are to broadcast to the former, then it is right that the broadcasts

should use the language of diplomacy, should avoid direct sharp criticism, and should keep off subjects which are likely to cause particular irritation. If to the latter, then our aim should be to provide information, including, of course, information on the communist orbit and on British opinion on communism ... My impression is that it is much more often concerned with the first of my imaginary audiences than with the second, and I believe this to be profoundly wrong. (19)

If Schapiro's assessment of our output in the 1950s was right, I would agree with him. The pontificating style of some of the commentaries, reminiscent of The Times's editorials of the time, would support Schapiro's argument. I do, however, believe - on the basis of my reading - that there was never any doubt that the target audience was not intended to be 'official circles' but the questing, inquisitive intelligentsia, both the newly educated technocracy and those with older roots in the intellectual life of Russia. If our approach, at the time, was in any way uncertain, this must, in part, have been due to the fact that we did not yet know whether shortwave sets were easily available to ordinary citizens and had little idea how widespread listening to western radio was becoming. Goldberg himself saw the discussion over correct target audiences differently. He wrote that the target audience should be the intellectuals as distinct from the actively dissident minority who were small and had little influence. Any change that would occur in Soviet society would come from the intelligentsia.

Soviet analysts themselves have repeatedly said that it appeared to be the BBC's policy to concentrate on the Soviet technical intelligentsia, 'Those who play an important part ... in scientific and technical progress in our country,' (20) which I read to mean that this was the group on which they thought we were making the most impact. In fact, audience research statistics show that the situation is more complicated: although a higher proportion of the better-educated people listen to the BBC, this does not mean that they outnumber the less well-educated in our total audience. Take Poland - for which we have more reliable statistics than for the Soviet Union - 42% of people with secondary education or more listen to the BBC. Only 22% of people with less than secondary education do. However, these less-educated make up 61% of our audience. It is a familiar conundrum for programme planners.

To revert to The Spectator controversy, in practical programme terms the argument seems to have centred on a question of tone: how aggressively condemnatory of the Soviet system and how hard-selling of an alternative social system, should BBC broadcasts be? I think our consistent intention has been better summarised by Radio Liberty than by ourselves: 'to be a guest in the living room'. I cannot see any evidence that in 1957 our broadcasters spoke like polite guests at a Soviet diplomatic reception. The Soviet attack upon Hungary, for example, and their opposition to free elections in the two Germanies were condemned in forthright terms. Professor Wiles, in The Spectator controversy, argued that too many of the basic assumptions of Marxism were being accepted as a basis of discussion by our commentators, especially by Goldberg. Goldberg himself - in an internal BBC discussion paper - countered that a root-and-branch condemnation of communism - i.e. that nothing could change in the Soviet Union so long as its leaders remained communists - would be a disastrous policy: the feeling of hopelessness conveyed to listeners would be resented by them. It would also make nonsense of the western attempts at reaching some understanding with the Soviet Union. Every East-West conference would a priori be condemned to failure. Moreover, it was untrue: important changes for the better had occurred in the Soviet Union since Stalin's death. It would be folly to ignore these developments. (21) The controversy dragged on for several months.

The BBC management did not come out of this controversy with much credit. They moved Anatol Goldberg out of his job as Russian programme organiser and made him a commentator - on the grounds that he was not a good administrator but that he was a brilliant commentator. Both true. But one cannot help wondering whether this would have happened if he had not been the target of this sustained and sometimes malicious campaign in The Spectator. Anyway, he went on to become the BBC External Services' chief commentator and his name became a household word in Eastern Europe.

May I now pull together the strands of this policy, which I have tried to illuminate by examining some of the more interesting attacks made upon it over the years. Since our approach is pragmatic, i.e. we react in a journalistic way to the events of the day, and do not go in for 'ideological plenums', this did not come easily. At the basis of our practice is the thinking that the power of propaganda has been grossly overrated by authoritarians - communist and fascist - throughout this century and even some non-authoritarians. Neither cadre parties nor supermen nor the slickest of advertising men can 'mould masses like clay' - as Mussolini claimed to be able to do.

'On what basis can one reach a conclusion about the real thoughts and feelings of real people? Clearly, there's only one such basis: the actions of such people.' The quote is from Lenin. I quote it with approval. What are the actions of Soviet people after 67 years of communist propaganda? Low labour discipline, low productivity, massive theft and corruption, nostalgia for the past, widespread alcoholism and persistent attempts by millions to listen to alternative ideas and uncorrupted news from foreign sources, despite the disapproval of their rulers and despite massive jamming. The masses have not been moulded in the planned image. There is little evidence for the evolution of a new Soviet man, but strong evidence for widespread alienation. The tone emanating from Andropov's Ideological Plenum 'class implacability towards bourgeois propaganda', (22) 'propaganda interventionists', 'subversive onslaught' etc shows it.

I do not wish to claim they have been totally ineffective in changing public attitudes. They have, for example, largely succeeded in changing attitudes to buying and selling for profit. Very many Soviet citizens would now regard this as 'speculation', and as immoral, whereas few would have had that attitude in 1917. But their successes are modest. So why should we, in the West, seek to imitate their style of propaganda? This is something which the BBC External Services have consistently tried to avoid - despite pressure from emigres and occasionally from some of our own politicians. Permit me to quote a favourite anecdote. It comes from Simon Ley's book Chinese Shadows. In the 1960s an elderly Chinese emigre was asked what he knew about Yugoslavia. 'Yugoslavia?' he said, 'a pseudo-socialist country run by revisionist hyenas in the pay of capitalism'. And now that he had left the Peoples Republic, where would he prefer to live? 'In Yugoslavia, for instance'. Why? 'It seems that in a pseudo-socialist country run by revisionist hyenas in the pay of capitalism, oil and cotton cloth are not rationed.' Reality appears to speak louder than propaganda.

We in the BBC have been reluctant to preach democracy but prefer to demonstrate it in action by exposing debate and controversy in our own ranks. Certainly this does disorientate some naive listeners brought up in a very different society. I recall that after a particularly lively discussion about East-West relations broadcast in our Polish service, a listener wrote in quite scandalised because the participants had disagreed and argued. Less naive listeners are affected differently by exposures of disagreement and even protest within our society. I recall interviewing a Bulgarian industrial worker who had defected to the West. He had, prior to his defection, been a listener to the BBC for many years. When had he started listening? I asked. After he had first heard about the BBC from friends in Plovdiv. They had told him that the BBC had reported something they considered amazing: someone had thrown a pot of ink at the British Prime Minister. (The incident happened in January 1972 when the Prime Minister, Edward Heath, went to Brussels to sign the Treaty of Accession to the European Community and a German woman threw a bottle of ink at him, which delayed the signing ceremony.) I do not suppose the BBC's news editors gave it a single second's consideration before reporting the incident. Yet this Bulgarian worker knew that his own media would have repressed such an item had it happened to a Bulgarian minister. As a result he started to think seriously about truth and credibility.

I would argue that we are effective in explaining ourselves when we act unselfconsciously, following the mores of our society. By exposing free debate in Britain (and elsewhere in the West) - the clash of opinion over the abolition of the Greater London Council, debates over privatisation of industry, controversy over the Falklands campaign, over the invasion of Grenada, over US policy in Central America and so on - we demonstrate democracy.

To sum up: I have touched upon the need for journalistic integrity unsullied by 'reasons of state'; upon the need for respect for the good sense of ordinary people; the need for a sympathetic, non-aggressive tone; the need to demonstrate democracy (warts and all) rather than to preach its advantages; the need to publish a wide variety of ideas rather than to become the mouthpiece of one faction; the need to break down the intellectual isolation of our audiences.

There is still one danger I have not touched upon: faced with abuses of human rights in Eastern Europe and elsewhere, each of us is in danger of giving way to anger. But if we give way to anger - however righteous - our voices become shrill and we communicate less clearly.

One final anecdote: in the 1970s the London underground rail network was covered with graffiti in a language I took to be Arabic. I asked Arab colleagues what these meant. They were as puzzled as I was. 'It's not Arabic,' they said. 'It seems to be Farsi'. I asked Persian colleagues. Yes, they expained, these were slogans denouncing the Shah, the Anglo-American imperialists alleged to be his paymasters, his secret police - 'may they be strung up from the nearest lamp-post' - and so on. Many millions of people pass through the London underground each week. A mere few hundred of them can read Farsi. What, I pondered, was the point of slogans that only communicated with a tiny minority? No, said my Persian colleagues, the purpose of this graffiti is not to communicate but to ventilate the anger and frustration of the slogan writers.

All of us who communicate across the iron curtain are occasionally in danger of such self-indulgence - of ventilating our own anger at brutality and inhumanity and of forgetting that our real purpose must be to communicate; to set out facts clearly; to cause listeners to think. If we lose sight of that purpose, we too condemn ourselves to ineffectiveness.

Notes
1. Callum A. MacDonald, 'Radio Bari: Italian Wireless Propaganda in the Middle East and British Countermeasures 1934-8', Middle Eastern Studies (May 1977). *
2. Gerald Mansell, Let Truth Be Told (Weidenfeld and Nicholson, 1982), p.51.
3. Mansell, Truth, p.239.
4. Vadim Kassis and Leonid Kolosov, 'Aerials Directed Eastwards', Moscow Home Service, 27th July, 1983.
5. Pravda, 25th August, 1983. See also Igor Fesunenko, Televideniy i Radioveshchaniye, no. 10, October, 1983.
6. Mansell, Truth, p. 218.
7. Ibid, p.220.
8. Krasnaya Zvezda, 16th February, 1980.
9. Vladimir Artemov and V. Semonov, The BBC - History, Apparatus, Methods of Radio Propaganda (Moscow, 1979). And V. Artemov and V. Semonov, Historical Journal of Film, Radio and Television,

vol. 4, No. 1, 1984.
10. Vladimir Artemov, 'The BBC is Fanning Psychological Warfare' Tiesa, 17th and 18th November, 1983.
11. Gazeta Robotnicza, Wroclaw, 7th April, 1983.
12. G.N. Vachnadze, Aerials Directed Towards the East, (Political Literature Publishing House, Moscow), 1975.
13. V. Bolshakov, Pravda, 23rd September, 1980.
14. V. Bukovsky, interviewed in On Air (Radio Liberty house magazine) no.3, 1983.
15. Margaret Thatcher, interviewed in the BBC TV programme World This Weekend, 4th May, 1980.
16. Gerald Mansell, interviewed in the BBC Radio Four programme World at One, 5th May, 1980.
17. Sir Ian Jacob, quoted in Mansell, Truth, p.217.
18. Peter Wiles, various contributions to The Spectator between 21st July, 1957 and 3rd January, 1958.
19. Leonard Schapiro, The Spectator, 16th August, 1957.
20. For example, M.S. Solovyez, Leningrad Home Service, 5th May, 1974. Also in Sovietskaya Latvia, Turkmenskaya Iskra and others.
21. Anatol Goldberg, BBC memo dated 9th January, 1958, and others.
22. Leonid Zamyatin on Soviet TV, 20th August, 1983. Also BBC Monitoring Service, 6th August, 1983 and 11th June, 1984 (quoting Chernenko).
23. Alexander Solzhenitsyn, 'About the World of the Russian Section of the BBC', Kontinent, no.8, 1976.

Chapter Eight

DEUTSCHE WELLE'S RUSSIAN SERVICE, 1962-85

Botho Kirsch, head of East European Service, Deutsche Welle

It was Erich Honecker's Neues Deutschland that described the modern mass media as the 'real key industry of the 20th century'. Citing Lenin, the East German Party organ characterised the press and the radio as being always and everywhere the underlying basis of political organisation. They forge the communicative link that combines whole groups of like-minded people, directing their activities towards a common goal. Those who control the mass media, therefore, decisively guide and organise the political life of a country. The resumption by the Soviet government in August 1980, after a seven years pause, of deliberate jamming of Voice of America, BBC and Deutsche Welle Russian language broadcasts reflects the high esteem in which communists hold the mass media. A substitute for jamming has been the continuous propaganda effort from the inception of these broadcasts to discredit foreign radio stations and to 'immunize' Soviet citizens against them.
   Although the total weekly output of Russian language programmes beamed from Cologne to the USSR is only 35 hours, Deutsche Welle occupies a prominent place on the list of what Moscow radio regards as hostile stations. If the effectiveness of Russian language broadcasts is measured by the Homeric tirades of communist counter-propaganda, an increase in the response to western broadcasting over the iron curtain is hardly imaginable. In the abusive language employed by Soviet media, Deutsche Welle is a 'wolf changing clothing but not its habits'; the programmes broadcast from Cologne are 'unbridled, distinctively hostile and virulent'. Deutsche Welle commentators look at the Soviet Union 'through the spectacles of a lunatic and the prism of the most obdurate prejudice'. They are a bunch of 'writers of empty words' and a 'Goebbels breed', 'masters of espionage

and psychological warfare who should not be allowed within a gunshot's range of a microphone'. A Novosti correspondent who, on the day of the invasion of Czechoslovakia, crashed over Prague in a helicopter, in one of his last despatches singled out Deutsche Welle, together with its elder and bigger brothers BBC and VOA, as the 'real masters of the black heavens'. The head of the CPSU's information department even raised the so-called western radio propaganda to the rank of a fourth sphere of state policy – alongside the armed forces, diplomacy and trade. Only recently Army General Epishev, chief of the Soviet army's political department, blamed the West for organising against the Soviet Union a 'real interventionist propaganda campaign' using radio waves and television channels as an instrument of political warfare. Whatever pretext the Warsaw Pact countries may have had for their invasion of Czechoslovakia in 1968, the real enemy against which their tanks were sent in, was the freely spoken and written word. As <u>Neues Deutschland</u> said 'The trouble did not start with turmoil in the streets. It all started with unlimited freedom of the press.'

Since June 1963 when the Soviet Union ceased jamming of the VOA, BBC and Deutsche Welle, the only unlimited 'press freedom' for the Russian people was on the air. One year earlier, in August 1962, Deutsche Welle had started broadcasting Russian language programmes to the Soviet Union. As a relatively late newcomer to the international broadcasting community its Russian service, right from the start had to cope with numerous handicaps – an unfavourable time schedule, a weak power base and staffing problems. But it soon caught up with its competitors in the air and firmly established its place with other major western broadcasters to the area.

Originally founded in 1953 as a joint venture of the domestic radio network ARD, the association of West German radio stations, Deutsche Welle constituted itself as the shortwave radio station of the Federal Republic of Germany with headquarters in Cologne. It broadcasts 94 programmes daily with a total output of over 100 hours, of which roughly five hours are in Russian. In 1960 a federal law was passed by the Bundestag, the West German parliament, establishing Deutsche Welle as a public corporation in its own right. Funds to operate the station are appropriated by the federal Government, but Deutsche Welle is not a government institution. Its operations and programming are supervised by the administrative council and the radio council respectively, constituted of representatives of the legislative bodies, government agencies and the churches. The corporation is managed by the general director who has overall responsibility for the running of the organisation.

The mission of Deutsche Welle broadcasts is set forth in the federal radio legislation enacted by the Bundestag. It is their purpose to 'provide listeners abroad with a comprehensive picture of political, cultural and economic life in Germany and to present the German viewpoint on important issues'. The essence of Deutsche Welle's programme policy has always been to present the government's point of view on an equal footing with that of the opposition. This goes to say that government policy should not only be presented, but also critically assessed from the standpoint of the opposition. Beyond these more general provisions of the Federal Radio Law, special guidelines were issued to assure the compliance of day-to-day programming with the long-term foreign policy objectives of the Federal Republic. Thus, Deutsche Welle broadcasts are designed to support independent personal judgement. They shall not unilaterally favour a political party, a religious creed, a trade or profession. The moral and religious values of listeners must be respected. News coverage should be comprehensive, accurate and impartial. Materials made available for broadcasting use must be thoroughly verified as to facts and sources. Editorial opinion shall clearly be distinguished from news, commentaries must be identified as personal contributions.

Although Deutsche Welle concentrates on reflecting news and views of West German society, reporting and commenting on domestic issues and developments in target areas is welcomed, provided it is related to the interests of the Federal Republic of Germany and its broader foreign policy objectives. However the tone, language and manner of such broadcasts should be fair and reasoned, avoiding polemical or biased treatment of the material involved. Newscasts, commentaries and press reviews reflecting a broad spectrum of German and international opinion account for about half the time allotted to Deutsche Welle's Russian service. The rest is made up of correspondents' reports, news analyses, interviews and feature programmes. Roundtable discussions, preferably with the participation of outside experts, provide a useful means of presenting different views to the audience.

Deutsche Welle's Russian Service

The backbone of the daily programme schedule are the 10-minute newscasts at the beginning of each of the three daily Russian broadcasts of Deutsche Welle. These include a dozen or so items in German, selected from the major international news agencies, electronically edited and transmitted to the translator's desk. Daily news is supplemented by fresh newscasts on repeat programmes late in the night and early in the morning. Outstanding events, such as national elections or the Olympic Games, are covered live. A continuous stream of spot news emerges from the monitoring of international media and Deutsche Welle correspondents in Bonn, West Berlin and Brussels. Russian music, theatre and literature have always attracted the German mind. This is to a certain degree also reflectd in Deutsche Welle's Russian broadcasts to the USSR, in which the great cultural heritage of the Russian people is especially cherished. Ample airtime is devoted to cultural programmes, such as book reviews, including the review of Russian emigre journals, extensive coverage of theatre and opera performances on the West German stage and open air concerts as well as a constant check on the international pop music scene. Regular contributions come from such outstanding literary figures as writers Lev Kopelev, Vladimir Voinovich, German Andreevy and Boris Khasanov.

The cornerstone of the Russian service and a major component of programme advance planning are feature programmes. They are organised either in magazine format or consist of news-related scripts centrally edited and ranging from 12 to 25 minutes respectively. Their topics cover a wide spectrum of human knowledge, keeping the Russian audience informed about important developments in history, economics, sociology and Sovietology. Contributors to the feature programme are Deutsche Welle staff writers and outside specialists. As a particularly valuable programme category, features justify spending about one third of the Russian service budget. Additionally, there are regular spots on sports, women, youth, agriculture and ecology. Religious programmes are common on weekends and on church holidays. Special German language lessons are broadcast to Siberia and Central Asia on high frequencies, in order to escape jamming which is particularly bothersome to language courses transmitted on short waves. They are designed for ethnic Germans who were deported during the war from their homelands in the Volga region to remote parts of the Soviet empire. Special emphasis is placed on weekend programmes. Many middle-class Russian city-dwellers prefer to spend the weekend on their dachas, or little wooden cottages, in the countryside, where overall jamming is less obtrusive. Carefully selected material, such as reviews of the international and German periodical press, and readings from tamizdat-literature (Russian books published only in the West) make up for the bulk of weekend programmes. Besides, a substantial share of Deutsche Welle's Russian programme is devoted to readings of protest letters, petitions and essays from uncensored samizdat sources, a unique collection of independent Russian thinking.

Significant assistance to programme quality controls of Russian language programmes is rendered by the audience survey and research department. Linguistically qualified experts review tapes and prepare programme summaries on a month-to-month basis for screening by the senior management and members of the radio council. For nearly two decades, auditor reports have attributed to the Russian service of Deutsche Welle a high quality, professional integrity and an overall effectiveness, although programmes were occasionally lacking linguistic glamour. Detailed programme evaluation has enabled programme managers to make periodicial adjustments in schedules, format and content as well as to correct blunders or broaden the scope of the service.

Over a period of seven years between 1973 and 1980, shortwave broadcasts from Cologne were free from interference, apart from selective jamming in the spring of 1974 when Solzhenitsyn's book Gulag Archipelago was read over Deutsche Welle. Yet, the rise of the workers' movement in Poland sparked off the jammers - the KGB jazz - again. It is estimated that the cost of jamming western broadcasts to the USSR is at least twice as high as the funds appropriated by western governments to produce and transmit them. Listening can virtually become impossible when regional 'sky-wave' jamming is being overlapped by one or more 'ground wave' stations located in Moscow, Leningrad or Kiev. Experience shows, however, that the effectiveness of jamming varies: at times it can block a signal in the city and fails to do so a few miles away in the flat country. The use of high power transmitters - nine of them are located in Wertachtal in the southern part of Germany - can overcome some jamming, as well as the use of high frequencies at daylight. From the evaluation of reception reports and personal observations made on package tours through the USSR, it can be concluded that jamming practices were considerably refined in the last years and have been intensified to a degree hitherto unknown. As Viktor Nekipelov notes, 'Near almost every larger city, on the mountain passes of the Caucasus and the Crimea stand powerful generators ejecting every hour and every minute decibels of meaningless noise, a cacophony of savage and superfluous sounds, a barbaric pollution of the air waves.'

In spite of heavy jamming, Deutsche Welle broadcasts in Russian continue to remain audible at least on one of the four to six frequencies employed. Evening programmes are more severely jammed than transmissions in the early morning, when the signal is clearer. High frequencies are less susceptible to interference than the lower ones. This could also explain the relatively stable pattern of listeners tuning in to programmes from Deutsche Welle daily. They obviously belong to the class of the intelligentsia which can afford to buy highly-prized radio receivers, preferably foreign made, with high frequency broadcasting bands between 15 and 21 mHz. On the other hand, owners of mass consumption radio sets within the reach of 6 to 11 mHz tend to be discouraged by jamming and tune in on other stations with a stronger signal relatively free from interference or discontinue listening to foreign radio altogether. It is among these listeners that a rather marked decline in Deutsche Welle's Russian audience was registered after a long period of a steady rise, whereas losses with regard to regular listeners were, for the reasons mentioned, less significant.

To cope with the effect of jamming, Deutsche Welle's Russian programme schedule has been adjusted to changing needs. An unusually high proportion of airtime is devoted to repeat broadcasts from earlier programmes. First run transmissions constitute roughly 40 per cent of the total output of the Russian service. Beyond these immediate priorities, airtime was increased several times as jamming intensified: by 35 minutes in the autumn of 1980 when jamming was reimposed in the wake of the Polish crisis, and again by 50 minutes in October, 1984 – following a stepped-up jamming effort after Andropov's death and Chernenko's takeover.

Despite the enormous investment of money and transmitting power, the Soviet government has not succeeded in cutting off its populace from uncensored information over the air. According to the latest findings by RFE/RL's SAAOR's Paris research staff, listenership to Deutsche Welle's Russian programme has, on the whole, remained remarkably stable over the various jamming periods. An estimated 7.5 to 11.2 million Soviet citizens - among them 2.2 millions daily - listen to the radio voice of Deutsche Welle from Cologne. 'The importance of foreign broadcasting in the Russian language is inestimable,' says dissident writer Viktor Nekipelov. 'These broadcasts are listened to by all strata of Soviet society: university professors and students, workers and peasants, former political prisoners and state officials; even party functionaries, journalists, justice officials and regular army officers huddle around radio sets more and more often.' The typical Deutsche Welle listener appears to be well educated, belongs to the 16-29 age group (with a solid share of the 30-49 years old age group) and is a city-dweller; only 2 out of 10 listeners are women. Communist party members listen to Deutsche Welle at a higher rate than non-party members. Listening rates are highest in the Ukraine, the Moscow and Leningrad regions, Belorussia, and the Baltic republics. Russian listeners usually tune in on Cologne radio at home during evening hours, often in the company of their family or friends, listening for up to 40 minutes daily, reception conditions allowing. The newscast ranks highest in preference among the audience, followed by commentaries, roundtable discussions and readings from samizdat sources.

I came across several of these listeners in 1978 and 1982 travelling in the European part of the USSR. Going by train from Vilnius to Pskov, I switched on my portable radio set to the wavelength of Deutsche Welle and had a fine reception. From the neighbouring compartment a curious Russian fellow traveller dropped in to listen to the programme I had prepared myself the day before I left Cologne for Leningrad. The talk was devoted to a review of Roy Medvedev's book October 1917, a German translation of which had just been published. The author, a prominent Marxist dissident living in Moscow, gives a vivid account of events going on in Petrograd on the very day of the glorious October revolution. According to Medvedev, life on 7th November was quite normal, with theatres playing and restaurants opened. An elegantly dressed crowd was flocking over famous Nevsky Prospect. Lenin, who had always mocked German workers for their unrevolutionary spirit, afraid to trespass on railway platforms without a ticket, bought himself one. Then he took the next tram to the Smolny Institute to put himself at the head of a coup d'etat which was directed against a Socialist-led provisional government – a rebellion that was, by the way, quite an unbloody affair.

I handed over my radio set to the unknown listener who immediately withdrew to the neighbouring compartment where a further three Russians, one of them the train conductor, were already waiting. After a while, my transistor set was returned to me with many compliments. 'Ochen interesno' (very interesting). On another occasion our travel group was shown around a model factory. Suddenly, in a lit corridor, a man with tinted glasses on his eyes approached our company and addressed himself to the man from Deutsche Welle. 'I often hear you on the radio', he began. 'Oh, how do you like our programme?' I asked. 'Not bad,' he replied and disappeared as quickly as he had turned up. A couple of days later, shortly before we were to depart to the railway station, the same man came to our bus and bade our guide from Intourist – a KGB controlled travel agency – to step aside, so that he could speak to the Deutsche Welle reporter in private. Obediently the guide complied, and the man introduced himself as a high local official. 'I would never have believed to meet some one from Deutsche Welle during my lifetime,' he said grasping my right hand. He shook it enthusiastically muttering all the time, 'Thank you, thank you for what you are doing to us.' In a low voice he added, 'Please, do speak more about Russia!'

In Kalinin, the old merchant town of Tver, our travel company was housed in a motel outside the city. In the evening the motel's dining hall was crammed with young folk dancing to the sound of a beat band called 'My Vas lyubim' (we love you). I would not trust my ears when towards midnight, all on a sudden, the band intonated – it is true, for a few seconds only – Deutsche Welle's signal tune The brother seeks his brothers', a famous motif from Beethoven's opera Fidelio. The spell was broken, and the Russian hosts began to fraternize with their west German guest – 'brothers' until long after midnight. About two months later a listeners' symposium in Vienna confirmed how popular Deutsche Welle's Russian broadcasts are with the Soviet audience. Taking part were 40 to 50 intellectuals – artists, writers, scholars and journalists – who had recently emigrated from the USSR and were now waiting for their immigration visa to western countries. Summing up his listening experience in the years past, a young Leningrad mathematician declared that,

> Comparing Deutsche Welle to the Voice of America and the BBC, one can explain the impact of foreign broadcasting with the following formula: the VOA newscast is the most comprehensive and the most operative. Whenever something happens in the world the other broadcasters fail to report on, one tunes in to the Voice of America. The highest cultural standard is achieved by the BBC, a true voice of culture, even of a certain intellectual sophistication. Deutsche Welle, on the other hand, seems to me the most intelligent radio station in the way it analyzes international politics.

Such judgement is obviously shared by large segments of the academic community in the Soviet Union. Dissident writer Victor Nekipelov lauds Deutsche Welle's Russian programme for its remarkable ability to combine logic and feeling. Another listener, writing from Obninsk, a scientific centre south-west of Moscow, pleaded that, 'information is death to Communism. Do not give up providing us with truthful information, and you will live to see within eight to ten years' time the fruits of your just deeds. Only 10 to 15 years ago we were complete fools. Now we have grown to be real human beings.' Professor Isaac Kaplan, now teaching in the sociological department of New York City University, expressed his gratitude to Deutsche Welle for its 'most useful programmes'; he was writing on behalf of a group of well-known scholars from the Economics Institute of the prestigious Academy of Sciences, the Scientific Labour Research Institute with the State Committee of Labour, and the Higher Trade Union School in Moscow. He stressed that overall jamming only strengthens the desire to listen to western broadcasts. 'Many of my former colleagues,' he continued, 'used to go to places outside Moscow to be able to listen to your broadcasts. Others who live farther away, make short summaries of your transmissions.' In her best-selling book, <u>Doors Only Open Slowly</u>, writer Raisa Orlova, wife of famous novelist Lev Kopelev, makes an ardent plea to Russian programme organisers not to be content to present their Russian audience with mere facts. They should also try to explain their point of view to a public not used to contradiction and discussion of conflicting views. (1)

Thanks to the effectiveness of international shortwave radio, modern tyrants can no longer operate in an air-tight public opinion vacuum. While seeking to sustain their absolute power monopoly, they have become increasingly sensitive to public pressure from the human rights movement, religious and national minorities, independent peace groups and workers associations. It is through western radio that millions of listeners in the Soviet orbit have become aware of their own situation, their plights and deprivations, their longings for truthful information and an objective evaluation of events abroad, as well as in their own countries. As a result, Russians nowadays are far better informed about their own situation and the world at large than at any other time in modern Russian history. The effect of this cannot and will not fail to make itself felt in the historical perspective. As former Under Secretary of State, George Ball has remarked, 'it is a sound principle that governments can be trusted that trust their own peoples; for an informed public opinion is the most reliable barrier against foolish or aggressive behaviour on the part of governments'. (2) The special impact of Deutsche Welle broadcasts to the USSR can be supported by many examples, a few of which are presented here:
1. One of the main instruments of Soviet policy to tame disobedient satellite countries and suppress domestic opposition has been the bogy of a revival of German <u>revanchism</u>, striving to recover the lost territories in the East by force and thus plunge the world into a new war. Deutsche Welle has not only raised its voice to disclaim the truth of all such charges. At the same time, it has avoided striking a purely defensive or polemical tone on this particular issue. The most effective way to combat Soviet-inspired propaganda campaigns of this sort has proved to be the presentation of a modern Germany as a democratic country with freedom of speech and the press, free elections and the right of individuals and nations to self-determination; an affluent society, not without internal strain and social contradictions, but firmly embedded in the community of free nations, following a policy of good neighbourhood with all countries in East and West, solely bent on the pursuit of purely economic goals, and which has definitely broken with the past.
2. A moving example of listenership reaction to Deutsche Welle's image-building of a new, democratic Germany has been the letter received from Professor

Deutsche Welle's Russian Service

Aleksandr Lerner, one of the leading Jewish activists in Moscow. 'I listened to your broadcast reporting the reactions of German viewers who had been shown on television the US-produced <u>Holocaust</u> film', wrote Professor Lerner whose three and five year old daughters were murdered by the Nazis during the war. 'I listened to the words of German viewers expressing feelings of shame and horror as to the massacres committed on completely innocent women, old men and children. I heard Jews being called upon to pardon Germans for the shocking crimes of their compatriots. And I listened to the sincere emotions that were expressed by good and honest people confronted with the cruel past of their country.' Professor Lerner then went on to say that this kind of reaction on the side of German public opinion to the <u>Holocaust</u> film constituted an 'important turning point in the evaluation of the terrible past by the German people.'

3. An important feature of Deutsche Welle's programmes to the USSR are 'rectifications' of the historical truth distorted by offical Soviet media. A small, but significant example occurred in May 1984 when Foreign Minister Hans-Dietrich Genscher was on an official visit to Moscow to discuss German-Soviet relations with the Kremlin leaders. When <u>Pravda</u> published the text of Genscher's dinner speech it was full of distortions. Deutsche Welle's broadcast laid particular stress on the omitted passages, especially on those where the Minister underscored Germany's peace-loving aspirations. 'Nobody wants war, and nobody is preparing a war', said Genscher with a view to the Kremlin's mounting campaign against the alleged resurrection of the spirit of <u>revanchism</u> in Western Germany. He praised the West's willingness to return without preconditions to the Geneva negotiating table, and he stressed Washington's preparedness to negotiate a ban on the nuclear arms race in space. All this was omitted by <u>Pravda</u>, which also left out Genscher's plea against war ever starting from German soil again.

4. A highlight of Deutsche Welle's programming to the USSR was the decision in January, 1974 to read substantial parts from Solzhenitsyn's gruesome tale of Stalin's concentration camps <u>Gulag Archipelago</u>. Over a period of six weeks, Russian listeners could receive day by day Solzhenitsyn's message of the blessings of defeat. Using the language of today, the Nobel Prize winner preached to his fellow-countrymen the old Christian virtues of tolerance and compassion. 'Victories are good for governments,

defeats are good for peoples. Victories only demand more victories; after defeat there is a thirst for freedom.' Peoples must suffer defeat the same way as individuals must endure pain and poverty. This is - according to Solzhenitsyn - the only way leading to a deeper spiritual life and moral elevation.

5. A glaring example of the suppression of spiritual life by the Soviet authorities was broadcast by Deutsche Welle in 1979, after a tape recorded religious service interrupted by a KGB raid had been smuggled to the West. One could hear children and women sobbing when the fists of KGB men banged against the door of a private home in the Ukrainian city of Kharkov, where the service was being held to celebrate the return of the parish priest after a five year absence in a concentration camp. Supported by a loudspeaker van, KGB officials asked the believers to disperse and go home. Instead, after some bewilderment, a mighty chorus of Eastern Church hymns arose to take up the battle with the barking police megaphone, until the noise from the street died away and was eventually drowned by the jubilant voices praising the Almighty Lord.

6. In August, 1983 Deutsche Welle's Russian Service was the first to broadcast the full text of the sensational Novosibirsk paper on economic reform after it had been leaked to western correspondents in Moscow. Originally presented by Academician Tatyana Zaslavskaya at a closed seminar organised by the economics departments of the Central Committee, the Academy of Sciences and the State Planning Commission, the paper allowed a valuable insight into the state of the debate on economic reform going on behind closed doors among senior specialists. A lively plea for experimenting with new forms of a socialist market economy and its dissemination by radio was surely likely to spur public discussion on a wide range of vital issues. By broadcasting this document to the Soviet Union, Deutsche Welle encouraged publication of, at least, a short summary of the paper's content in the Academy of Sciences' official bulletin <u>Social Sciences</u>.

In his Nobel Prize lecture, Alexander Solzhenitsyn called the 'suppression of information' between the parts of the planet a 'rampant danger' to international peace. 'Suppression of information', he said, 'renders international signatures and agreements illusory; within a muffled zone it costs nothing to reinterpret any agreement - to forget it, as though it had never really existed. A muffled zone is, as it were, populated not by inhabitants of the earth, but an expeditionary corps from Mars; the people know nothing intelligent about the rest of the earth and are prepared to go and trample it down in the holy conviction to come as liberators.'

All too readily it has been forgotten that tension in post-war Europe has repeatedly been whipped up over the human rights issue to a point where the Soviet Army has been 'forced' to intervene, in order to save socialism from a 'threat' their masters fear more than anything else. It is the 'wind of change' - to quote President John F. Kennedy - blowing over the iron curtain and instilling people behind it with new hopes. To stem the waves of historical evolution a wall had to be built in Berlin, tanks were sent into Czechoslovakia and martial law was proclaimed in Poland. Mass emigration of three million people from East Germany to West Germany, the unorthodox ideas of the Prague Spring and the rise of a trade union movement in Poland - all this was explained by hard-liner Soviet ideologists in terms of a huge conspiracy of the legendary imperialist forces seeking to undermine the foundations of socialist society. According to this view, the most important channel for ideological subversion is international shortwave radio, whose powerful transmitters are 'far-reaching guns' waging a psychological war against the socialist countries.

Actually, it is the other way round. Western ideas of freedom and democracy, self-government and ideological pluralism compel Stalin-type communist leaders to shut off their societies from all external influences they hold to be dangerous to their power monopoly. Liberalisation and democratisation in Eastern Europe are not the results of sinister imperialist scheming to subvert socialism, as communist mass media want to make their audiences believe. What is really happening in the countries of Eastern Europe is a complicated historical process with periodic setbacks to times which had long been thought passed. The power of the dogma of the medieval church, for that matter, was not thwarted in one single revolutionary act. It took centuries for democratic and liberal ideas to develop. Basically, the same historical process is now going on in the countries under Soviet rule. Apart from the West Slavs, the peoples inhabiting the vast stretch between the Soviet-Polish border and the shores of the Pacific Ocean have gone through a different course of history from the middle ages to modern times, without experiencing a gradual evolution of human rights and civil liberties. For centuries past they have been captives of orthodoxy - first of the Eastern church, then of Stalinist dogma.

It was not until Krushchev denounced Stalin's crimes on the 20th Party congress in 1956 that writers, scientists and philosophers in the Soviet-dominated bloc began to challenge, out of their conscience's anguish, the basic tenets of totalitarian rule. The discovery of the individual's conscience, however, is one of the roots of modern civilisation. Modern people want to think for themselves and act according to their own judgement without being told what to do by a higher authority, a 'big brother'. They want to decide for themselves which books to read, which films to watch and which radio programmes to listen to. It is for this reason that human rights activists in the Soviet orbit fight Stalinist dogma, the censorship and the Party's autocracy. From ancient times to our days, thinkers and philosophers have devoted their best endeavours to teach humankind their unalienable right to determine their own destiny. Such high aspirations have more than once been foiled by the dogma. But, in the long run, the values of a free society have always proved to be stronger than the power of the dogma that holds human minds in the bonds of ignorance and superstition. It is in this spirit that Deutsche Welle renders its contribution to international broadcasting over the iron curtain. Wherever it comes closest to its mission, it achieves its most powerful effect.

Notes
1. Raissa Orlova-Kopelew, <u>Die Türen öffnen sich langsam</u> (Hamburg, 1984), pp.177f.
2. George Ball, <u>Diplomacy for a Crowded World</u> (Boston/Toronto, 1976).

Chapter Nine

DEUTSCHLANDFUNK: BROADCASTING TO EAST GERMANY AND EASTERN EUROPE

Jürgen Reiss, director, Europa-Programm, Deutschlandfunk

A driver on the Cologne Autobahn who takes the Köln-Süd exit to reach the centre of town cannot miss seeing two skyscrapers standing next to each other; the buildings have been landmarks on the south side the Rhine metropolis since their completion at the end of the 1970s. The buildings are the broadcasting centres of Deutschlandfunk (DLF) and Deutsche Welle (DW). These two organisations have special status among broadcasting stations in the Federal Republic of Germany: both are corporations under West German federal law. All other broadcasting services in the Federal Republic are organised under state law, because each Bundesland, or federal state, has control over broadcasting within its boundaries. The distinctive elements of the German broadcasting system originated when it was created at the end of World War Two.

The first radio stations in post-war Germany were operated by the military occupation authorities and staffed by Allied personnel. German broadcasters were slowly introduced and finally became the sole members of staff and management.

In the Western Zones of Occupation, independent regional broadcasting organisations were eventually created within the framework of the Western Allies' German policy, which called for the establishment of a liberal democratic society. The regional stations were based on state law, fulfilling another tenet of the Allies' German policy: the idea of a new Germany organised as a federal republic. In order to guarantee that the broadcasting stations were independent of the state, political parties and special interest groups, they were conceived as non-profit, public corporations with the right of self-administration.

The radio stations' articles of incorporation

created safeguards to freedom of information and opinion through the establishment of supervisory bodies. These were composed of representatives of socially relevant groups, whose functions were to monitor the work of the stations. The legislation on the setting up and organisation of the broadcasting stations, as determined by the Western Occupying Powers, still governs the broadcasting system in the Federal Republic of Germany. The laws are supported by the majority of Germans, who have drawn lessons from the misuse of the broadcasting system as a propaganda instrument of the Nazi regime. (1)

While the Western Powers sought after 1945 to assure the independence of broadcasting stations in the part of Germany they occupied and to create the prerequisites for programming that reflected free and diverse opinions, developments in the Soviet-occupied part of Germany went an entirely different way as the broadcasting medium passed from the hands of one totalitarian regime into the hands of another. Immediately after the capture of Berlin, the Soviets set up the Berliner Rundfunk in the building of the former Deutschlandsender. Operated by Soviet-supervised German communists, it spread its propaganda beyond the region it dominated.

In 1948, Berliner Rundfunk began broadcasting to West Germany Wir sprechen für Deutschland (We Speak for Germany). It was directly controlled by the Central Committee of the Socialist Unity Party (SED) and transmitted on the clear and far-reaching 191 kHz longwave frequency of the former Deutschlandsender station. The Deutschlandsender, one of Nazi Germany's most important propaganda organs which the victorious powers decided should be silenced, was resurrected under communist direction. Although the German Democratic Republic (GDR) lost the longwave frequency of the Deutschlandsender when the Copenhagen Frequency Plan took effect, it received two no less efficient longwave frequencies from the Soviet Union on which, starting in 1951, it broadcast the programme Hier spricht die KPD (This is the Communist Party of Germany Calling).

The Federal Republic of Germany (FRG) had nothing with which to counter the East Zone effort. None of its stations, which were regional in nature, could cover all Germany; thus, they were unable to fulfil the commitment to national reunification, as set out in Bonn's Basic Law: to keep alive, at least through information, a feeling of unity among the people in both parts of Germany; and to inform them factually, impartially and comprehensively about

Deutschlandfunk

events in the world and all of Germany and thus break the information monopoly of the rulers in the communist-dominated part of the country.

Establishing a supra-regional radio station in the Federal Republic which could fulfil this function was a long and difficult process. It became an extended struggle between the opposition Social Democratic Party (SPD), the governments of the Bundeslander (Federal States), the Association of Public Broadcasting Organisations (ARD) and the Federal Government. The opposition suspected that the Federal Government, and especially Konrad Adenauer, wanted to create an instrument of state control with the supra-regional station. The Bundeslander wanted to protect their control over broadcasting rights, while the ARD saw itself as the trustee of existing broadcast organisations. The German government also demanded consideration of its interests. Although agreement was reached in the autumn of 1952 to establish a longwave station, Deutsche Langwelle - an ARD cooperative effort for transmitting programmes to all of Germany using the facilities of the then Nordwestdeutsche Rundfunk (NWDR) - the dispute was not over. There were further arguments as to where the final headquarters of the supra-regional station would be located, on its financing and the composition of its governing bodies. Until 1956, only music was heard on the Deutsche Langwelle station, but on 3rd November, 1956 - the year of the Hungarian uprising - hourly news broadcasts began. This was the result of a decision taken by Norddeutsche Rundfunk (NDR), 'in view of events behind the Iron Curtain'.

During the same period East Berlin had increased the power of its Deutschlandsender transmitter to 300 kilowatts. It had also installed one FM, a shortwave and two AM transmitters and started the Deutschen Freiheitssender 904 (German Freedom Station 904). The purpose of this massive increase in broadcasting capability was made clear in a 1953 speech to the Central Committee of the Socialist Unity Party by the Socialist Unity Party Politburo member Fred Oelsner: 'Radio is the most effective method for us to have political influence on the West German population. The responsible comrades in broadcasting must always remember that every broadcast to West Germany is a missile into the camp of the enemy, whose explosive force must be carefully calculated. We cannot use duds.' (2)

Four years after the first news broadcasts on Deutsche Langwelle, on 26th October, 1960, the

Deutschlandfunk

Federal Government's proposed 'Legislation on the Establishment of Broadcasting Organisations under Federal Law' was passed (with the SPD voting against) by the German Bundestag (federal parliament), therefore creating the legal basis for the establishment of Deutschlandfunk and the re-establishment of Deutsche Welle under federal Law. Deutschlandfunk was the successor to Deutsche Langwelle, but with an expanded mandate: in addition to programmes for all of Germany, it also was to transmit a European foreign languages service. Deutschlandfunk (DLF) went on the air for the first time on 1st January, 1962. As an all-Germany station, it had to contend over an area that was virtually smothered by the GDR.

Organisation and Legal Mandate
In section 5 of the law on the establishment of federal radio stations, Deutschlandfunk is mandated to broadcast to all of Germany and to Europe. It is, by law, a public interest organisation. Section 21 precludes government supervision. The station's executive bodies are the broadcasting board, governing council and the director general's office.

The broadcasting board consists of 22 members, with representatives from both chambers of the federal parliament (including a representative for the city-state of Berlin), the federal government, the Protestant church, the Roman Catholic church, the central council of Jews in Germany, employers' associations and the labour unions. The governing council is composed of seven members elected from the broadcasting board. The broadcasting board elects the director general, who is nominated by the governing council. The broadcasting board advises the director general on programming matters. The governing council supervises the director general's management and sets the budget.

The director general, who is elected for a six-year term in office, is responsible for the management of the station, including the organisation of programming. In consultation with the governing council, he is responsible both for the recruiting and dismissal of senior employees and for representing the station in public. The organisation's budget is governed by financing rules set by the station itself. The Federal Accounting Office audits the books. The station also sets its own internal operating rules.

Judicial supervision is exercised by the

Deutschlandfunk

federal government. Section 23 of the Legislation on the Establishment of Broadcasting Stations under Federal Law, which covers the organisation of programmes, specifies that:

> all of the programmes must correspond with the fundamental liberal-democratic order. They are to provide an independent formation of opinion. They may not be slanted to support one party, one religious group, one profession or one interest group; the moral and religious feelings of the listeners must be respected.

Section 24 of the legislation states that, 'All reporting must be comprehensive, truthful and factual.' All broadcast programmes have to be recorded and must be stored for four weeks. Thereafter, if there are no complaints, they may be erased.

Deutsche Welle and Deutschlandfunk are based on the same law. The wording allows the federal legislators to leave open some questions of jurisdiction. It is clear, however, that Deutschlandfunk is an all-Germany station that also serves neighbouring European countries, which gives it priority over Deutsche Welle to broadcast to the continent, especially to Central Europe.

Both stations took this into consideration when they agreed on a jurisdictional allotment for broadcasts to eastern and south-eastern Europe, which took effect on 1st January, 1977. I will discuss this agreement later. Another difference between the two radio stations, is that Deutsche Welle generally uses shortwave frequencies for its broadcasts, while Deutschlandfunk is heard primarily on long and medium wave frequencies. In addition, DLF has an FM transmitter in Bonn, and is expected to obtain further transmitters in this frequency spectrum, to be sited along the borders of the Federal Republic. Deutschlandfunk is financed 60% by the state and 40% by listener license fees from the Association of Public Broadcasting Stations.

According to law, the director general has programme responsibility, which he delegates in practice to senior management staff. The heads of the main programme departments - current affairs, Europe and culture - act as directors and editors-in-chief. Under them are the heads of the individual specialised departments and services, as well as the heads of the foreign language services. DLF's Studio Bonn reports from the capital of the Federal Republic

Deutschlandfunk

of Germany, while its Studio Berlin reports from the western sector of the former capital of Germany, with special emphasis on East Berlin and East Germany. The central news service has a special position within the current affairs programme section.

Deutschlandfunk is a member of the Association of Public Broadcasting Stations in the Federal Republic of Germany (ARD) and exchanges programmes with other ARD stations, particularly music and drama.

German Language Service
The programming principles set out by law for Deutschlandfunk are valid for both the German and foreign language services. The mandate to transmit German language programming includes the legislative order to organise radio broadcasts for all of Germany. The programmes exist to provide a comprehensive view of Germany.

The primary target audience are the populations of both German states. The inclusion of both is due in part to the reunification mandate built into the Basic Law. This mandate is of fundamental significance for the overall constitutional order of the Federal Republic, which the Federal Constitutional Court has often clearly noted - for example, in a decision given on 31st July, 1973 on the Basic Treaty which stated that, 'The existence of one German nation is embodied in the Basic Law.' DLF is not a station with an anti-GDR fixation. As a Deutschlandfunk publication puts it, 'Providing a comprehensive picture of Germany by DLF means nothing more than giving its listeners a picture of both the Federal Republic of Germany and the German Democratic Republic; that mandate has been given additional European endorsement since the introduction of the Final Document of the Conference on European Security and Cooperation, but does not neglect the special interests of the Germans in the two neighbouring states within the German nation.'

Truth, factuality and objectivity are the requirements for reporting about either the Federal Republic or the GDR. The right of criticism as a basic part of journalistic freedom of opinion is exercised toward both sides. The intellectual and political differences with the East's ideology have a place in the programmes, but generally indirectly. For example, a factual portrayal of living conditions in the free part of Germany and in the western world, although reserved and unobtrusive, enables listeners in the GDR to make comparisons and draw their own conclusions. This restrained and undogmatic critical style of reporting particularly disturbs the East Berlin regime, which all adds to the credibility of the station. This credibility evolves from its prudence - a prudence not found in the massive propaganda and indoctrination efforts of the communist radio stations.

The German language service of Deutschlandfunk is organised into two main departments: culture and current affairs. It is transmitted over medium wave frequencies: 1539, 1268, 756 and 549; there are also long wave frequencies 209 and 155kHz. The Bonn area is served by an FM transmitter on 81.9MHz.

The culture department covers the humanities and the arts, religion and church life, science and technology. It fills many parts of the daily schedule with regular news and information programmes on the worlds of art, music, literature, religion and churches, science, research and medicine. Radio plays are broadcast every week. Church services are carried on Sundays and religious holidays. Music programmes make up nearly 60% of the German service's daily schedule; every musical genre is broadcast but about two-thirds of output is light music, while the remaining third is devoted to classical.

The political element of the German language service is provided by the current affairs department. These broadcasts reflect - as the name suggests - the major political events of the day. News is broadcast around the clock, every hour on the hour, with news every half-hour during peak morning listening times. Live interviews are regularly scheduled. Separate from the news - in compliance with the legal mandate - are commentaries and reports. Press reviews include extracts from newspapers in the Federal Republic and the international press. The selection covers the broadest possible political spectrum. There is also a programme of quotations from the East Berlin press.

The current affairs schedule is flexible enough to handle news as it breaks. The schedule begins at 4.05a.m. with a commentary on mainly GDR and all-Germany topics, produced by the East-West department, and timed to reach people in the GDR before they go to work. That is followed by a morning magazine programme with reports, interviews and music. Then come reviews of newspapers in the Federal Republic and East Berlin. An agricultural programme is broadcast at 11.50a.m. The midday block is more reports and interviews, plus an international press

Deutschlandfunk

review. One of the afternoon programmes covers business and industrial news. At 8.05p.m., two major topics of the day are commented upon. A current affairs documentary is transmitted at 9.40p.m., and a final commentary follows the midnight news.

In addition to the Monday to Friday schedule there are specific weekly programmes, such as political features or a discussion of the week's events. Although topical, these are not necessarily about day-to-day political events, but attempt to give an overall picture of current happenings. Sport is also featured. Saturdays, Sundays and holidays bring schedule changes, with a mix of church services, a great deal of serious and light music, cultural and sports broadcasts. A significant Sunday morning programme is the 25-minute interview of the week.

Deutschlandfunk cannot conduct listener research in the GDR, so it cannot provide statistical data on how extensively its programmes are listened to in the other part of Germany. The following methods allow indirect estimates of the audience size. First, there are listeners' letters. Sending a letter from the GDR is a risk; not all get past the censor; so the number of letters received by the German language service is astonishing. Other important indications come from interviews with visitors from the GDR, with westerners who have made official or private visits to the GDR, and the impressions gathered by correspondents accredited in the GDR. All of this information indicates that Deutschlandfunk, along with the Berlin stations, is the most listened-to western radio station.

Deutschlandfunk is also the western radio station most denounced by the GDR's ruling Socialist Unity Party, and that is a further indication of the effectiveness of its broadcasts. If they were not being heard, the rulers in East Berlin would not bother. There is a permanent campaign in the GDR media against Deutschlandfunk's programmes - mostly attacking differences of opinion rather than facts reported in the programmes. Most illuminating are the publications which deal with the Deutschlandfunk broadcasts: Stefan Frohmader, <u>Semantic Manipulation in FRG Broadcasting to Falsify Socialist Reality in the GDR, as Epitomised by Broadcasts from Deutschlandfunk</u>; Jurgen Frenzel, <u>Eclectic Mixing of the Political and Non-Political as Methods of Manipulation, A Survey of Deutschlandfunk Broadcasts</u>; Michael Lichtenberg, <u>Development and Main Tendency of the Ideological Diversion and Meddling</u>

Deutschlandfunk

Policy of FRG Broadcast Media After the Conference on Security and Cooperation in Europe, as Portrayed in The Press Review From East Berlin Newspapers in The Morning Programme of Deutschlandfunk. The list is endless. Most significant are the terms used by the GDR press to describe Deutschlandfunk: 'ideological diversionary station', 'Centre for psychological warfare', 'main station of ideologial diversion against the GDR and the NVA (Volksarmee)'. Comments such as these indicate that the programmes of Deutschlandfunk are a major thorn in the side of the Socialist Unity Party - because free journalists are articulating factual, critical and, therfore convincing opinions.

The European Service
The foreign language sections of the European service department of Deutschlandfunk are legally mandated to organise radio programmes for European countries. Until 1st January, 1977, Deutschlandfunk's European Service consisted of 12 editorial departments, broadcasting 30 and 45-minute daily programmes in 14 languages, on the medium wave frequencies of 1539kHz and 1268kHz. There were the seven West European services: Danish, English, French, Italian, Dutch, Norwegian and Swedish, and five East European services: Polish, Romanian and Hungarian, while the Yugoslav and Czechoslovak services broadcast in two languages each.

However, since 1953 - long before its 1960 conversion into a Federal Law radio station - Deutsche Welle had also been broadcasting to East Europe, including to Czechoslovakia, Yugoslavia, Poland and Hungary. When Deutschlandfunk was established, there was double programming to those countries. In order to make their work more efficient, Deutschlandfunk and Deutsche Welle entered into an agreement on 23rd April, 1975. Taking effect on 1st January, 1977, the agreement allowed Deutschlandfunk to retain its medium wave broadcasts in Polish, Czech, Slovak and Hungarian; DLF also assumed editorial responsibility for Deutsche Welle's shortwave broadcasts in these languages. Deutsche Welle retained its shortwave broadcasts in Serbian, Croatian and Romanian, and took over editorial responsibility for Deutschlandfunk's medium wave programmes in those languages. The agreement called for both stations to retain the original scope and concept of their programmes. The broadcasters of the East European services remaining with Deutschlandfunk saw a considerable increase in their programme responsibility with the assumption of the added shortwave broadcasts. As a result, the Polish service now broadcasts four programmes for a total of two hours 35 minutes a day; the Czechoslovak service has five daily broadcasts totalling 3 hours 20 minutes; the Hungarian service has a total broadcast time of 2 hours for its three programmes. All of the broadcasts are transmitted on 1539kHz medium wave and in the 31, 41 and 49 meter bands shortwave.

The European service, like the German service, is legally mandated to present a comprehensive picture of Germany to other European countries. This mandate to portray German reality has expanded, because the Federal Republic has become a full member of the international community and a full participant in efforts to find solutions for global problems. The growing number of international obligations is now a basic part of political reality in the Federal Republic. Including this expanded international contact in its commentaries and features is part of the job of Deutschlandfunk's foreign language services.

The European service operates truthfully and avoids glossing over things. It is obligated to refrain from interference in the internal affairs of its target countries, to avoid ideological or political controversy. It is the conviction at DLF that programmes designed to avoid contention and present the truth, difficult though this is, complement liberal democratic principles. Objectivity and fairness build credibility.

Unlike most international radio stations, Deutschlandfunk's European services are not supplied with uniform programme scripts from a central service. The individual foreign language department heads have broad autonomy in designing their programmes for their specific target areas. The foreign language programmes of DLF are mostly spoken-word broadcasts. Although there are features in which music is presented and discussed, as well as hit parades and request concerts, music is generally only a short link item between individual segments of the broadcast.

All of DLF's general identification announcements indicate that Deutschlandfunk is a station for Germany and Europe.

The broadcasts usually consist of two segments: the first covers day-to-day news events, while the second is a broader current events bloc, with more

Deutschlandfunk

in-depth reporting of general topics. The first segment consists of three regular sections: news, a political commentary and a press review. All of this material, as well as much of the material in the second part of the broadcast, originates in German, editorially adapted to meet the needs of the audience and then translated into the appropriate language.

Each broadcast begins with the news. While the German service broadcasts news every hour on the hour and can be up-dated as needed, this is not possible for the foreign language services; the important news, as seen from the viewpoint of the target audience, is selected and presented as a daily news review. The duty news editor evaluates the news agency reports and makes selections based on their importance, topicality and relevance to the target country. Where necessary, items are expanded or rephrased so the listener can understand the context.

News and commentary are strictly delineated. The commentary is always on the outstanding political event of the day. Because it offers a special way of clearly presenting the German political scene and to elaborate on the German viewpoint of political events, its author is nearly always a German journalist. There are special criteria for commentaries in the European service programmes. For example, pure opinion pieces are discouraged because foreign listeners are not interested in the commentator's opinion so much as the event. The commentator is briefed to explain and give the pros and cons of the issue before indicating his opinion. DLF's European services have to assume that its listeners are not comprehensively informed about conditions in Germany, and further, that they may be ignorant or even misinformed. That is especially true of East European listeners, who are faced with the massive influence of propaganda and do not have the multiplicity of information sources that are available to people in the democratic states. They are often uninformed about their own country. Topics for comment and by whom are chosen by the director of the European service. Individual language services are given a choice of scripts on various topics and select according to what they think best suited to their audience.

The press review section quotes the German and international newspapers. The section is balanced and covers the full spectrum of political opinion.

The second half of the European services' broadcasts comprises reports, features and interviews on political, cultural, economic and social life. During a typical week of programming, the individual services present features on science and technology, culture and art, business, labour and social affairs, sports, women and youth segments, magazine programmes about Germany, plus reports from Berlin and Bonn. A portion of the second half of the broadcast includes features and reports written in the broadcast language by members of its editorial staff. Many items are taken from the German service but all scripts in German are adapted to meet audience needs before being translated.

Another major segment of the foreign language broadcasts is a joint project of the DLF European Service and the Deutsche Welle with the assistance and cooperation of the Foreign Ministry and the Goethe Institute: the radio language teaching series <u>Familie Baumann</u>. First broadcast by DLF in 1970, the six-part course of 26 lessons in each course has been repeated once. The course used a lively and didactic way of showing the life of a German family; 130,000 listeners followed the language course. A new language course, called <u>Auf Deutsch gesagt</u>, which also had strong listener interest, began in 1983. In addition to providing the basics of the German language, the language courses are designed to give general information about Germany.

In order to discover the size of its audiences the European service departments hold quizzes with prizes, which have proved to be popular.

Listeners' Mail to the European Services
The number of listeners' letters received annually by DLF's European services varies, depending on whether they come in response to quiz programmes and promotional activities in western countries, or whether the volume reflects the political climate in the eastern bloc states: 57,000 letters in 1977; 48,000 in 1978; 39,000 in 1979; 46,000 in 1980; 60,000 in 1981; 38,000 in 1982 and 55,000 in 1983. Letters from Eastern Europe quite often make up half the annual total. Two examples of how political climate influences listeners' mail: the Czechslovak service received in 1969 - the year after the Prague Spring - 58,000 letters, but the next year there were barely 1,000. The Polish service received 21,000 letters in 1980 and 31,000 in 1981. After martial law was imposed in Poland the figures dropped to 9,000 letters. In 1983, after martial law was lifted, the number of letters doubled - to 18,000.

Interesting information on audience size comes

Deutschlandfunk

from studies made by the East European Audience and Opinion Research department of Radio Free Europe in Munich (see Chapter 13). The department's results are based on interviews with travellers from East Europe and projections are made from the information. The results that follow are for the years 1976 to 1980: the number of people listening in East Europe to western stations equals 82% of the population in Czechoslovakia, 76% in Poland and 68% in Hungary. Deutschlandfunk is listened to by 15% of the people in Czechoslovakia, 13% in Poland and 9% in Hungary. That means a total audience of 5.6 million people. This audience share compares favourably with those of the BBC and Voice of America.

Outlook
Broadcasting is in the midst of a technical revolution. Within the ARD, as well as in Deutschlandfunk, there is discussion on making radio more widely available through satellite distribution, direct broadcast satellites or the use of cable networks. However, plans run into the difficulties of West Germany's federal structure on one hand, and financial stringencies on the other. As of September 1984, no decision has been made on the use of satellite radio. Although this would be an interesting supplement to terrestrial transmissions, in the years to come satellite broadcasting will not be in a position to replace land-based transmitters.

Notes
1. Private broadcasting, which is just beginning in the country, will mean basic alterations in the organisation of the broadcasting system in the Federal Republic.
2. Quoted from Rolf Steininger, <u>Deutschlandfunk - die Vorgeschichte einer Rundfunkanstalt, 1949-61</u>.

Chapter Ten

RADIO IN THE AMERICAN SECTOR, RIAS BERLIN

Donald R. Browne, University of Minnesota, Twin Cities

In a world of dozens of multi-language, worldwide coverage international radio stations, RIAS Berlin would hardly seem to count. It broadcasts in one language only, German, and to one primary target area, East Germany (the German Democratic Republic). However, it has done so for nearly 40 years, and the ways in which it has attempted to cope with changing socio-political situations in its target areas, and with change and resistance to change within its own internal structure over that period, have broader implications for international radio stations, especially those formed in or substantially reshaped by the cold war. My investigations of VOA, BBC, Deutsche Welle, RFE, Radio Liberty, Radio Moscow and Radio Berlin International, as well as RIAS, (1) indicate that many of the RIAS programme strategies and problems are characteristic of the other stations. Because RIAS is a monolingual, 'one-target' station, the strategies and problems often appear more clearly and more quickly than they do in the more complex stations, making RIAS something of a bellwether among international radio services.

Brief History (2)
RIAS began life in February, 1946 as a US military government-supported wired radio service for the US occupation sector in Berlin, largely as a means of supplying the German population of that sector with information they would need in their daily lives (for example, stocks available at food distribution centres) as well as education on such subjects as the evils of the Nazi era. It began to operate its first over-the-air transmitter late in 1946, and thus began to be heard in other parts of Berlin, including the Soviet occupation zone. When in 1948 the Soviet

government imposed a blockade on land and water routes leading from US, British and French occupied zones of Germany to Berlin, the station's power was increased considerably and it began to devote the major share of its broadcast time to material designed particularly for listeners in Soviet-occupied Germany. It added a second programme service in 1953, a third programme service in 1955, and its staff and budget grew accordingly. Many of those staff members left Soviet-occupied Germany to join RIAS. By the end of the 1940s, it had a full range of programme material, from news and commentary to musical request programmes, quiz show and broadcasts for schools. It saw itself, in the words of some of its staff, as 'the sort of station listeners in Soviet-occupied Germany would want if they had a choice in the matter'. It appears to have been the first international broadcast station to have taken this approach, and those who were considering the foundation of what would become Radio Free Europe looked upon RIAS as a model for the future RFE. (3)

In serving as a surrogate radio station for the 'other' Germany, RIAS had several advantages. Travel between the western and eastern parts of Berlin was quite easy, and East Berliners, as well as some East Germans (4) living outside the city, made day trips to West Berlin and even worked there during the day. They supplied a fairly steady flow of information on occurrences in their daily lives. Newspapers and magazines from throughout East Germany were quite easy to obtain. And radio broadcasts, not only from the central stations in East Berlin but also from the stations in Dresden, Leipzig and other cities (5), could be received in West Berlin. It was even fairly easy to conduct public opinion surveys among East Germans who would come to West Berlin for such major attractions as the annual Green Week agricultural fair.

The station acquired considerable popularity among its East German listeners during the 1950s, not least of all because of its well-informed comments (some of them delivered in political satire shows) on matters the East German media would not cover. The station also strove to make its listeners aware of the various respects in which citizens of the other East European socialist states enjoyed greater liberties and privileges than East Germans, so that the latter might press for similar treatment on the grounds that it couldn't be 'anti-Communist' to receive it. RIAS was careful to avoid direct encouragement of anti-government demonstrations, and, on the occasion of the 1953 uprising (largely in East Berlin), cautioned listeners to consider their personal circumstances carefully before deciding whether to take part.

By the end of the 1950s, however, it was quite clear that the liberation policies proclaimed by some US political figures, most notably by Secretary of State John Foster Dulles, would not involve US military intervention to support any spontaneous uprisings in Eastern Europe. RIAS began to emphasise gradual and peaceful evolution, and paid more attention to economic, social and political developments in western Europe, in both socialist and capitalist economies; the hope was that East Germans would not want to see themselves falling too far behind, and would press for reforms, even as Hungary was doing.

The erection of the Berlin Wall in 1961 cut off RIAS from its easy access to information about daily life in East Germany. Radio monitoring continued, but other forms of communication were reduced to a trickle. As this occurred after the decision to place more emphasis on life in the west, its effects were not as devasting as they might have been, but it did mean that RIAS would have very little indication of how many listeners it was attracting and what they thought of its programmes. Indirect indicators, such as East German media attacks against the station, became more important as evidence that RIAS was touching a sensitive nerve, and served to show that the East German government continued to consider the station dangerous enough to be worth attacking.

In the late 1960s, RIAS moved to a programme scheduling concept familiar to North American listeners, but which was becoming increasingly common for West German radio: block programming. The earlier RIAS schedules had included a certain amount of general appeal programming, but it was interspersed with specific programmes for specific audiences, for example, the daily five minute programme for East German border guards (Five Minutes for Twenty Thousand). Starting in 1967, larger blocks of airtime for broader categories of listeners, such as those in their teens and twenties, would become the mainstay of the schedule, and programmes for specific audiences by and large would disappear. This was thought to be more in line with what the majority of listeners in East Germany (and West Berlin) would want to hear.

While popular music predominated, there were frequent insertions of newscasts, commentaries and features, but they sounded less and less as if they were intended primarily for East German listeners. That appears to have been a recognition that East Germans in the 1960s had access to a wide variety of German language stations from outside East Germany, as several West German stations could be heard with relative ease, while Austrian and Swiss stations were audible at night, and the BBC and other international services in German were available for a few to several hours per day. East Germans also had better domestic radio than in the 1950s, at least where music and other entertainment formats were concerned. As more and more East German households acquired television sets, that became another competing element, especially since the East German government, after a series of largely futile attempts to discourage people from watching West German TV, seemed to give up the battle, countering with a second TV service of its own in 1969.

The 1970s saw relatively few changes in programme practices at RIAS, but by the end of the decade it was apparent that television was occupying an increasing share of the time East Germans spent on the broadcast media. The German inter-state treaty of 1972 made it much easier for West Germans, including media reporters, to report first-hand from East Germany, so that RIAS was able to regain some of the contact it had lost in 1961, but it also meant that West German television stations could carry more reports about life in the GDR, giving East Germans a further reason for watching West German television.

As of the mid 1980s, RIAS seems to be undergoing an internal agonising reappraisal (to borrow a favourite US Secretary of State Dulles phrase from the cold war period), with expressions of concern by some of its staff members over its continued ability to attract and to hold East German listeners. (6) It continues to offer large amounts of block programming, and about 60% of the schedule is music, more of it popular than classical (US and Western European rock, for the most part). News is broadcast hourly, usually for five or ten minutes, and there are three or four commentaries a day on current events, as well as a roundup of excerpts from West German and other newspapers. RIAS 1 offers a full 24-hour schedule, while RIAS 2 simulcasts RIAS 1 for about 12 hours a day. RIAS 3 no longer exists as such, but does offer a separate transmission once a week over the station's shortwave transmitter - a repeat of the hour-long music request programme (Music Knows No Boundaries) from RIAS 1.

Radio in the American Sector, RIAS Berlin

When one compares RIAS programming for the period 1948-67 with programming in recent years, the major difference is that the station now sounds more like other West German radio stations. If listeners knew nothing about the original purpose of RIAS, they would have few obvious clues that the station was intended primarily for East German listeners. The East German jamming that once interfered with RIAS broadcasts ended in 1978. The station long since stopped identifying itself as 'RIAS Berlin - a free voice of the free world.' The broadcasts for specific audiences in East Germany have ceased, although music request shows actively solicit requests from East German listeners, and there are approximately 100-150 such letters per month from East Germany, and additional letters sent by East Germans but mailed from other countries. (7) A Sunday musical quiz attracts 100-200 letters from East Germany per broadcast. There are also telephone calls from East Germany (direct-dial services exist between the two Germanies), and the station receives 300-400 such calls a month, most of them music requests and dedications. There is no way to assess more accurately how many listeners the station has, whether the number is rising or falling for the population in general or for specific target groups in particular and, therefore, whether fears that the station may be losing some of its appeal for East German listeners are justified.

Present Issues
The fact that RIAS has modified its programming over its nearly 40-year history is hardly surprising. Most radio stations today, domestic or international, bear little resemblance to what they were 40, 30 or even 20 or 10 years ago. They have changed for a variety of reasons, but many have something to do with the activities of competing stations. In the case of RIAS, the competition comes from several sources within and outside East Germany, and comes from both radio and television. RIAS also has had to consider the changing political, economic, social and cultural situation within East Germany itself, and the changing foreign policies of the two Germanies, the United States, the Soviet Union, the NATO alliance and the Warsaw Pact. In other words, life is more complicated for RIAS than it is for most domestic broadcast stations and for many international broadcasters, but probably little more complicated than it is for Radio Free Europe, Radio

Liberty, Radio Marti or any other station that attempts to provide a surrogate domestic broadcast service for listeners in another country. The issues that follow apply not only to RIAS but to many other international stations.

1. **Who Are the Target Audience?**
A station which is on the air 24 hours a day and which has a multitude of broadcast frequencies (three AM, four FM, one shortwave) and plenty of signal strength with which to reach all corners of the target nation, as RIAS does, can afford to consider the possibility of reaching more than one audience. According to administrators and staff, the two primary targets at present are government officials and young people in East Germany. The assumption is that the two groups have largely different tastes. In theory, young people should be attracted by the large amounts of rock music presented by the station, (8) while government officials will want to fill in the gaps in the news presentations of the East German media. But once those audiences are attracted, will they remain tuned to the longer background reports and commentaries which contain much of the material that makes the station truly different from its competition? And do attempts to reach those audiences alienate still others, e.g. teachers, farmers or tradespeople who could be important to the station's overall objective of insuring that East Germans retain a sense of contact and even perhaps a common purpose with the west?

This is not just a matter of programme formats; it is also a matter of presentational style. Young East German listeners may be amused to hear rock music presented by an American whose German accent leaves much to be desired (The Ric DeLisle Show), but will it perhaps lead them to take other material presented by the station less seriously? Government officials might secretly appreciate the implied criticism of a phrase in a commentary which refers to 'the old men in the Kremlin' (Dettmar Cremer, Kommentar, 9th September, 1984), but would younger people respond positively to it? It isn't that there are correct answers to either of those questions, but rather that the questions don't appear to be raised very often. Furthermore, although the station should be in a good position to seek to reach more than one audience at a time, thanks to the existence of both RIAS 1 and RIAS 2, there is very little difference between the two services, aside from the slightly greater amount of classical music and radio drama on RIAS 2.

2. How Does the Station Know Who It's Reaching?

Because RIAS does not have the opportunity to conduct surveys within East Germany, and because East German surveys on radio listening usually do not cover western radio, the station has little notion of how many listeners it has, who they are and what they think of the programmes. A series of surveys conducted by the West German research firm Infratest gives a broad indication of audience size and overall listening trends, but fails to supply specific detail on the audience and its programme preferences.

Radio Stations Heard at Least Occasionally in East Germany*

	1970	1976	1978
RIAS	39	37	39
SFB (Sender Freies Berlin)	32	31	36
DLF (Deutschslandfunk)	46	46	30
Luxembourg	not included	23	19
NDR (Norddeutscherundfunk)		17	19
WRD (Westdeutscherundfunk)	32 (combined)	8	11
HR3 (Heissicherrundfunk)	not included	5	11
BR3 (Bayrischerrundfunk)	not included	9	10
Others	16	15	12

*Per cent of population. Figures obtained from West German tourists interviewed concerning listening habits observed by them in East Germany.

While these surveys do seem to indicate that RIAS is listened to fairly widely in East Germany, they also indicate that various West German stations, particularly Sender Freies Berlin and Deutschlandfunk, are strong competition. Surveys conducted in the 1950s showed far higher figures for RIAS, but in those days there was only one East German TV service (and it wasn't particularly interesting to watch), viewing of West German TV was strongly discouraged,

Sender Freies Berlin wasn't created until 1954, and Deutschlandfunk didn't exist (it began to broadcast in 1962).

There is also some question as to how accurately the Infratest surveys reflect actual audience viewing behaviour. They are conducted among East Germans who have left East Germany by one means or another and among West Germans who have visited relatives there and thus are in some position to report on media consumption habits in those households. In other words, the data are drawn from something other than a random sample, although that has been the case for surveys done for RIAS throughout its history.

Still, there are other ways for RIAS to gather information on its effectiveness in reaching and pleasing East German listeners. It receives anecdotal reports from visitors to East Germany. Phone calls and letters from East Germans sometimes mention specific reactions to programmes. The East German media sometimes react in general or specific terms to RIAS broadcasts, as in an <u>Armeerundschau</u> (magazine for East German military personnel) article in July, 1984, entitled <u>RIAS, schalt dein Radio an</u> ...' (RIAS, turn on your radio), in which listeners (presumably young soldiers) are warned against the insidious ideological influence of a seemingly harmless offering such as the RIAS pop music request programme <u>Treffpunkt</u>. None of these sources lends itself to systematic analysis, although they acquire more power if they converge on certain points to reinforce one another.

There are two further means of assessing the station's probable, if not actual, impact but neither is employed at present. A more systematic and thorough questioning of those who have left East Germany could yield useful data on listening habits, if not preferences and opinions on specific programmes. These are sometimes as many as a few thousand people a month, most of them old age pensioners whose relatives in West Germany have agreed to receive them. RIAS would have to take into account the demographically skewed character of the sample, as well as the tendency of those who are moving from one country to another to overpraise various aspects of life in the new country, including its mass media.

Content analysis of the programming schedules and styles of the major competitors among radio stations (DLF, SFB, Luxembourg, NDR and WDR) could give RIAS a set of patterns against which to measure its own strategies. That could be particularly helpful if done in conjunction with the sort of survey mentioned above. For example, if the analysis showed that there were pop music request shows from three or four of the stations at the same time, and if survey data showed that more serious listeners found little on any of the frequencies to interest them, RIAS might consider shifting its schedule to accommodate them, or might ensure that there was a serious alternative on one of its two channels.

3. **Programming for Mass or Specialised Audiences?**
Thanks to its two channel system, RIAS could cater to a mass audience (young or otherwise) on one channel and to more specific (and presumably smaller) audiences on the other. However, the station seems in recent years to have concentrated more heavily on mass audiences, especially young listeners. Lacking studies on how listening habits of young East Germans evolve over time, RIAS does not know what might induce them to remain faithful to the station as they grow older. Still, it would seem safe to assume that their tastes for information and preferences for certain styles of presentation differ even while they are in their teens. Studies of the evolution of listening habits among West German teenagers might yield some clues to possible lines of approach for their East German counterparts. If such studies reveal diverse tastes and preferences, RIAS could develop special features and series for various subgroups, e.g. those with scientific, political, recreational or other interests, and promote those features during the mass programmes, perhaps with brief previews.

The older generation of RIAS listeners has presumably continued with the station from earlier years and holds some degree of basic loyalty to it and faith in it. But their listening schedules may be even less predictable than are those of teenagers, especially with increases in leisure time, in activities on which to spend it and in disposable income. Here, a possible strategy might be to increase the amount of repeated programming, especially of political, economic and cultural features. Some features are currently repeated once. There would be nothing wrong with repeating them two, three or even four times, on different days of the week and at differing hours, given the likelihood that any single broadcast would reach only a fraction of the listeners who would wish to hear it. A further advantage of repeats is that, if RIAS announces the scheduled times of presentation at the end of the original broadcast and the first and second repeat broadcasts, those who hear them can pass the word to potentially interested acquaintances.

As RIAS 2 presently simulcasts RIAS 1 for about 12 hours a day, it would be possible to use some of that time for repeats rather than simulcasts. In its earlier years, RIAS could count on listeners planning their days around the station's broadcasts, because its information seemed vital to their interests and there were few alternative sources. Those days are gone, and the station will have to work harder to reach audiences which are now unwilling to make as much effort to seek it out.

Whether the senior programming administrators have the flexibility to carry out such changes is another question. There does appear to be a widespread realisation among RIAS staff in general that the station needs to undertake a major reconsideration of its programming strategies, and the appointment of a new <u>Intendant</u> (station manager) and new US director in mid-1984 has already led to formal discussion of change. But there are a number of highly placed, quite powerful German staff who see little need for reconsideration of programming strategies that they devised many years ago, and that still seem appropriate for the East Germany of the mid-1980s. Resolution of differences will not be easy, partly because of the constraints on flexibility imposed by West German broadcasting employment practices.

4. How Will RIAS Reconcile Flexibility with Employment Law?

Although RIAS was established at the time of the Allied occupation of Germany, and although West Berlin remains under a (loose) form of occupation government, the station itself has always been a German operation, with more or less US supervision of programme output. As the West German broadcast system solidified in the 1950s, RIAS cooperated more and more with it, and became an adjunct member of the West German broadcasters' cooperative organisation, the ARD. As West German labour law developed, and as it was applied to broadcast organisations, RIAS by and large came under that law. Its essential element is that, once a broadcasting staff member has been in work for a certain amount of time, it's almost impossible to dismiss her or him, and quite difficult to move her or him to another position. Habitual and repeated non-performance of duties might constitute grounds for dismissal; disappearance of the specific job for which the person was hired probably would not. Even freelance contributors whose services are contracted by a station over a long enough period of time may be able to claim the same protection under law as full-time staff members.

Setting aside any consideration of whether such protection is justifiable, the fact remains that, unless a station has an excellent retraining programme or a large enough budget to hire additional staff for new programming ventures while keeping 'redundant' staff on the payroll, such labour laws will almost certainly limit a station's ability to implement programming changes. The RIAS budget has not allowed for much expansion of staff in recent years, and the situation is unlikely to be much different in the future. (9)

One result is that it becomes harder to retain vitality in one's approach to programming. As staff members grow older, some become more resistant to change. The labour laws have had one especially interesting effect for RIAS: employment of staff members who live in East Germany has slowed to a trickle. Granted, it has been fairly easy for RIAS staff to visit East Germany since the signing of the inter-state treaty, and some have been permitted to record programme material there. But the experience of having lived in the country, quite common among earlier generations of station staff, has been a distinct rarity in recent years. Potential staff members would not be easy to locate, given the East German government's restrictive policies on emigration, but they are available.

5. Who's in Charge and What Do They Hope to Accomplish?

RIAS is funded by both the US and West German governments, but the bulk of the money - anywhere from 80 to 90 per cent, depending upon the prevailing rate of exchange - is West German. Both governments must approve the appointment of the Intendant, and she or he is almost certain to be affiliated with the ruling political party or parties in the West German federal government. (The present Intendant, Peter Schiwy, is a Christian Democrat; the CDU is the present majority party at the federal level.) Although there are two US officers appointed by the US Information Agency to supervise the station, they don't concern themselves with all aspects of programming but concentrate on translating and discussing general US policy guidelines with RIAS staff (there are two formal editorial meetings each day), meeting individual staff members as the need arises (and often at the wish of the individual staff member), and taking various sorts of action to see to it that problems don't recur. They also have numerous diplomatic functions, such as meeting visiting dignitaries.

Certain US directors of RIAS have been reluctant to question the judgement of the Intendant and the programme director, on the grounds that a German has a more instinctive feel for how to approach the audience, whether West or East German or both. While it's undoubtedly true that a German would usually have a better idea of how to approach a German audience than would an American, it's also true that RIAS was established to serve certain US policy interests, and that that remains one of its primary missions, even with the diminished US budgetary contribution and smaller US 'supervisory' staff (there were seven US officers until the early 1960s.) A discussion I had with a former US director revealed a sense of frustration on his part that, although he felt that occasional news features carried on RIAS distorted or failed to reflect the official US viewpoint, there was little he could do to rectify the situation, aside from talking to the reporter or the editor about it. He might or might not be supported by senior German staff, some of whom appeared to resent any direct involvement by US officers in programming matters.

What makes supervision more difficult is that it isn't just the station's news and public affairs programmes that carry policy-related messages. RIAS has many cultural programmes that for the most part sound like cultural programmes anywhere else, with details on the lives of artists, coming events, etc. Yet two of the more recent controversies involving programme policy centred on a classical music show (Klassik fur jedermann, or Classics for everyone) and a literary review (Lesezeichen or Bookmark). The moderator of the first of these, Rainer Clute, dedicated his 19th October, 1983 show to the peace movement and played music to illustrate the tragic side of war, such as Prokofiev's Field of the Dead section from Alexander Nevsky. He also spent more than the usual amount of time talking about the music and much of that talk was about the need for peace. The moderator of the literary review, Hans-Georg

Radio in the American Sector, RIAS Berlin

Soldat, used his 18th September, 1983 broadcast to deliver a travelogue on present-day Nicaragua, interspersing this with various of Pablo Neruda's thoughts. The programme was pro-Nicaraguan, but not blatantly anti-American. (10)

Both men were disciplined for have exceeded their authority, Clute because he talked so much on a show that 'normally didn't contain much talk', and Soldat because his broadcast 'had nothing to do with literature'. Several East German writers, living in both West and East Germany, signed a petition deploring the RIAS disciplinary action against Soldat, stating that it was impossible to separate literature and contemporary political life. As of late 1984, both men continue to work for the station, but are under closer supervision than formerly.

What makes these two cases interesting is that the reasons for disciplining their producers do not appear to have taken into account the effects of their broadcasts on listeners. One could imagine the need for discipline if Soldat's programme had been strongly anti-American, in that both East and West Germans hearing it might have wondered whether US policy had suddenly shifted or whether a form of propaganda sabotage had been committed! As the programme raised questions about large power-small power relationships, however, it could have been very useful from a policy standpoint, in that it could cause East Germans to ponder afresh the relationship between the Soviet Union and Afghanistan or, for that matter, East Germany itself. Clute's programme could have been similarly provocative for East German listeners, since the peace movement in East Germany is small and functions under severe restrictions, but is attempting to express itself. Granted, neither man specifically claimed that his broadcast had been made for that purpose, and granted, a station such as RIAS cannot allow its staff completely free rein. Still it's entirely possible that both broadcasts actually added to the station's prestige among its East German listeners. Certainly the East German broadcast services would not have provided comparable fare.

A fair amount of any given RIAS broadcasting day is devoted to material that East Germans are unlikely to hear over any other station, their own or those coming from outside the country. For example, the Ost-Politik (East German Political) department prepared a news analysis in mid-September, 1984 that deftly contrasted several East German statements, one by a high-ranking SED (Socialist Unity Party) member, one by an East German professor of international law, and one made several months earlier by Erich Honecker, the East German President, on the concept of reunification. The comparison pointed out that the East German government itself, although seeming in some ways to reject the concept, at least as it would apply to the two Germanies, seemed in other ways willing to accept it, if it were more on their terms.

However, in my last three visits to the station (1972, 1980 and 1984), I have been conscious of a greater awareness of possible West German or US government interest in what the station broadcasts. The awareness seems to be causing station staff at times to consider programme decisions in light of West German or US government reaction. As that possible interest is accompanied by budgetary support, the station could hardly ignore it. But if in doing so it were to lose sight of the need to make its East German listeners' interests its primary concern, RIAS would have abdicated its responsibility. I emphasise that it appears to have those interests firmly in mind much, and even perhaps most, of the time but that there is the possibility of erosion.

What adds to that possibility is that there appears to be an increasing tendency on the part of RIAS production staff to identify with the interests and approaches of their counterparts in West German broadcast stations. Many RIAS staff members have moved on to work for other West German stations, but there isn't much reverse flow. For better or worse, some see RIAS as an excellent training ground for the larger ARD stations. By that token, they seem anxious to establish their credentials as West German broadcasters, which may mean that they attempt to bring out the political party perspective a bit more sharply, as is commonly done over the West German stations, (11) or that they abandon the role of enquiring interviewer and become actively involved in supporting the particular viewpoint of an interviewee. This happened with an interview conducted in mid-September 1984 by a RIAS freelancer with a reporter from the Hessischer Rundfunk (Frankfurt) who was condemning the damage caused during Allied military manoeuvers being conducted in West Germany at the time.

Finally, there is the question of how the station can serve two masters. At present, US and West German policy coincide quite closely. If the policies of the two countries were to diverge in any important way, say over the placement of medium-range nuclear missiles in West Germany or over the possible reunification of the two Germanies and the concessions needed to attain that goal, what would RIAS do? It could not ignore the issues, since most other broadcasters would be covering them, and it probably couldn't limit itself to straightforward news items on the situation, since its policy from its earliest days has been to carry backgrounders and commentaries on important events. Despite what I have already stated about the German character of the station, its likely decision in such a case is not a foregone conclusion, and I would not rule out the possibility of compromise, but it would not be a comfortable situation for the staff, and it might result in broadcasting material that would confuse East German listeners.

The planned-for visit of East German President Honaecker to West Germany in September, 1984 served as a very modest test case of potential conflict over foreign policy. Discussion of the visit touched off renewed speculation in West Germany (and may have done so in East Germany, although there were fewer visible signs) about the prospects for reunification. Leaders of the ruling Christian Democratic Party (CDU) seemed especially interested in the possibility. On the other hand, the US government, as well as several other NATO members, were somewhat less enthusiastic. RIAS maintained a 'low profile' on the issue, but did pay some attention to discussion of those prospects, adding a little of its own. Conflict never arose, but it appeared difficult for the station to make any very clear statements about the pros and cons of reunification.

Conclusion
Throughout this article the assumption has been that RIAS continues to have programmes that its audiences want to hear, and that those audiences are important to the foreign policy considerations of the US and West German governments. I have introduced the possibility that the audiences might have less interest in the station if it sounds more and more like other West German stations. They might continue to listen, but not so much for the material that made RIAS unique in the past, especially if that material now seemed to be in shorter supply, or more ambiguous.

In 1984, East Germany celebrated the 35th anniversary of its existence as a sovereign nation. Talk of reunification notwithstanding, there seem to be few West Germans, especially among the younger generation, who think that East Germany is about to disappear, either through some sort of merger (which younger people seem to regard as highly unlikely) or through western support for an internal uprising (even less likely, given what did not occur in East Germany in 1953, in Hungary and Poland in 1956 and in Czechoslovakia in 1968). The standard of living there is the highest in Eastern Europe, consumer goods are increasingly plentiful and of ever higher quality, and people generally seem to be increasingly relaxed and even quite proud of what they have accomplished over those 35 years. Does RIAS still have a place in this atmosphere or is its useful life just about over?

If the station had been emphasising over the past 15 years the sort of material it had broadcast over the previous 20, it would clearly be anachronistic. Its emphasis on problems in East Germany, deficiencies on the part of the East German leadership and general weaknesses in the communist world, though based almost entirely on selected factual material, presented a rather depressing picture of the East German present and future; nor was there any very feasible solution offered for those problems, especially after it became clear that the west was not about to intervene militarily in any internal uprising. Even the move to an emphasis on western economic development in the 1960s seemed at first to be a bit heavy on the 'look what we have that you don't' angle.

But RIAS moved away from that approach too, and towards a tacit acceptance of a relatively prosperous and sovereign East Germany. Following the signing of th 1972 interstate treaty, there was all the more reason for the station to broadcast from that perspective. However, that was also the period when the station came to resemble its West German counterparts and to lose some of its uniqueness.

Certainly, RIAS continues to broadcast more information about life in East Germany than any of the West German radio stations, although the West German government-financed Deutschlandfunk runs it a reasonably close second in that regard. It also is possible that the station presents material about life in the west in a manner that makes it especially understandable, attractive and meaningful to East German listeners, although that is only speculation. (Certainly many station staff members feel that they attempt and accomplish this.) The station has symbolic value as a tangible indication of the US

Radio in the American Sector, RIAS Berlin

presence in West Berlin and US interest in East Germany. It may sound like other West German stations much of the time, but the East German media frequently remind their consumers that RIAS is backed by the US government. The symbol may not be as powerful now as the West German government carries the lion's share of the financial load (the East German media underscore that fact, too), but it is still present.

RIAS almost certainly is not as important to most East German listeners as it once was, but it retains importance because it appears to be relied upon by many for the accuracy of its reporting, the insight of its backgrounders and commentaries, and the balanced viewpoints (no clear-cut rights and wrongs) of much of its programming. In times of crisis, internal or external, there continues to be anecdotal evidence, as there has been throughout the station's history, that many East German listeners turn to RIAS first to verify the crisis and to obtain an accurate picture. It helps, of course, that the station has such a superb location for reaching all of East Germany, and that it is able to operate two services on several frequencies.

RIAS also retains special status as a 'bargaining chip' of considerable value in East-West relations. There is little doubt that the East German government would still like to see it removed from the airwaves, although its attacks on the station have generally been less virulent in recent years. However, the uses of that 'chip' could cause differences in opinion between the West German and US governments: it isn't out of the question that West Germany, in seeking closer relations with East Germany, might consider the station expendable if its removal brought a correspondingly large East German concession. The frequencies on which RIAS broadcasts are assigned to West Germany, not the United States, and of course the vast majority of the RIAS budget comes from West Germany.

Many of the problems the station faces – flexibility, need for 'fresh blood,' the difficulty of reaching audiences in what has become a more TV-conscious age, problems of internal supervision and in determining goals for programming – are common enough among international broadcasters, especially those of the 'surrogate' variety such as Radio Free Europe and Radio Liberty. They may emerge more clearly in the case of RIAS because it is a very specifically targeted operation, but how the station deals with them in the future may offer useful guidance for many of the larger stations.

Notes
1. See especially Donald R. Browne, International Radio Broadcasting: the Limits of the Limitless Medium. (New York, 1982).
2. See Donald R. Browne, 'The History and Programming Policies of RIAS: Radio in the American Sector of Berlin', unpublished PhD dissertation, University of Michigan, 1961; and 'RIAS Berlin: a Case Study of a Cold War Broadcast Operation', Journal of Broadcasting, Vol. 10, no. 2 (spring, 1966), pp.119-35, for a more detailed history of the station.
3. See Sig Mickelson, America's Other Voices: Radio Free Europe and Radio Liberty (New York, 1983), p.25.
4. Actually, there is no formal distinction between East Berliners and East Germans, and in this article the latter is generally used for both groups. In the East, they are more apt to be called 'citizens of the German Democratic Republic' or, less formally, simply 'Germans'.
5. The stations outside Berlin have limited amounts of broadcast time each day in which to cover local and district news, special events, etc.
6. Discussions with several RIAS staff members, September, 1984.
7. There is censorship of the mail in East Germany, and an East German aspiring to or holding a position of responsibility in the country would think twice before writing to RIAS.
8. See a paper by Peter Wicke of the German Democratic Republic entitled 'Young People and Popular Music in the GDR: social realities and some theoretical views', presented at the annual conference of the International Association for Mass Communication Research, Prague, Czechoslovakia, September, 1984. Wicke discloses that over three-quarters of all East Germans in the 15-18 year old range have their own radio sets, and over half have their own audio cassette recorders.
9. When one contrasts the situation at RIAS with the situation at the Voice of America, the difference in approaches to the matter of job security becomes quite apparent. VOA staff members have some general protection under civil service regulations, but there isn't much protection against removal from a specific job. The Reagan Administration, after coming to office in 1981, was

able to move (or remove) dozens of VOA staff to other positions and appoint individuals more favourably disposed to the Administration's policies. Whether one agrees or disagrees with the Administration, it's clear that VOA has more flexibility in staffing than RIAS.

10. Details on these episodes are contained in 'Mit "Frieden" Sendungscharakter zerstort?,' Evangelische Presse Dienst, West Germany, 11th November 1985; and 'Schaden angerichtet', Suddeutscher Zeitung, 13th February, 1984.

11. For a discussion of the politicisation of West German broadcasting, see Arthur Williams, Broadcasting and Democracy in West Germany (Bradford University Press, Bradford England, 1976), chapters 7 and 8.

Chapter Eleven

GERMAN DEMOCRATIC REPUBLIC CENSORSHIP AND WEST GERMAN BROADCASTING

Gerhard Wettig, Bundesinstitut für ostwissenschaftliche und internationale Studien, Cologne

Impact of West German Electronic Media on the GDR

Radio broadcasts have always been able to be heard all over Germany. West German broadcasts can be received in East Germany and vice versa. Ever since Germany was partitioned after World War Two, both sides have tried to communicate news and ideas to those on the other side of the divide. (1) In East Germany, the Deutschlandsender was set up as a political instrument to disseminate eastern propaganda under the catchword of national unity amongst West Germans. When the West German Bundeswehr was created in the mid-1950s, two radio stations specialising in 'anti-militaristic' propaganda among West German soldiers was added.

On the western side, the US occupation power founded the West Berlin RIAS radio station in 1946-7 which allowed a western voice to be heard in East Germany after the outbreak of the cold war. RIAS soon became both popular amongst East Germans and the target of the East German leadership's anger. The uprising of 17th June, 1953 was, according to official East German comments, the result of 'subversive activities' by RIAS. The truth is that the information spread by RIAS on the events in East Berlin and then in various parts of the GDR, helped to make people feel they could finally do something about their grievances - despite the fact that RIAS did not exhort action and, in many cases, gave express warnings against it.

The impact of RIAS was strong throughout the 1950s and 1960s. East German jamming could not do much about it. Other West German radio reporting was also a source of apprehension to the leaders of the GDR. Since the late 1950s, West German television has become a political factor of increasing importance in East Germany. At a time when the communist leaders of the GDR still felt that the German drive for unity would work in their favour and that their broadcasts might have a decisive political impact on the West German public, they opted for a television system identical to that of the Federal Republic and different to that of the other East European states. Since then, almost the whole GDR - with the exception of two minor strips - has been able to receive television programmes from West Germany. It was only during the 1950s, when television watching expanded and East Germany's failure to be attractive to Germans on both sides of the East-West divide became obvious, that GDR leaders realised they had made the wrong choice. West German TV was becoming increasingly popular in the GDR, and much more so than East Germany's. The leaders of the GDR began to perceive the broadcasts from West Germany not only as competition but as a serious challenge likely to undercut their information monopoly (something they saw as an indispensable component of goverment monopoly).

The GDR's leadership did not repeat the all-German choice when colour television was introduced in the mid-1960s. Together with the Soviets and the rest of the East Europeans, they decided in favour of the French SECAM system and against the West German PAL. East Germans, as a result, cannot receive West German programmes in colour without a special adapter (which is not provided by the state-owned industry). But whether the West German broadcasts are watched by black and white or adapters are procured privately, TV 'from the west' has not lost its attractiveness. In the 1960s, the GDR leadership repeatedly made attempts to put an end to the population's exposure to the West German 'class enemy'. Groups of communist party youth went into action to reset domestic television aerials so that they could no longer pick up television broadcasts from the west; schoolchildren were put to drawing the TV clock - the parents of those who automatically drew the western clock were presumed to be watching western television at home and severely reprimanded. In the long run, however, such measures have not prevented the East German population from preferring West German television to that of the GDR.

Eastern Action against Western Broadcasting
Failures at home have made the East German leaders seek a solution to their problem outside their frontiers. The first indication of this was a

memorandum from the GDR Minister of the Interior to the West Berlin Senate on 12th December, 1967. Under the Potsdam Agreement the Senate was required, said the GDR politician, to 'prevent all neo-Nazi activity and propaganda,' to 'extirpate all Nazi influence,' and to 'put an end to all policies emanating from West Berlin which are directed against East Germany and other socialist states and which are inimical to peace'. The insinuation that 'the machinations of the neo-Nazis' enjoyed Senate approval pointed to aims that went beyond the mere elimination of the expression of neo-Nazi or right wing opinions. (2) The attack was aimed at the spread of information undesirable to the East German leadership.

On 10th March, 1968, the GDR Ministry of the Interior openly used the alleged virulence of neo-Nazism in West Berlin as a pretext for restrictive action against the city. (3) The Soviet government supported its ally's demands for good conduct on the western part, declaring that the GDR was 'not only justified but duty-bound by existing international agreements to take action against the Nazi, revanchist and militaristic activities of the Federal Government in West Berlin'. The three western powers were called upon to intervene in the situation that had arisen. (4)

The line of thought underlying these pronouncements was explained in a quasi-official study by Gunter Görner. (5) Görner drew on two fundamental principles. First, each state is absolutely obliged to maintain unlimited control over information in its own territory. Secondly, the right of transit which two states maintain across a third may be permitted only where precise requirements with regard to 'peacefulness' are met. Görner felt that the West disregarded 'East German sovereignty in the field of radio and telephone communications,' because much 'news is passed between West Germany and West Berlin of a kind which not only threatens the security of East Germany but is directed against the peaceful coexistence of all peoples'. As an example of lack of respect for East German sovereignty, Görner quoted 'television programmes of a tendentious and revanchist kind which are exchanged between West Germany and West Berlin'.

If that argument had been put into practice, West Berlin, an enclave territory in the midst of the GDR, would have been deprived of the possibility of receiving any radio or television programmes from the Federal Republic not authorised by the East German authorities. Any such regulation would have put an immediate end to West Berlin's role as a source of free uncensored radio and television services, which could also be received in the GDR.

As for the 'peaceful' nature of transit, Görner construed this in the sense that the party which desired a right of transit over the territory of the GDR, was obliged to take measures to prevent 'the resurgence on its territory of war propaganda carried out by private persons, organisations, etc.'. Otherwise the country which was expected to grant transit over its territory, would not be in a position to do so. Both West Berlin and the Federal Republic, which wanted the right of transit from the GDR, were to be 'held responsible' not only for 'illegal utterances' on the state radio but also for tolerating 'attacks carried out by free private radio stations'. Accordingly, Görner saw the GDR as 'fully justified in demanding that West Germany suppress the dissemination of news which threatens the peace and the security of the GDR'. All future agreements on transit rights were to be based on absolute 'respect for the sovereignty of the GDR in the field of radio and telephone communications'. The message was clear: West Berlin could not exist without making use of traffic and communication lines which run through East German territory. It therefore had to assume the obligation vis-a-vis the government of the GDR henceforth to ban the broadcasting of all information likely to be offensive to the East German leadership.

The offensive stance taken by the GDR leaders followed the hard line the Kremlin was beginning to develop. The kind of reformed Communism emerging in Czechoslovakia came as a shock to the Soviet leaders. Moscow's first reaction was to pronounce that, according to the laws of history, deepening detente was bound to be accompanied by an 'ideological struggle' that would become continuously more intense. The practical conclusion to be drawn from that was the need to protect eastern societies against uncontrolled influences from the west. Information dissemination across the West-East dividing line ranked highly in that context. It is no coincidence that the first efforts by ruling communist parties in the East to coordinate their information policies vis-a-vis the West, started in 1969. The foundations of a common strategy to block the free flow of information were laid down by the Warsaw Pact powers (excluding Romania) at various international symposia. The first symposium was held in early 1969 and attended by representatives of the Polish and East German Parties. It was devoted to 'problems of psychological warfare waged against the socialist states by the mass media of imperialism'. In the autumn of the same year, communist representatives from 15 European countries met in Jablona near Warsaw for another conference. Under the banner of European security, action against 'hotbeds of cold war propaganda', such as Radio Free Europe and Radio Liberty, was discussed. (6)

Early in 1970, an international congress was held in Moscow, the declared aim of which was to organise the joint efforts of the Warsaw Pact states in the struggle against 'anti-communist subversion'. Taking as their point of departure the Prague proposals drawn up by the Foreign Ministers on 31st October, 1969, (7) the participants debated the concept of peaceful coexistence and renunciation of ideological warfare, a concept which they applied exclusively to western reporting and presentation. The pattern was set for demands that the West give up unilaterally all dissemination of information. The participants of the congress (on which again the Romanians were not represented) organised themselves into committees which took responsibility for the joint coordination of anti-western measures, and for directing their practical implementation. The East German representatives urged joint investigation of what they called 'West German psychological warfare'. All participants agreed that it was necessary to train cadres in order to cope with the 'diversionist actions' of the West. (8) Since then, the ruling parties in Eastern Europe - with the exception of Romania - have coordinated their efforts to keep out influence from western societies.

During the 1970s quadripartite negotiations on Berlin, Soviet ambassador Abrassimov tried to make West Berlin's good conduct towards the GDR in the field of broadcasting a topic of discussion. The point of departure was the basic Soviet position (sharply rejected by the western powers) that the USSR was unilaterally and exclusively competent to have a say in decisions concerning West Berlin. (9) If that had been made to stick, it would have opened the doors to muzzling West Berlin's mass media. The Soviet delegation expressly suggested that, in return for Soviet concessions, West Berlin should pledge itself to refrain from the dissemination of 'hostile propaganda' against the GDR and other communist states. (10)

On 26th May, 1971, ambassador Abrassimov presented a draft agreement which contained corresponding provisions. (11) This specified that everything should be avoided in West Berlin which 'in accordance with the generally accepted norms of international law, could be regarded as interference in the domestic affairs of other countries, or which could disturb common order and security'. This was primarily directed against aspects of the Federal German presence in West Berlin which, from the Soviet standpoint, represented acts of interference in contravention of international law, and which threatened security in the Berlin area. It was equally clear that Abrassimov's words could be used against alleged interference by Western-based telecommunications media in the internal affairs of the GDR - for example, to block the dissemination of undesirable information. It was also stipulated that the state organs of the Federal Republic must no longer be allowed to 'use the territory of West Berlin against the interest of other states'. Finally, the Soviet side wanted to make the three western powers give assurances that 'all necessary measures' would be taken 'to ensure the prevention in their fields of competence of neo-Nazi or similar activities which might be detrimental to public order or might give rise to tension in this area'. It is likely that there was an express request - at least informally - that radio and television activity in West Berlin should not run counter to Soviet and East German demands. When the Western powers rejected these proposals out of hand, the Soviet negotiators dropped the whole matter. (12) Accordingly the Quadripartite Agreement of 3rd September, 1971 contains no provisions to limit the right to disseminate information from West Berlin. (13) The GDR demand, that transit to and from the city over East German territory had to be made dependent on good conduct by western radio and television did not bear fruit.

During the negotiations on the Basic Treaty on the Relationship Between the Two German States, the East German government again tried to obtain a legal basis for prohibiting the transmission of undesirable information from West Germany to its people. The draft that the GDR negotiator presented to his West German counterpart in summer 1972, envisaged that the parties to the treaty should 'desist from all activities which are calculated to disturb the peaceful coexistence of the peoples.' This aimed at, among other things, the inclusion of a good conduct clause in the field of information - defined 'good conduct' to be defined by Eastern criteria. The stipulation, 'That the sovereignty of each side shall be limited to its own state territory' could have supported subsequent demands that West Germany should discontinue its alleged interference in its neighbour's affairs, since the words 'all measures that contradict this basic principle must be given up' were used to clarify the meaning. (14) In the event, neither formula was included in the treaty.

East German Struggle Again West German Broadcasting in the 1970s

The December 1972 Basic Treaty on the Relationship Between the Federal Republic of Germany and the GDR has marked a turning point in intra-German relations. West Germany was keen to substitute peaceful togetherness and cooperation for past antagonism. The following requirements for the new relationship were implemented: diplomatic relations between the two German states were established on the basis of equality; barriers to diplomatic recognition of the GDR by other countries were dismantled; the GDR was accorded economic benefits in exchange for cooperation in intra-German matters of particular West German interest. At the same time, the government of the GDR is under a contractual obligation to honour the commitments contained in the follow-up regulations to the Quadripartite Agreement and in the Basic Treaty aiming at improvement of contact and communication across the intra-German border. One of the annexes to the Basic Treaty stipulates free working conditions for mutually accredited correspondents. West German journalists were allowed to be continuously present in East Berlin and in the GDR for the first time: henceforth, Germans on both sides of the dividing line were to be provided with better information about one another.

West German expectations ran high that a new era of intra-German public communication was beginning. However the Basic Treaty proviso for free journalist access was in the context of the legal provisions of the host country, and this limitation gave ample opportunity for the GDR government to restrict the West German correspondents. The GDR leaders were quick to take their chance. One and a half months after the Basic Treaty had been signed, the East German government decreed that the correspondents were to be held responsible for what they or their editorial boards at home reported and that sanctions ranging from reprimands over explusions to the closing down of their office altogether, were to be applied in order to forestall unacceptable information being issued. (15) The uproar which followed in West Germany seems to have contributed to the GDR leaderhsip's initial reluctance to make full use of the legal instrument it had created. The East German functionaries also seem to have underestimated the impact which relatively free reporting by West German correspondents could have had on the society of the GDR.

Clearly, the developments in the years that followed were more far-reaching than they had anticipated. A news chain took shape which, in the eyes of the ruling Socialist Unity Party (SED) officials, gradually assumed alarming proportions. Via correspondents accredited in the GDR, West German media were gaining faster and more detailed access to information about events in the GDR on which a veil of silence had been lowered and about problems that had been treated as taboo. Since 1973, not only deviationists such as Robert Havemann but thousands of ordinary GDR citizens began to approach West German correspondents with problems for which they were unable to gain a hearing elsewhere. The undesirable news items (undesirable from the regime's viewpoint) were often relayed straight to East German homes by electronic media in the Federal Republic of Germany and West Berlin. Such information proved particularly effective when accompanied by on-the-spot television coverage to prove the point. East German current affairs coverage by the West German media soon came to be the main topic of political debate both within the family and at work. West German television began to provide a substitute in the GDR for the free market in public opinion that had been suppressed by the regime.

The East German leadership had given up attempts to prevent the population receiving West German broadcasts. Early in 1973, a secret public opinion survey, conducted by an institute of the SED central committee apparatus, finally made clear that official efforts to discourage people from watching had utterly failed. Seventy per cent of the population generally preferred to switch on to West German programmes. (16) On 28th May, 1973, SED Secretary General Erich Honecker publicly announced that everybody in the GDR was free to listen and watch whatever they wanted. (17) In the late 1970s, the East German leadership also decided that it was no longer worthwhile jamming RIAS radio broadcasts.

Official East German acquiescence to West

German broadcasts did not mean that the leaders were in any way content. They made abundantly clear that they felt that some correction had to be made. Erich Honecker used the opportunity of his conversation with Chancellor Helmut Schmidt when the CSCE Final Act was signed in Helsinki, for vivid complaints about 'the continuing interference by mass media of the Federal Republic in the internal affairs of the German Democratic Republic'. It was possible, Honecker claimed, 'to observe from one month to the next an intensification of the hostile campaign against the GDR'. Honecker expressed the hope that 'now that the seal has been set on the Helsinki Agreement, we may look forward to changes in this sphere also'. (18) On 14th February, 1976, he publicly reproached western, and especially West German politicians and mass media for contravening the non-intervention principle, and for having recourse to slander against East Germany, the Soviet Union and other East European states. (19)

Leading GDR officials were unwilling to accept the trend towards a free market in public opinion, which had begun to be set in motion. They began to take restrictive actions against West German journalists accredited in East Berlin. These intensified as the mood in East Germany grew worse, in the wake of economic difficulties and the repercussions of the human rights concessions in the Helsinki Accords. GDR authorities sought not only to penalise the reporters on the spot but to exert pressure on news desks in West Germany to toe their line and spike news and footage that might cause dissatisfaction and unrest in the GDR. Fresh regulations governing foreign correspondents were issued in April 1979 and June 1979 by the GDR Volkskammer, the parliamentary surrogate. (20) In direct contradiction of assurances given when the Basic Treaty was negotiated, western correspondents were practically forbidden to gather news that was not officially supplied and controlled, while GDR citizens who offered aliens news ran the risk of a treason trial.

Problem of West German Broadcasts
Political and social problems encountered by the SED leadership in dealings with visitors and journalists from the Federal Republic of Germany seem to indicate that the GDR's political difficulties lie deeper than questions of retarded living standards. Freedom of contact and unhampered dissemination of information

across the intra-German border has become so alarming to the representatives of the Soviet-style regime that they have resorted to repression and seclusion in order to secure a measure of control over their subjects. Statements made externally, and particularly for internal consumption by leading party functionaries, including those of the Secretary General, indicate that they still regard the Federal Republic of Germany as the class enemy; or simply, as 'the enemy' (as Erich Honecker expressly noted in his speech of 22nd June, 1979).

The problems that unavoidably arise for a repressive regime when there is interaction with a pluralistic, liberal country come to assume the character of 'ideological subversion' when they are evaluated by SED officials. The presence of West German journalists in the GDR is seen as a deliberate ideological offensive launched by West Germany which can only be countered by repressive measures to isolate the East German population from contact with the pluralistic western news system. The reaction had to be toned down in view of the international situation in general and the wording of intra-German agreements in particular. The East German leaders cannot afford to contravene the agreements openly on a wide scale. The GDR leaders do not want to call into question either detente in Central Europe or the inter-German relationship, largely because such a policy would endanger the economic advantages West Germany provides. East German repression and seclusion has to be realised whenever possible by indirectly sidestepping treaty commitments rather than by directly contravening them. Opportunities of contact and information across the intra-German border in accordance with the terms officially negotiated are nullified, whenever possible, by means of intra-state counter-measures.

Ties with a country run on western democratic lines, such as the Federal Republic of Germany, inevitably represent a serious challenge to a regime that is based on central control and strict discipline and accustomed to repression as a means of maintaining its monopoly of government and information. State and society in West German constitute, in the circumstances and from the SED's point of view, an antagonistic counter-system with hostile and dangerous effects on the GDR. Domestic difficulties of its own making are attributed to the West German 'class enemy', (21) a convenient scapegoat SED officials can blame for their own shortcomings. This viewpoint makes relations between the two parts of Germany difficult. Regardless of the economic benefits enjoyed by the GDR, the Federal Republic of Germany continues to be cast in the role of originator of serious political problems in the GDR. The logical consequence for the East German leaders is that seclusion towards West Germany must be maintained and intensified by almost every means available. Erich Honecker has repeatedly referred to the Federal Republic of Germany as an imperialist foreign country. On 22nd June, 1979 he reiterated clearly and unmistakably the tenet of progressively intensified class struggle between the two German societies.

The sore point of the intra German quid pro quo has been the withdrawal of contractual contact and information concessions by the GDR without a corresponding withdrawal of concessions by the Federal Republic.

There are many reasons why the GDR has seen fit to renege on its treaty commitments. One is that an irrevocable quasi-recognition was part of the price paid by West Germany for agreements reached in connection with the 1972 Basic Treaty. Were Bonn to waive economic advantages so far enjoyed by East Berlin but not unmistakably classified as counter-concessions that might be repealed if the GDR failed to keep its part of the bargain could well call existing intra-German relations into question in their entirety. This is a prospect in which the Federal Republic of Germany has no interest whatever, both because of the difficult position of West Berlin and in view of intra-German contacts that are still possible. A further difficulty is that the SED leadership does not usually breach its contractual commitments directly. It prefers to offset them by domestic measures. The East German technique of making successive amendments to negotiated agreements presents West Germany with a problem that, so far, has not found a solution which satisfactory to the western side.

Development of West German Broadcasting
West German broadcasting to the GDR is circumscribed by a number of fundamentals which have prevailed in Central Europe since the end of World War Two. The division which has emerged in Germany is not the result of a natural development or national decision, so the territories are not neatly separated. Extensive overlapping makes the broadcasts of one side easily receivable on the other. The insular

position of West Berlin within the GDR provides an asymmetrical pattern, for East Germany is more exposed to West German broadcasting than vice versa.
The people in both parts of Germany share language, nationhood and culture. Such broad commonality makes for much understanding of, and interest in, each other and there is considerable receptivity to information from and about the other side. Again, the patterns are asymmetrical. East Germans tend to be more attracted by the messages of the West German media than vice versa. This has, of course, to do with the poor scope the GDR leadership allows for pluralism and spontaneity. Uniformity seems indispensible to political domination - and the audience responds negatively. For East German listeners and watchers, West German broadcasting is a unique possibility to rest from the familiar information cliché. The East German leadership views the intrusion of the West German electronic media into its sphere with resentment. In Soviet-type communist theory and practice, the information monopoly of the ruling circles is a corollary of their power monopoly. Any deviation seems akin to loss of control, as Soviet and East German reactions to the Prague Spring of 1968 demonstrated. It is not simply propaganda, therefore, which motivates the East German leadership to call the intrusion of the West German electronic media into the GDR an interventionist encroachment into their sovereignty.
The nature of the challenge with which the East German leadership has felt confronted has changed over time. In the early post war years, it was radio broadcasting from West Germany and West Berlin. There was little the East Germans could do, as any diplomatic protests which Moscow (not East Berlin) might have made would have been certain to go unheeded under the conditions of the cold war. The situation changed gradually with television. West German television could not be asked to stop broadcasting, even if a more relaxed East-West relationship provided diplomatic leverage in western capitals. Television, however, was technically more complicated than radio - which provided the East German regime with the opportunity to identify watchers and exert pressure on them. Both East Berlin and Moscow tried to exploit West Berlin's dependence on transit traffic through the GDR to impose 'good conduct' on the City's broadcasters. Those attempts came to nothing. By the time the Basic Treaty on the relationship between the two German states was concluded at the end of 1972, the East German leaders

had realised they had to acquiesce to broadcasts from West Germany and West Berlin. They were willing to accept West German and other western correspondents in East Berlin and to give them contractual guarantees of suitable working conditions. This was perceived as part of the GDR's normalisation effort: East Germany, which had finally come close to international recognition and to generally being accepted as a normal state in the international arena, would also host foreign correspondents like other states. Nobody in East or West at the time foresaw that this was soon to create an additional challenge to the East German leadership's position.

It made a tremendous difference whether the West German media reported GDR events and development in general terms, or whether they were on the spot. Reporting on the GDR became more comprehensive and more precise once West German correspondents were there, could seek information wherever they wanted, were able to talk freely to East Germans, and had the opportunity to film what they saw. It was not only the scope of the information that broadened. At least as important was the authenticity of West German television for the East German watchers, now that they could see directly on their television screens what was being talked about. The wealth of information which West German correspondents gathered in the GDR, was made possible largely by the population's willingness to cooperate. People with grievances, or who simply felt that they knew something that a larger public should be aware of, primed the West German correspondents with stories and hints of where to look for news. This is consonant with what journalism is expected to do in western countries, but seen from the political perspective of a Soviet-type regime, it was subversive and led to 'spying out state secrets'. The news chain that emerged was perceived as dangerous by the East German leadership. Events and developments of vital interest to GDR citizens, which were normally hidden from the public according to the leaders' desires, were almost certain to come into the open sooner or later. The East Germans were finding an outlet for making public what they wanted to become public. The West German correspondents confined their information to the West German media, but as West German television programmes were on the screens of most East Germans every evening, within one or two days everybody in the GDR knew about it. The news would arouse heated discussion not only at home but at work. The authorities, who were used to manipulating information for political purposes, were by-passed. Public opinion independent of the ruling circles began to emerge, much as in western countries.

East German Reaction to the Challenge
The East German leadership was disturbed at the prospect of its information system becoming irrelevant and West German broadcasting was creating an independent East German public. Something had to be done to stop the process. According to Lenin, a chain must be broken at its weakest link. In the case of the new news chain, the weakest link was the West German correspondents who lived in East Berlin, who could be put under pressure by the GDR authorities. The East German leaders complained that the correspondents were spoiling good-neighbourly relations between the two states and that the mutual cooperation which Bonn sought in order to ease contact across the dividing line would be seriously impaired. The general caution delivered to West German correspondents in February 1973 was followed by restrictive measures. For some time, the East German authorities hoped the problem had gone away, but the tactics of reprimand and expulsion did not provide the intended result. The correspondents were not intimidated.

The East German leaders finally decided, in 1979, that they had exhausted all means other than full-scale restrictive legislation. They first issued a regulation which subjected the western correspondents (in practice the West German correspondents, as the most dangerous element) to isolation as far as unauthorised reporting (on a case by case basis) was concerned. A few months later, any GDR citizen who contacted a West German correspondent and passed information, could be prosecuted. The offence ranked as a major crime, similar to treason, even if the information had been taken from a source which had been made officially public. (22) The measures were designed to deter, which they did. The extreme punishment did not actually have to be applied.

Why did the authorities wait so long before they took repressive action? One reason has to do with the GDR's 'non-recognition complex'. Once international recognition of the state had been secured after more than 20 years, the leaders were reluctant to jeopardise the newly-won international prestige by action which would be regarded as repulsive. Another reason is that, during the 1970s, the East German rulers developed an increasingly strong interest in intra-German cooperation, as they urgently needed the economic benefits Bonn was offering. The West German government, however, had always been outspoken with regard to the improvement of intra-German communication and reporting. Restrictive East German action would have been bound to cause serious repercussions in Bonn and might also have put in jeopardy the new economic benefits. The outrage provoked by the February 1973 regulations in the Federal Republic seems to have restrained the East German leadership for a time. It was only gradually that the leaders of the GDR found that there were ways of disassociating communication from other aspects of the intra-German relationship.

The restrictions placed on West German reporting from the GDR resulted in considerable 'de-sharpening' of television programmes beamed into East Germany. Since then, the East German leaders have found it tolerable to live with the information challenge from the Federal Republic. Official GDR sources even have claimed that the authorities of the country practice 'openness to the world' to such an extent that they enhance reception of West German television. (23) If that should indeed be verified, the reason for this much have been to bolster what is known to be a particularly low professional and political morale in those few regions of the country where West German TV cannot be received. The people there perceive their being deprived of what citizens elsewhere enjoy, as a kind of discrimination which they strongly resent. It has also been argued that the regime feels the West German TV's prevailing critical attitude towards life in the Federal Republic to be an asset which can be exploited for mitigating discontent in the GDR.

The harsh restraints imposed on West German reporting in the GDR and the resulting blurring of the impact of West German television, does not mean that the East German leadership regards such broadcasts as harmless. A delicate balance has emerged between the ability of the West German broadcasters to bring their programmes to an East German audience, and the ability of the East German leaders to restrain West German reporting of events in the GDR. Contrary to its professed need for unlimited control over mass information, the East German leadership sees itself in competition with the West German society which is constantly being created on the television screens. However, it finds solace in that West German television neither adequately reflects society in the Federal Republic nor has the means to explore much of what is kept hidden in the GDR. Accordingly, the East German leadership regards West German broadcasting as a phenomenon it not only has to live with, but one that can be lived with for the time being.

Basic Issues at Stake
The French leftist philosopher André Glucksmann has made the point that good and evil cannot be distinguished out of context. Because people tend to believe that what is good for themselves is good in general, a criterion for a more objective judgement has to be found. Glucksmann feels that the comparability criterion meets the need. Those who make others suffer for their own benefit, can perceive that to be good as long as they do not compare their well-being to the suffering of the other. When the comparison is made between making another suffer and having to endure suffering personally, the second comes out as far worse. The final balance between inflicting suffering and enduring it is negative. Inflicting suffering proves to be predominantly evil despite the benefits one of the two sides is able to reap.

Any judgement, however, depends on a comparison being made. So, there is a requirement of visibility. Those who are to compare the relative merits of an action must have before their eyes both results which they are to compare. That means that the two results have to be on record - i.e. that they must not be hidden from people's eyes. You can't condemn, you can't fight a phenomenon you have not become aware of. This is why publicity is indispensible if the good is to be promoted and the evil restrained. The kind of control to be exercised <u>vis-a-vis</u> the ruling circles, was the basic issue for the struggle for freer communication in the GDR which the West German electronic media had rendered possible. The struggle was lost in the end. That meant also that a chance for peaceful change had been lost. One should not underrate the importance of this. Those who plead for a closer relationship with the eastern regimes, usually justify their case by asserting that doing so is the only way of inducing peaceful change which will eventually ease the strains of East-West antagonism and help the eastern peoples to have better living conditions. If peaceful change can be barred by the eastern regimes at will (and there is certainly the desire to do so), the whole concept of creating peace and justice by government-to-government East-West cooperation has to be thought out again.

The failure to make a decisive stop toward emancipating the public from leadership tutelage in the GDR, prompts the question of what kind of East-West relationship can be made to prevail - the Soviet or the Western one. In Soviet perception, East-West relations are performing at two different levels: the government-to-government and the intra-societal levels. Moscow's intent is that at the intra-societal level (which comprises the activities of the mass media), different normative principles are to apply in western and eastern countries. The political struggle which, according to Soviet philosophy, has to be waged between 'socialism' and 'imperialism' (i.e. the western democracies), must take place both between eastern and western countries and within western societies, but it shall not be allowed within the societies of the east. (24) The Soviet concept implies a basic asymmetry to the detriment of western democracy. In the optimum case, the status quo between East and West is being preserved; in all other cases, the eastern side will change the balance in its own favour. Thus the western expectation that there will be peaceful change one day will remain a pious hope, while Soviet-type ideological struggle in the west will be practised; the potential result is political damage to the West - a prospect which had been clearly demonstrated by recent Soviet fostering of the anti-missle deployment opposition in many West European countries. (25)

In particular, the western countries have to decide whether they are willing to accept the two biases the Kremlin offers. Are they willing to allow government-to-government relations to be totally separated from relations at the social level, so that Moscow can arbitrarily indulge in intra-Western 'ideological struggle', while reaping fruits of pragmatic East-West cooperation at the same time? Are they willing to allow for highly asymmetrical influence patterns at the societal level, so that the Kremlin can strive for political advantage in western countries without taking any risk within its own power sphere? The answer to these questions will determine western policy towards broadcasting over the iron curtain.

Notes

1. For details on the development of intra-German broadcasting see Douglas A. Boyd, 'Broadcasting Between the Two Germanies', Journalism Quarterly, vol.60, no.2 (summer 1983), pp.232-9; George Quester, 'Transboundary Television', Problems of Communism, September-October, 1984, pp.77-9. The factual development of inter-German communication since 1972 is presented in detail by Rolf Geserick and Arnuld Kutsch, Möglichkeiten und Behinderungen des Informationszuganges für westdeutsche Korrespondenten in der DDR seit 1972', Publizistik, 3-4/1984, pp.455-91.
2. Aussenpolitische Korrespondenz, 52/1967, pp.410-12.
3. Aussenpolitische Korrespondenz, 11/1968, p.90. The East German Minister of the Interior added that in future, 'Members of the NPD and those active in the neo-Nazi cause' would be debarred from transit rights between the Federal Republic and West Berlin.
4. Aide-memoire from the Soviet government to the government of the Federal Republic, 5th July, 1968 published in Moskau-Bonn. Dokumentation, ed. Boris Meissner, part 2, Köln: Verlag Wissenschaft und Politik, 1975, p.1133.
5. Gunter Görner, DDR gewährleistet friedlichen Westberlin-Transit, Berlin (East): Staatsverlag der DDR, pp.34, 36, 41, 69ff.
6. O. Bures/H. Kittlemann/H. Künzel, Aggressionssender, Verlag fur fremdsprachige Literatur, Prague, 1971, p.5.
7. Pravda, 1st November 1969 (Russian text).
8. Interview with Janusz Kolczynski in Gazeta Poznańska, 13th and 14th May, 1972.
9. Statement by the Soviet Embassy in East Berlin of 31st January, 1970, in Pravda, 2nd February, 1970.
10. This has been reported by DPA correspondent Walter Marquart on 4th November, 1970 and also by Der Spiegel of 9th November, 1970, pp.29 et seq.
11. Reproduced (slightly shortened) in Quick, 4th August, 1971.
12. Hans-Ulrich Kersten, Fulbrights Attacken, gegen RIAS Berlin, in Basler Nachrichten of 30th March, 1972; 'Geheimniskrämerei um den Sender RIAS', Frankfurter Rundschau, 29th April, 1974.
13. Das Viermächte-Abkommen über Berlin vom 3. September 1971, ed. Federal Press and Information Office, Bonn, September 1971, pp.179-98 (English text).
14. See Quick, 25th October, 1972.

15. For text of 21st February, 1973 regulations see <u>Texte zur Deutschlandpolitik</u>, ed. Federal Ministry of Intra-German Relations, Bonn, vol.13 (1973), pp.194-9.
16. Werner Kinnigkeit, 'Duldung der Ochsenköpfe', <u>Süddeutsche Zeitung</u>, 18th January, 1974; 'SED-Chef gibt Empfang westlichr Rundfunk- und Fernsehsendungen frei', <u>Tagesspiegel</u>, 30th May, 1973.
17. Report of SED Secretary General Honecker to the Politbureau of the SED given on 28th May, 1973, printed in <u>Erich Honecker</u>, <u>Reden und Aufsatze</u>, ed. Institute for Marxism-Leninism (attached to the SED Central Committee), vol.2 (Dietz Verlag, East Berlin, 1975), p.235.
18. Interview with SED Secretary General Honecker, <u>Neues Deutschland</u>, 6th August, 1975.
19. <u>Informationen</u>, ed. Federal Minstry of Intra-German Relations, 4/1976, p.3.
20. For the text of 11th April, 1979 amendment to 21st February, 1973 regulations see <u>Neues Deutschland</u> of 14th April, 1979. The text of the 28th June, 1979 Volkskammer resolution is contained in <u>DDR-Report</u>, 9/1979, pp.610-11.
21. Cf. the characteristic October 1978 comments by the GDR Minister of State Security, reprinted in extracts by <u>Der Spiegel</u>, 26th February, 1979, p.30 et seq. Similar but more restrained comments are to be found in Erich Honecker's 22nd June, 1979 speech, reprinted in <u>Neues Deutschland</u> of 23rd and 24th June, 1979.
22. The GDR leaders are anxious to withhold from the West actually published news. An obvious example is the fact that the provincial newspapers may not be exported to the Federal Republic and other western countries.
23. In those areas of the GDR which are outside the reach of West German television, the East German authorities allegedly have begun cabling apartment houses so as to allow West German TV programmes to be received there. See Manfred Schell, 'Der Kampf gegen das West-TV geht zu Ende', in <u>Die Welt</u>, 19th December, 1983. A more detailed evaluation is contained in George H. Quester, 'Transboundary Television' in <u>Problems of Communism</u>, September-October, 1984, pp.78-9.
24. The claim has been expressly made by the Kremlin's Nr.2 in 1973 (see speech of Mikhail Suslov on 13th July, 1973, in <u>Pravda</u>, 14th July, 1973) and upheld ever since.
25. The 'peace movement' which opposes US

missile deployment in Western Europe, may not have been too far from reaching its goal (as indeed the Soviet leaders felt quite confident to expect). Despite its ultimate failure, it has succeeded in making some political inroads into the societies of countries like the Federal Republic. For the Soviet attitude and behaviour towards the West European 'peace movement' see Gerhard Wettig, 'The Western Peace Movement in Moscow's Longer View', in: Strategic Review, XII:2 (spring 1984), pp.44-54.

Part Three

IRON CURTAIN AUDIENCES AND PUBLIC OPINION

Chapter Twelve

SOVIET AREA AUDIENCE AND OPINION RESEARCH (SAAOR) AT RADIO FREE EUROPE/RADIO LIBERTY

R. Eugene Parta, director of Soviet Area Audience and Opinion Research at RFE/RL.

It was recognised early in the history of Radio Liberty that knowledge of the station's audience was essential if RL were to perform its mission well. In 1956, Dr Max Ralis, a Russian-speaking sociologist from Cornell University, was appointed head of the newly formed audience research division. To safeguard its objectivity, the new division was from the outset structurally independent of the broadcasting activities. It was established as an independent unit, reporting directly to the president of the organisation, Howland H. Sargeant.

The challenge was immense. If the USSR had wished to learn about the audiences to its broadcasts to the west, it was free to hire a western survey research firm to carry out a study. As this means was closed to western broadcasters to the Soviet Union, others had to be found, and an entirely new survey methodology elaborated.

The first task of audience research was to find out whether Radio Liberty did in fact have an audience in the USSR. An early attempt to establish the listeners' existence was by soliciting mail. Requests for letters broadcast over the air provoked a massive response. Well over 6,000 items of mail have reached Radio Liberty since its inception, including over 1,000 during the peak year of 1964 alone. Soviet censorship and the mail interception techniques employed by the Soviet authorities (frequently invoked by the letter writers themselves) led audience research analysts to believe that the number of letters and cards despatched to the station was probably considerably higher than the quantity received. Mail tests carried out confirmed this assumption. These letters constituted an invaluable piece of documentary evidence attesting to the existence of an audience for RL in the Soviet Union in the days before other methods of audience research became feasible.

A second means of determining Radio Liberty's impact was by analysing attacks on the station that appeared in Soviet media. Although RL was subjected to attacks from almost the first day it went on the air, the denunciations reached a peak during the years 1965-74, when they appeared in over 1.5 billion copies of various Soviet publications. (If it had been possible to screen the local press as well, this number would probably have been higher.) Although media attacks betrayed official concern about Radio Liberty's impact on the Soviet population, they were of no use in helping the station understand more about the size and nature of its audience.

The third approach, which in time allowed general inferences to be drawn about the audience, was to gather empirical evidence of listening habits to Radio Liberty and other western stations, by interviewing Soviet travellers in the West. The first major interviewing effort took place at the Brussels World Fair in 1958. Over 300 Soviet citizens were contacted, of whom 65 turned out to be listeners to Radio Liberty. Interviewing of Soviet visitors continued through the 1960s, but it remained on an ad hoc basis. This meant that, while a good deal of evidence on listening to Radio Liberty was gathered, it was impossible to undertake any statistical analysis of the findings and project them back onto the Soviet population.

As the number of Soviet citizens allowed to travel to the West steadily increased, it became possible to envisage the development of survey procedures and analytical techniques that would permit generalised estimates of the audiences to western broadcasts in the USSR. From 1970 onwards, the audience research division began to systematise its data collection methods. Interviews were entrusted to survey research institutes, and a standard questionnaire was developed. By late 1985 a computerised data base of almost 25,000 interviews was in existence. At present, about 4,000 interviews with Soviet travellers to the West are conducted annually by a dozen independent survey research institutes. This has paved the way for sophisticated analysis of western radio listening habits in the USSR, and even detailed analysis of the reliability and validity of the data itself. (1)

Systematic data collection and computerised procedures to analyse the data developed side by side. One of the pioneers in this area was the late

SAAOR at Radio Free Europe/Radio Liberty

Professor Ithiel de Sola Pool of the Massachusetts Institute of Technology. In the early 1970s, Professor Pool used Radio Liberty audience research data in the MIT Communist Communications project and provided the first estimates of the size and composition of western radio audiences in the USSR. Drawing on techniques developed by the Harvard statistician, Professor Frederick Mosteller, he constructed a computer simulation model of the Soviet population. Although this model has since been expanded, it is still the basic instrument used to project audience research data onto the Soviet population. (2)

SAAOR has for many years maintained close working relationships with leading academics and other specialists in the Soviet field. New methodologies aimed at improving audience estimates in areas where the original computer simulation model is inadequate (ethnic, as opposed to geographic, composition of audiences, for instance) are currently under study both at Harvard and at MIT, with which SAAOR maintains a direct computer link and where its computerised data is stored.

After the merger of Radio Liberty and Radio Free Europe in 1976, the audience research division of Radio Liberty was rechristened Soviet area audience and opinion research (SAAOR). The new name reflected new research capabilities that had developed as a by-product of the interview project. Interviewing Soviet respondents on western radio listening provides SAAOR with a unique opportunity to gather data on a wide range of public attitudes in the USSR at the same time. Studies based on these data include attitudes toward events in Poland and Afghanistan, opinions on a range of civil rights issues, views on the downing of the Korean airliner and feelings about the increased danger of nuclear war. One of the main aims of these studies is to investigate whether respondents who have access to western information through radio broadcasts view topical issues differently from those who do not. It has appeared consistently throughout that western radio plays an important part in the formation of attitudes diverging from the official Soviet position.

In addition to interviewing Soviet travellers, SAAOR carries out research among Soviet emigrants from the USSR. These data are not used for the purpose of estimating audiences to western broadcasts in the USSR since they come from an atypical subset of the population. However, the more open interviewing situation allows us to gather detailed information on listening and audibility conditions. The emigrant data also provide an independent sample against which to crosscheck.

Ever since the data collection procedures were systematised in the early 1970s, it has been a matter of principle to ensure that research covers all of the major western stations broadcasting to the USSR, and not just Radio Liberty. Field work and questionnaires have been developed that avoid bias towards any one station. The data obtained are shared with other western broadcasters to the Soviet Union and SAAOR has developed close working relationships with most of the major western stations.

Although SAAOR provides Radio Liberty with services such as programme reviews, background reports and various types of analysis, the keystone of its research is estimating the size of western radio audiences in the Soviet Union. Listening estimates are updated annually on the basis of discrete samples. The most recent estimates (for 1984) indicate that the Voice of America has the largest audience of any western broadcaster to the Soviet Union. VOA reaches between 14% and 18% of the adult population in the course of an average week. Next come Radio Liberty with 8 to 12%, the BBC with 7 to 10%, and Deutsche Welle (DW) with 3 to 6%.

These percentage estimates translate into millions of listeners, most of whom tend to be young, well-educated, city dwellers: in short, an elite audience. They bear witness to the vital job that western radio is doing by communicating with the better-educated elements of the Soviet population, despite the obstacles erected by the Soviet government in the form of jamming, media attacks and other types of discouragement.

Demographic Composition
The demographic composition of audiences also varies. Listening to western radio is most prevalent among educated urban males (see Table 12.1), but there are otherwise divergences between the four stations in terms of their relative appeal to different age groups. All stations draw their highest ratings in the 30-49 year-old age group. VOA is most widely heard by listeners under 30, as well as among the over-fifties. Deutsche Welle has relatively little appeal to the younger generation.

All four stations have higher ratings among better-educated listeners. This trend is particularly noticeable in the case of Deutsche Welle. None of

Table 12.1: Weekly Audience Ratings for the Major Western Broadcasters January-December 1984*

	RL %	VOA %	BBC %	DW %
Overall Rating	8-12	14-18	7-10	3-6
Age				
16-29	5-7	10-12	5-7	1-3
30-49	14-20	18-24	11-15	5-7
50+	3-7	11-15	3-7	3-7
Education				
Less than secondary	5-9	8-12	4-8	2-5
Secondary plus	16-18	25-31	13-15	7-9
Sex				
Men	14-18	23-27	13-17	6-10
Women	3-7	7-11	2-4	1-3
Residence				
Rural	5-9	6-10	2-6	1-3
Urban	10-14	19-23	10-12	5-7
Geographic Region				
European RSFSR**	7	13	8	5
Moscow & oblast.	9	19	15	7
Leningrad & Obl.	8	16	12	7
Siberian RSFSR	6	14	4	3
Baltic States	14	20	12	5
Belorussian SSR	9	12	6	3
Caucasian SSRs	17	21	9	3
Central Asian SSRs	12	17	5	2
Moldavian SSR	10	12	8	4
Ukrainian SSR	14	19	11	2

*Source: See AR 2-85 <u>Trend Report: Radio Liberty's Audience in the USSR, January-December, 1984</u>. Ratings are the percentage of the population aged 16 or over in each category which hears a given station in the course of a given week. The overall rating is the percentage of the total adult Soviet population to hear the station during an average week.

** Excluding the cities and oblasts of Moscow and Leningrad.

the four major stations appears to have had much success in reaching the lesser-educated members of

Soviet society. Relatively few women in the USSR appear to listen to western radio. BBC has the highest ratio of male to female listeners at 3 to 1, and DW has the lowest at 7 to 1. The notorious 'double burden' of work and home shouldered by Soviet women is most probably the principal cause of these uniformly low listening rates as the combination of domestic chores and full-time jobs would leave little time for leisure.

Rural residents listen at about half the rate of urban dwellers, except in the case of Deutsche Welle, where the ratio of urban to rural dwellers is as high as 6 to 1. Probable causes of the low ratings are the lack of adequate radio sets, the absence of privacy, and the relative lack of interest in national and international affairs that frequently corresponds to a low level of education.

The Ukraine, the Baltic states, and the Belorussian and Caucasian Soviet Socialist Republics are all areas with high rates of listening. The urban areas of Moscow and Leningrad also show high listening rates, except in the case of Radio Liberty, which obtains its highest ratings outside the European RSFSR which excludes the cities and oblasts of Moscow and Leningrad. One reason for this is the concentrated heavy jamming of RL, which is particularly effective in large urban areas. Inversely, Radio Liberty's extensive programming in Soviet nationality languages boosts its ratings in non-Russian areas.

Western Broadcasts and Attitudinal Patterns

During the late 1970s, SAAOR gathered survey data on a range of questions broadly related to civil liberties. These data provide an opportunity to measure attitudes toward the Soviet system in general. SAAOR has constructed a scale of attitudinal types classifying the urban population into five categories - liberals, moderates, the indifferent, conservatives and hardliners - using statistical methods such as factor analysis and the MIT mass media simulation programme. (3)

It emerged that the population groups most likely to hold liberal values are men, the under-30s and the better-educated. In geographic terms, the Baltic and Caucasian areas appear the most liberal, and the provincial areas of the RSFSR the most conservative. Overall, it is estimated that about 13% of the adult urban Soviet population could be labelled liberal while 29% could be described as moderates. (4) At the other end of the spectrum of opinion, about 28% take a conservative stand on civil rights, and 12% a hardline position; 19% of respondents were indifferent to or uninterested in these concepts. About one in seven of the adult urban population can therefore be seen as receptive to basic western ideas of civil liberties, a figure that would be considered low by the standards of most modern industrial societies.

Use of western media for information varies considerably between the different attitudinal categories. Seventy-nine per cent of the liberals use western radio as a source of either international or national information. Newspapers, the domestic source most widely used by this group, come in second place with 70%. Moderates also make widespread use of western radio as an information source, but at a rate almost less than half that of the liberals: 40%. The indifferent, conservative and hardline elements turn to western radio at considerably lower rates: 19%, 22% and 10% respectively. Persons in the hardline category often cite such reasons as 'knowing what the enemy is saying' to justify their listening. Clearly western radio has been most successful in reaching citizens who are to some degree critical of the Soviet system. However, the relatively high proportion of moderates who listen suggests that thinking people in the USSR have generally come to rely on western sources to supplement domestic media in obtaining the information they need.

Table 12.2: Stations Heard, by Attitudinal Type

	Liberal %	Moderate %	Indifferent %	Conservative %	Hardline %
BBC	28	18	13	10	5
Deutsche Welle	21	14	6	10	4
Radio Liberty	45	12	5	3	5
VOA	54	35	24	16	10

Totals may exceed 100% due to multiple response.

Preferences for different western broadcasters are apparent among the different attitudinal categories. The liberals have the highest rates of listening to all four major stations (see Table 12.2). Voice of America and Radio Liberty are the stations most frequently sought out by this group, with BBC and DW in third and fourth place respectively. Among the moderates, VOA remains in first place, but BBC moves into second place and Radio Liberty drops to fourth. The other three attitudinal groups show somewhat lower listening rates to all the stations. VOA is the station most widely heard by all attitudinal groups, but among the conservatives BBC and Deutsche Welle exert a certain appeal as well. (5)

Table 12.3 gives an attitudinal profile of the audience to each of the four stations. It appears that fully half of Radio Liberty's audience belong to the liberal camp and another 30% are classified as moderates. Audiences to the other stations are more balanced, with the largest single attitudinal group being that of the moderates (a finding that reflects to some extent the greater weight of the moderates in the overall adult urban population). VOA and BBC have a very similar audience profile. Deutsche Welle shows a different pattern, since it draws a relatively high proportion of its audience (25%) from the conservatively-minded group. Since DW enjoys a reputation for good programming on science and technology, it is possible that many of its listeners are tuning in less for political than for technical and professional information.

Table 12.3: Composition of the Audience of each Western Station

	BBC %	DW %	RL %	VOA %
Liberal	25	25	50	25
Moderate	35	36	30	37
Indifferent	18	10	8	17
Conservative	18	25	8	16
Hardline	4	4	5	5
	100	100	101	100

To sum up, western broadcasters to the USSR have had considerable success in reaching the educated urban stratum of the Soviet population as a supplement to domestic media sources. They reach listeners of all ages within this group, though with different types of programming. Western radio is more attractive to men than to women. Although western stations are heard throughout the USSR, Radio Liberty and VOA dominate the audience outside the RSFSR due to their extensive broadcasting in non-Russian languages. Western radio clearly appeals most to the more critically-oriented and independent-thinking strata of Soviet society. Although it has made some inroads among regime loyalists who tune in to 'hear what the adversary has to say', or who need western information to function professionally, it is of limited interest to either the politically apathetic or the hardline elements in Soviet society.

Four Case Studies
Earlier in this article we mentioned that SAAOR conducts surveys of topical issues in order to obtain a better understanding of the role and effectiveness of western broadcasters in the complex area of attitude formation. We will now briefly examine four such issues: The downing of the Korean airliner in September 1983, the war in Afghanistan, the perceived threat of nuclear war, and the events surrounding the phenomenon of the Solidarity trade union movement in Poland.

Korean Airline Incident. The Soviet downing of flight KAL 007 on 1st September, 1983 provided a clear test of the efficacy of western radio in communicating to Soviet listeners a version of events almost diametrically opposed to the Soviet view. In the two months immediately following the incident, SAAOR queried 274 Soviet citizen travellers on their reactions to the incident and their sources of information. (6)

From the outset, western broadcasters to the Soviet Union gave heavy coverage to the KAL incident. Soviet media, however, during the first week of September, restricted their discussion of the affair to a series of cryptic hints indicating that a foreign plane had violated Soviet airspace. Not until 7th September did Pravda acknowledge that the Korean Airlines plane had been shot down by Soviet air defence. This was the signal for the launching of a full scale media and agitprop campaign aimed at mobilising domestic opinion in support of the government position. In view of the sheer volume of commentary on the incident, it is not surprising that only three, of the 274 travellers questioned, claimed to be unaware of the event.

Table 12.4: Sources of Information on KAL Incident

N = 164*	%
Agitprop meetings	62
Soviet television	48
Western radio	45
Soviet radio	44
Soviet media (unspecified)**	32
Word of mouth	24
Soviet press	19

Total exceeds 100% because of multiple response.

*Includes cases of ascertainable information only.
** Some respondents indicated that they had obtained information from 'domestic media' without specifying whether they meant radio, television or the press. Figures for 'unspecified Soviet media' have been included in this table to give a more equitable picture of Soviet media consumption. Even though we have no way of dividing up these responses between Soviet press, radio and television, it should be remembered that they are cumulative.

Table 12.4 lists all the sources used by respondents to obtain information on the KAL incident. Western radio was mentioned by almost half the respondents included in the table, and thus compares very favourably with Soviet TV and radio. The most important source of information, however, were agitprop meetings. These meetings, which are usually organised at the workplace, are a common feature of Soviet life, and they apparently proved to be an effective means of rallying support among the population. The Soviet press was cited by only 20%, which may reflect the confused coverage in the immediate aftermath of the incident, coupled with a possible government decision to emphasise television and agitprop to make its case. Some respondents also noted that they had acquired information on the airplane tragedy in the course of conversations with foreigners during their travels abroad, or from the foreign press; this category, however, has not been included in Table 12.4.
A striking dichotomy of attitude between western radio listeners and non-listeners is evident

in Table 12.5. The Soviet version of events was accepted by nearly 80% of non-listeners to western radio, as against fewer than 20% of western radio listeners. Inversely, a far larger proportion of listeners than non-listeners tended to believe the western view of the incident. However, it was evident from respondents' comments that many people had reservations about adopting one version or the other down to every last detail.

The percentage of "Don't knows" was almost twice as large among listener respondents compared to non-listeners. Possibly this greater reticence stems from the fact that western radio listeners had been exposed to two conflicting accounts of the incident, and consequently found it more difficult to reach a conclusion. However, holding a position of 'don't know' may already indicate a reluctance to accept the official version of events.

Table 12.5: Credibility of Different Versions of Events

	Western radio listeners N=110* %	Non-listeners to western radio N=114* %
Soviet version most credible	18	79
Don't know	30	16
Western version most credible	52	6
Total	100	101

*Includes cases of ascertainable credibility only.

The attitudes expressed in Table 12.6 mirror closely the credibility patterns shown in the previous section. Just as some 50% of western radio listeners accepted the western version of events, nearly 50% also disapproved of the Soviet action. Inversely, the non-listener group is dominated by respondents who approved the shooting down of the aircraft. While the percentage of Don't knows stays much the same for the listeners to western radio, the figure has increased slightly among non-listeners, possibly because acceptance of the official version of events is not tantamount to condoning official violence.

Table 12.6: Attitudes Toward Downing of Aircraft

	Western radio listeners N=74* %	Non-listeners to western radio N=125* %
Approval	22	70
Don't know	31	20
Disapproval	47	11
Total	100	101

*Includes cases of ascertainable approval only.

While the sample size used in this spot survey is both small and unrepresentative of the Soviet population as a whole, the dichotomy that emerges between listeners and non-listeners to western radio is instructive and is consistent with our SAAOR research. Some scepticism of the Soviet version of events may well have existed without western radio information sources. But it is doubtful that an 'alternative opinion' could have been formed. For this, outside information was necessary. It is interesting to note that in the first week or so following the downing of the aircraft, most respondents showed a good deal of confusion over the matter. At this stage, their natural response was to voice support of their government. Only after the western version of events had been consistently repeated, while the Soviet version came out in halting and at times contradictory form, were opinion changes noticed.

War in Afghanistan. A major analysis of Soviet citizens' perceptions of the Afghan war was undertaken by SAAOR, using a data base of almost 3,000 respondents interviewed during 1984. (7) The MIT computer simulation programme was used to project this data onto the adult urban segment of the population.

The projected data indicated that only one quarter of the Soviet adult urban population expressed approval of Soviet policy in Afghanistan; another quarter disapproved of that policy, while half the adult urban population was either ambivalent or held no opinion. Similarly, only a quarter of adult urban Soviet citizens expressed confidence in the eventual success of official policy in Afghanistan. One quarter foresaw no clear Soviet success there, while a half was either ambivalent or ventured no prognosis. This lack of active popular support for, and faith in, Soviet policy in Afghanistan suggests a potential political problem for the Kremlin.

Disapproval of Soviet policy in Afghanistan ran highest in non-Russian areas of the Soviet Union, particularly in the Baltic States, Central Asia and the Caucasus, and among non-Russian national groups. Conversely, residents of the RSFSR, particularly in Moscow and Moscow oblast, expressed the greatest approval for official policy and were the most optimistic about its success. Residents of Central Asia and the Central Asian nationality groups present a special case in that they displayed both high approval and disapproval of Soviet policy in Afghanistan. This may be attributed to a split between, on the one hand, Central Asians whose sense of affinity with the Afghans leads them to disapprove of the Soviet presence in Afghanistan, and, on the other, Slavic residents of the region and assimilated indigenous residents who have a more patronising attitude toward the 'primitive' Afghans.

Listeners to western radio disapproved of Soviet involvement in Afghanistan at a rate nearly three times as great as that of non-listeners. Inversely, non-listeners displayed three times more approval of official policy than listeners. This dichotomy suggests that information from western radio broadcasts plays a considerable role in the formation of opinions which diverge from the official version of events.

The Soviet press was the most frequently cited source of information about Afghanistan. Soviet television was the offical source least cited for news of Afghanistan, although it was usually the preferred medium for information on international affairs. News passed by word of mouth clearly occupied an important role in informing Soviet citizens about events in Afghanistan; it would appear, moreover, that such information is quite negative. Nearly half of the citizens who specifically cited word of mouth as a source of information on Afghanistan disapproved of official policy, compared with only 20% who approved.

In an area where the Soviet press has been

reluctant to provide detailed coverage (in fact it was not until the summer of 1984 that press dispatches began to speak openly of the problems facing Soviet troops in Afghanistan), western radio has clearly filled an information void and, in so doing, has contributed to the formation of attitudes which are either questioning or critical of official policy.

Nuclear Threat. Research conducted by SAAOR in 1983 showed that 56% of the survey group of 2,983 felt that the danger of nuclear war had increased over the past few years; 22% did not feel there had been any such increase, while the remaining 23% did not hold an opinion on the question. (8) These findings remained constant across all demographic categories. The reason most commonly cited in support of an increased nuclear threat was 'aggressive western policy', followed by 'uncontrolled arms race between the superpowers'. The period of the survey coincided with a shrill propaganda campaign waged in the Soviet press against the installation of Pershing 2 and cruise missiles in Western Europe. Although this campaign was supposed to have been aimed chiefly at western audiences, it is evident that there was a domestic backwash effect. What started out as a campaign to frighten Western Europeans succeeded in scaring the Soviet population as well. Both western radio listeners and non-listeners in the sample argued in support of an increased nuclear threat at the identical rate of 56%. However, the reasons cited varied considerably. Only 23% of the western radio listeners evoked western aggressivity as the reason for a heightened danger of nuclear war, compared to 65% of the non-listeners.

A follow-up survey on the topic during the period January 1984-May 1985, based on a sample of 3,354 respondents, indicated a slight increase in the proportion of those who felt the threat of nuclear war had increased: 61%, compared to 24% who did not think so. (9) As in the previous survey, these responses were generalised across all demographic categories. Perceived causes of the increased danger, however, underwent some modification in the more recent period. Whereas the earlier survey group tended to blame an aggressive US and western policy for the danger, the latter group shifted the blame to causes such as the arms race. As in the previous survey, western radio listeners cited different causes for the increased danger to non-listeners.

Only 13% of listeners cited western policy as the cause of the nuclear threat, whereas 40% of the non-listeners did so.

This would seem to indicate that in a context of international tension, when the messages of both domestic and foreign media reflect that tension, listeners and non-listeners to western radio will perceive the dangers of the situation in much the same way. However, the causes of the situation are likely to be assessed very differently by those whose access to outside sources of information has given them a more sophisticated understanding of the issues at stake. Once again, this is a clear demonstration of the importance of alternative sources of information.

Solidarity Movement in Poland. The Solidarity movement in Poland was perhaps the most complex of these four issues for western broadcasters to convey to the Soviet population. During the period September 1980-May 1982, SAAOR surveyed 1,719 Soviet citizens on their attitudes to the events in Poland. During the autumn of 1980, as many as 24% of those surveyed (unweighted figures) supported liberalisation in Poland. In the post-martial law period after December 1981, this figure dropped to 15%, while those opposed to liberalisation climbed from 44% to 71%.

During the first year of the Polish developments, western radio listeners showed more inclination to support liberalisation than non-listeners (by 26% to 14%). Radio Liberty listeners were more favourably inclined than others (42%) but this finding is linked to the more critical orientation of RL's audience which has already been noted. These general tendencies continued into the post-martial law period, although the overall drop in favourable attitudes to liberalisation affected western radio listeners as well. More striking, however, was the finding that virtually none of the non-listeners to western radio (3%) were favourable to Polish liberalisation during the martial law period.

Although there is a high correlation between liberal attitudes and western radio listening, the data suggest that western information on Poland failed to strike a responsive chord outside the critically-oriented stratum of Soviet society, and that even there it possibly did no more than reinforce previously held viewpoints. Elsewhere, Soviet propaganda seems to have successfully mobilised opposition to Solidarity around three major themes appealing to the emotions and perceived self-interest of Soviet citizens: the danger of strikes, portrayed as a counter-revolutionary activity leading to social breakdown or chaos; the latent dislike of Poles shared by much of the Slavic population of the USSR; and the threat to national security. (10) The lesson to emerge from this case study is that western radio is less able to influence the Soviet population than domestic media when the direct interests of the average Soviet citizen are made to appear threatened.

Conclusions
The foregoing examples indicate that western radio, by providing information unavailable from domestic sources, plays a role in the process of shaping Soviet listeners' opinions on the events of the day. For the approximately one in eight of Soviet urban adults who are critically disposed to the system, western information may primarily serve to reinforce critical positions. For others, especially the 30% of urban adults we have characterised as moderates, western radio provides an alternative and supplemental source of information without which a critical thought process could hardly even begin.

Western radio is in communication with the more critically thinking element of Soviet society, but its audience is not limited to those groups. It is also widely heard among the elite of Soviet society, including members of the Communist Party who tune in not only to 'know the enemy', but also to obtain information which allows them to function effectively in their own society. Western radio has been less successful in reaching the politically apathetic, the lower educated Party members, other hardliners and probably never will have large audiences among these groups.

We have also observed that western radio communicates most effectively when the Soviet version of events is hesitant or contradictory (e.g. on the KAL incident), or when Soviet media palpably gloss over an issue on which information from other sources is available (news of the war in Afghanistan can be had from returning veterans, for instance). On complex emotional issues, such as Poland, where the perceived self-interest of the average Soviet citizen diverges from the message being transmitted by western radio, the results of western radio communication will be decidedly more mixed, as our research results show.

International radio communication in itself is not sufficient to bring about basic changes in a society. However, it is difficult to imagine the complex process of evolution toward a more pluralistic society in the USSR without the alternative information provided by western stations. Western radio has successfully established itself as an additional source of information used by the majority of the educated Soviet population. Its impact, whether in reinforcing previously held attitudes, or in opening new horizons, is already significant. It has the opportunity to expand its audience even further among the 'moderates' in Soviet society: educated people who are actively seeking out the information required by a modern technological society.

Notes

1. SAAOR Analysis Report AR 5-84, <u>A Study of SAAOR Data Validity: Behavior and Opinion Measurement</u>, by Mark Rhodes, issued April 1984.

2. For a more detailed discussion of this methodology, as well as data-gathering procedures, see 'The Shortwave Audience in the USSR: Methods for Improving the Estimates', by R. Eugene Parta, J. Klensin and I. de Sola Pool, in <u>Communication Research</u>, vol.9, no.4, October, 1982.

3. SAAOR Analysis Report AR 6-84, <u>Civil Liberties and the Soviet Citizen: Attitudinal Types and Western Radio Listening</u> by R. Eugene Parta, issued in September 1984.

4. These and other figures given in this article should not be viewed as point estimates, but mid-points in ranges. Our projection techniques do not permit us to speak with certainty about specific percentages. The results are given in percentage form to facilitate understanding of the general trends that emerge from the data.

5. The relatively high rating of VOA and BBC among the 'indifferent' group suggests that some of the respondents who gave 'don't know' responses to the questions in the survey might have been concealing moderate or even liberal tendencies.

6. SAAOR Analysis Report AR 4-84, <u>The Korean Airline Incident: Western Radio and Soviet Perceptions</u>, by Kathleen Mihalisko and R. Eugene Parta, issued April 1984.

7. SAAOR Analysis Report AR 4-85 <u>The Soviet Public and the War in Afghanistan: Perceptions</u>,

Prognoses, Information Sources, by Sallie Wise, issued June 1985.

8. SAAOR Analysis Report AR 1-84, Has the Nuclear Threat Increased: Some Soviet Citizens' Views by Dawn Plumb, issued February 1984.

9. SAAOR Analysis Report AR 5-85, Soviet Public Opinion and the Perceived Danger of Nuclear War: A Threat Persists by Sallie Wise, issued December 1985.

10. These points are developed at greater length in SAAOR Analysis Report AR 6-82, Soviet Citizen Attitudes Toward Poland Since Martial Law: Agitprop, Western Radio and the Evolution of Opinion by R. Eugene Parta and Mark Rhodes, issued in September, 1982.

Chapter Thirteen

PUBLIC OPINION ASSESSMENT AND RADIO FREE EUROPE'S EFFECTIVENESS IN EASTERN EUROPE

Mary McIntosh, chief, Statistics, Analyses and Attitude Research, East European Audience and Opinion Research, Radio Free Europe, Munich

For almost 25 years the audience and opinion research department of Radio Free Europe has been conducting surveys among Czechoslovaks, Hungarians and Poles. Surveys of Romanians and Bulgarians have been taken for shorter periods. For obvious reasons, those surveyed are not directly selected from the resident populations inside Eastern Europe. Samples are drawn from the large numbers of people - more than four million every year - travelling to different West European countries. Previous research has shown that people travelling to the West are similar, though we know not identical, to the stay-at-home populations.

Nine opinion research institutes are employed in six different countries to conduct independent surveys. Generally, each overall survey for a particular nation is based on at least 1,000 interviews. The samples consist only of East European nationals visiting the West who plan on a limited stay and who intend to return home. We do not interview refugees, legal immigrants, or other persons intending to stay in the West. About one in five travellers refuse to be interviewed.

Quota sampling is employed to ensure that all segments of the population are proportionally represented. In addition, results from several sampling institutes are continuously compared to ensure that the data from one country are consistent with data obtained in others. Data from each of the different institutes are judged reliable only if they reveal no statistically significant differences. Comparisons of our findings, taken over a number of years from many samples, have shown remarkable consistency.

Public Opinion Assessment

Audience Characteristics in East Europe
Employing these methods, Radio Free Europe has for the past quarter of a century sought to determine its broadcast effectiveness systematically. One way to gauge this effectiveness is by measuring the size of the RFE audience.

Our 1983 survey data indicates that western broadcasts reached anywhere from 56% of the adult population of Bulgaria to 85% of the adult population of Poland. In Hungary, Czechoslovakia and Romania, the average lies between 77% and 75%. These figures are based on interviews with nearly 6,500 East European nationals, taken between the spring of 1982 and early 1983.

Table 13.1: RFE'S Listening Audience 1982-83

	Adult Population %	
Czechoslovakia	37	= 4,370,000
Hungary	58	= 4,930,000
Poland	68	= 18,830,000
Romania	64	= 10,620,000
Bulgaria	33	= 2,340,000

Radio Free Europe
In four of the five countries previously mentioned, Radio Free Europe, or RFE, has the largest total audience. Only in Czechoslovakia do RFE and the Voice of America share an audience of approximately the same size (see Table 13.1).

An accounting of listenership cannot be regarded as accurate without consideration of the jamming practices of the regimes under which our target audiences live. Jamming clearly discourages listeners. In 1983, almost six out of ten Poles, half the Czechoslovaks, a third of the Romanians and Bulgarians, and a quarter of the Hungarians who did not listen to RFE gave one of the following reasons: RFE was jammed or their set couldn't receive RFE. Thus lower listenership patterns in Czechoslovakia and Bulgaria may be at least partially explained by the jamming of our signals by those countries. In Poland, however, RFE listeners are sufficiently motivated to make the effort necessary to receive our broadcasts, despite heavy jamming.

An examination of programme ratings, based on audience size, clearly reveals the overall appeal of RFE broadcasts. Not unexpectedly, newscasts

Public Opinion Assessment

attracted the largest audience cross-nationally. RFE is obviously fulfilling a critical need for uncensored, international news coverage.

A characteristic example of this occurred during the Korean airliner incident in 1983. When 1,685 respondents were asked how they first learned of the downing of KAL 007, over two thirds stated they first heard of the event over Western broadcasts.

Table 13.2: Station over which KAL 007 First Heard About

	Czechs/ Slovaks %	Hungarians %	Poles %	Romanians %	Bulgarians %
RFE	36	49	47	70	26
VOA	19	5	14	7	8
BBC	6	2	5	7	18
DW/DF	4	2	4	3	2
Domestic radio	29	42	33	15	46
Other	6	0	4	0	0
	100*	100*	107*	102*	100*

*Totals may exceed 100% due to multiple response.
RFE: Radio Free Europe; VOA: Voice of America; BBC: British Broadcasting Corporation; DW/DF: Deutsche Welle/Deutschlandfunk

When asked to evaluate the quality of the RFE and domestic coverage, only 4% of the respondents gave negative evaluations of RFE, compared to 65%, who judged domestic radio unfavourably.

Programmes which offer a more in-depth analysis of current events, both nationally and internationally, attract the second largest group of listeners. These data suggest that RFE is clearly effective and valued as a medium designed to impact the information flow between East and West. Entertainment programmes are also effective in attracting listeners.

Another, much less precise, but still very revealing way of gauging RFE's effectiveness, is by monitoring the regimes response to RFE broadcasts. The more protest, the greater the assumed impact of the medium. A current example of this is a statement on 14th August, 1984, by Jerzy Urban, the Polish government spokesman who stated, 'If you closed your Radio Free Europe, the underground would completely cease to exist.' This statement seems to confirm that RFE has the ability to affect listeners' opinions, at least in the eyes of the regime.

Although our listenership studies show that RFE has a broad appeal to East Europeans, there is a tendency for women, those under 25, and the university-educated to be less regular listeners than the rest of the population. As a consequence, these groups are potentially more difficult to impact than the others.

While RFE and other western broadcasters have a large following, it must not be overlooked that they are in competition with the domestic media for listeners and, therefore, potential impact on the audience. In East European countries, the population relies on regime-controlled stations primarily as a source of entertainment and relaxation, and secondarily as a source of official news, which they are expected to know as a matter of civic duty. So, while most listeners understand that their local radio is an instrument of the regime, it should be noted that it is still listened to more regularly and more frequently than western broadcasts.

Propaganda and Western Broadcasts

Of critical concern to the assessment of the effectiveness of western radio in East Europe is the perception by the audience of the objectivity and credibility in those broadcasts. Listenership depends, in part, on the presentation of information and ideas that are perceived to be accurate and believable. If listeners perceive that information is being disseminated that is distorted or manipulated, they assume that the station is airing its own prejudices, and reject both the station and the message. The challenge facing RFE or other western broadcasters, is to balance the role of objective reporter with the commitment to provide a forum through which traditional values and beliefs may be preserved, and the principles of western democracy affirmed.

In an attempt to understand how East Europeans perceive western broadcasts, the following question was asked: 'Of the following western stations broadcasting to your country, which do you feel is/are to some extent propagandistic? Voice of America or Radio Free Europe or BBC/London or Deutsche Welle/Deutschlandfunk?'

Public Opinion Assessment

Table 13.3: Perception of Propaganda in Western Broadcasts by Country*

	No Propaganda %	RFE %	Some propaganda			N/A %
			VOA %	BBC %	DW/DF %	
Czechoslovakia	54	20	14	8	12	20
Hungary	49	26	17	11	9	17
Poland	51	22	18	8	11	13
Romania	61	17	10	4	4	12

*Totals may exceed 100% due to multiple response

Two noteworthy observations may be drawn from these figures. First, while more than half the respondents did not feel that the western broadcasts were propagandistic, about one in four disagreed and cited one or more of the western broadcasts as biased. The second point of interest was the high degree of continuity in respondents' opinions across countries. This finding suggests that RFE projects an identifiable image that is similarly perceived by respondents from the surveyed countries.

A comparison of the responses given, relative to specific broadcasters, revealed that the two American stations, RFE and VOA, were most likely to be perceived as propagandistic. BBC and DW/DF were cited least often in this respect.

A favourable picture emerged when responses from RFE listeners were examined. Very few listeners perceived RFE as propagandistic. This was particularly true of regular listeners. Belief in the objectivity of western broadcasts increased in accord with frequency of RFE listenership.

Age and education were also indicative of a respondent's perception of propaganda. Younger respondents and those with university education, were most likely to characterise western broadcasts as propagandistic, whereas those over 50 and those with an elementary school education, were least likely to do so.

An analysis by country suggests that Hungarian and Romanian respondents represent two ends of the continuum reflecting perceptions of propaganda. These findings might be a reflection of the differing political environments in both Hungary and Romania. The relatively permissive society created under Kadar might, in part, account for the lack of affinity between some Hungarians and the western

Public Opinion Assessment

media. RFE's strong ideological stance is likely to be unappealing, and therefore challenged, by those who believe that the Kadarist version of socialism is a step in the right direction. In contrast Romanians, who live under one of the most oppressive regimes in the Warsaw Pact, are more likely to identify with the thrust of RFE's broadcasts. This identification is probably a reflection of the belief held by most Romanians, that socialism has no possibility of becoming a tolerable political system, and must therefore be altered.

These cross-national differences in political attitudes have been observed in other APOR studies which reveal that Hungarian respondents have been more likely to express a desire for meeker political commentaries and support for gradual political change. In contrast, Romanian respondents have favored more militant commentaries and sought radical political change. These findings, in conjunction with the data presented in this report, suggest a broader picture by which to gauge characterisations of propaganda in western broadcasts.

Opinion Formation

A principal measure of RFE's effectiveness is its ability to impact attitudes and influence opinions. In order to determine RFE's ability to exert influence on a listener's way of thinking, the following question was asked: 'Does listening to Radio Free Europe help you form your opinions, does it reinforce the opinions you already have, or does it have no influence on your opinions?'

Table 13.4: Listeners' Assessments of RFE's Influence on Personal Opinions

	Czechs/Slovaks %	Hungarians %	Poles %
Opinion formation	45	49	51
Opinion reinforcement	42	33	28
No such influence	12	14	20
No answer	1	4	1

Overall, RFE has been, and continues to be, regarded by its listeners as a significant communicator, either helping to form their outlook or reinforcing their views.

The table above shows that four-fifths of those interviewed felt that RFE had an effect on their opinions. Not surprisingly, there was a relationship between listening frequency and perception of RFE's influence. Those who listened least often felt that RFE had little influence on listeners' attitudes, while those that listened most often rarely expressed this view.

Of additional interest is the extent to which RFE influences public opinion on important internal and international political issues. Table 13.5 shows that a plurality of listeners were of the opinion that RFE has a certain amount of influence on public opinion as far as domestic and international political issues are concerned.

Table 13.5: Listeners' Assessments of RFE's Influence on Public Opinion

	Czechos-lovakia %	Hungary %	Poland %
None	6	12	11
Some	35	45	44
Considerable/very much	58	43	44

Overall, the findings set out in Table 13.5 reveal that listeners were more cautious about ascribing pronounced RFE influence on their country as a whole than about acknowledging this influence on themselves. This perception may be, in part, a function of the lack of substantive discourse among people, which is fostered by totalitarian regimes as a mechanism of social control. Thus, members of a totalitarian state are unlikely to know the true opinions of their fellow citizens.

It is significant to compare the respondents' perceptions regarding the influence of RFE broadcasts on themselves, on public opinion and on the regime. The majority of listeners were of the opinion that RFE had no influence on the regimes.

This was particularly true of Czechoslovaks, somewhat less so for Hungarians and least true for Poles. When respondents who felt that RFE influences the regime were asked how this was manifested, the most prevalent response was that RFE denies the regime the possibility of manipulating its own information entirely at will.

The primary point of interest in this study is that listeners perceived RFE's influence on themselves to be considerable but were more sceptical of the degree of RFE's influence on public opinion, and quite sceptical of RFE's influence on the regime.

Table 13.6: Listeners' Assessments of RFE's Influence on the Regime

	Czechs/ Slovaks	Hungarians	Poles
% of listeners ascribing to RFE no influence on the government of their country	72	65	51
% of listeners ascribing to RFE some or considerable influence on the government	18	33	37

Given the chasm that exists between the regime and those it governs, it is not surprising that these respondents feel that decisions are made by the regime in isolation from the opinion-formation process. These findings underline the hopelessness and frustration that is manifested in totalitarian states.

The findings quoted so far have sought to illustrate the characteristics and attitudes of listeners and to document RFE's effectiveness in opinion formation. The issue that remains is how East Europeans assess the political nature of their societies, and what their opinions are regarding socialism, democracy and political change.

Political Orientation

After a generation under Communist rule, there is not a great deal of evidence to suggest that the peoples of East Europe have embraced the socialist system of government. Table 13.7 suggests that there appears to be very little affinity for the Communist Party. These data are based on answers given to the question: 'Imagine that free elections were to be held in your country, and there would be five

Public Opinion Assessment

different kinds of parties from which to choose: Communist, Democratic Socialist, Christian Democratic, Peasant and Conservative. Which would you vote for?'

Table 13.7: Party Preferences in Hypothetical Free Elections

	1976-77 Average %	1981-82 Average %
Communist Party	6	3
Democratic Socialist Party	41	40
Christian Democratic Party	25	30
Peasant Party	14	7
National Conservative Party	7	8
Other/no answer	7	10

Responses have been remarkably consistent over time, varying only slightly at times with major change within a country. These data suggest that there is a small, stable group of Communist Party supporters, and a much larger group (over 80%) who would choose to live under a different type of political system, given the opportunity. The ideal of the great majority of respondents was a democratic system, with a centre-right Democratic Socialist party being the preferred choice in the latest survey.

Although there is remarkable similarity in political attitudes among East European peoples, a few differences are important to note, particularly because these differences suggest how the impact of western broadcasts is likely to vary due to the underlying political climate in each country. Presented below are the cross-national results for three time frames, beginning in 1968, and spanning 14 years.

Support for the Communist Party was greater among the Hungarians than among Czechoslovaks or Poles. This is a reflection of the somewhat more tolerable nature of the Kadarist regime, relative to the other East European regimes. Support for the centre-left Democratic Socialist party is much greater in Czechoslovakia and Hungary than in Poland. This is a new trend for the Poles, who appear to have become disenchanted with all things socialist and now favour the Christian Democratic party more than they have in the past. This new allegiance could well be a function of the success of the Solidarity movement, with its underlying religious orientation, and strong links to the church. The most recent Polish findings, obtained after the imposition of martial law, also clearly indicate the virtual disappearance of any support for the Communist Party, continued drop of support for a Democratic Socialist party, and continued increase of support for a Christian Democratic party.

Table 13.8: Party Preferences 1968-81

	1968-70			1974-77			1978-81		
	CS %	H %	P %	CS %	H %	P %	CS %	H %	P %
Communist	3	4	3	4	8	4	3	7	4
Democratic Socialist	37	31	27	43	42	46	43	42	35
Christian Democrat	21	29	33	25	25	28	29	26	34
Peasant	5	12	8	5	17	11	3	11	15
Conservative	8	6	7	7	5	4	8	9	7

CS = Czechs/Slovaks   H = Hungarians   P = Poles

Unwavering anti-Communist attitudes are shared by the young people of Eastern Europe. The latest survey showed that only 1% of those under 35 in Poland, 2% in Czechoslovakia and 6% in Hungary would have voted communist in hypothetical free elections. These figures are exactly in line with the national averages and reveal that communist indoctrination has failed. Indeed, it seems to enhance active resistance to communism - as amply demonstrated by the role of the communist-educated younger generation in the Hungarian Revolution, the Prague Spring and recurring Polish crises.

The Functioning of Socialism and Democracy

Undoubtedly, this lack of support for the socialist regimes of East Europe is partially a function of the unsuitability of Marxist-Leninist doctrine to successful economic management. The legitimacy of any political system rests, in large measure, on the ideological support of those it governs, and on its ability to solve problems and conflicts as they arise. So, any examination of the viability of a

Public Opinion Assessment

Figure 13.1: How Well Democracy Works

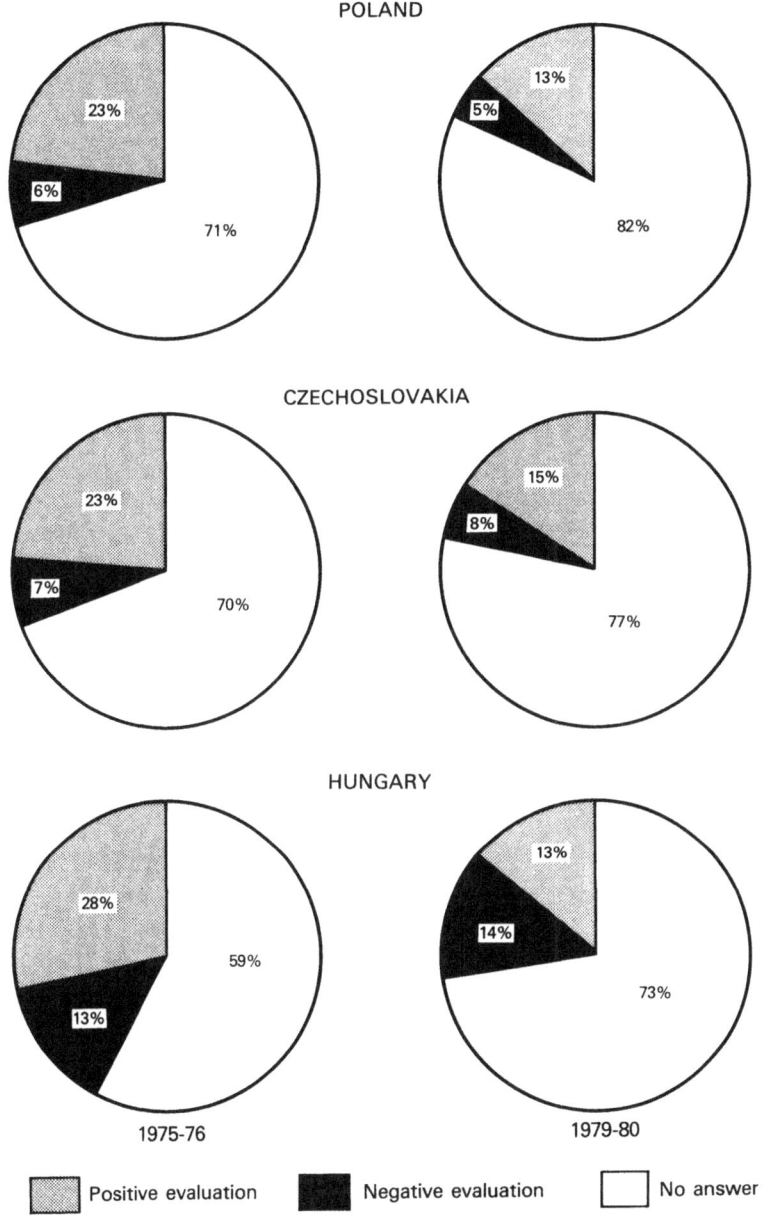

Public Opinion Assessment

Figure 13.2: How Well Socialism Works

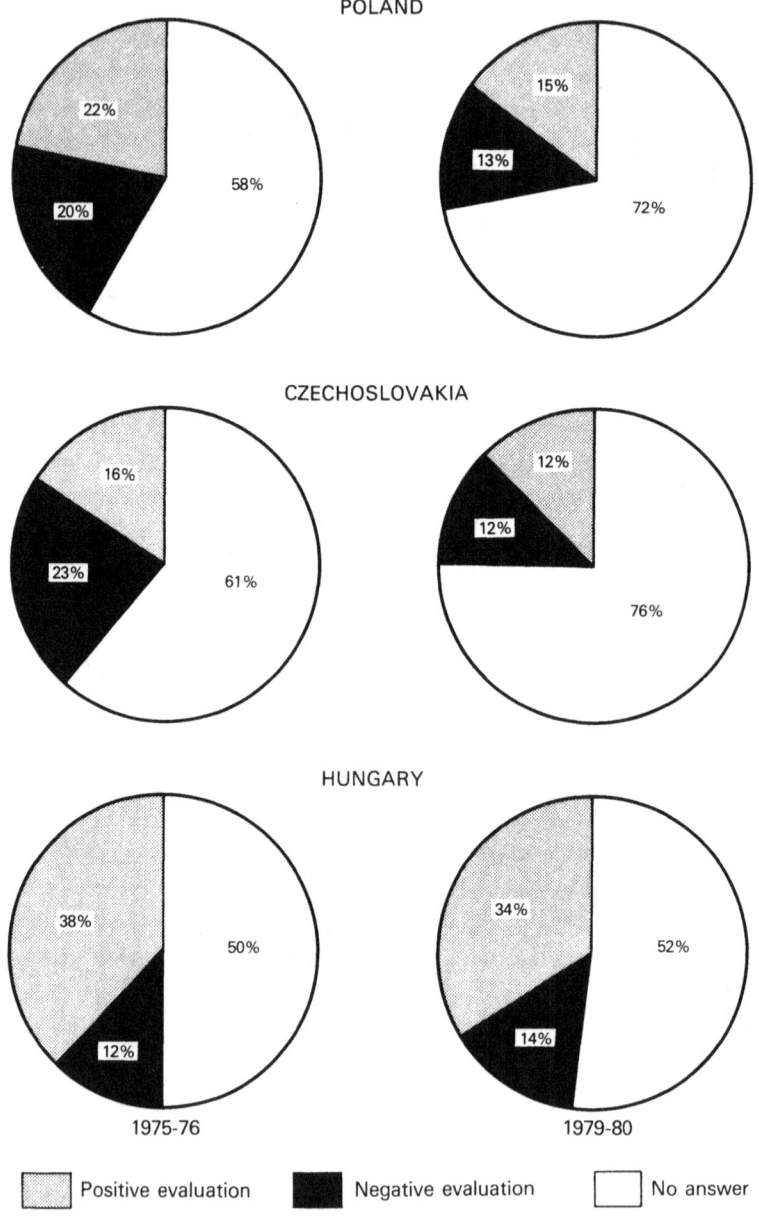

system must include a discussion of how well it is thought to be functioning from the viewpoint of the population. Figures 1 and 2 illustrate the results of the question: 'How does socialism work out in practice in your country?'

The data from questions addressed, in 1975-76 and 1979-80, to samples of western visitors from Hungary, Czechoslovakia and Poland (the 1979-80 data were collected on the eve of the crisis which brought forth Solidarity) are presented in Figures 1 and 2. The percentage of those who evaluated socialism in a negative light increased in time in Czechoslovakia and Poland, but hardly at all in Hungary. A third of the Hungarian respondents felt that socialism was working positively in the 1979-80 survey period.

When asked to state what the important influences were on their attitudes toward socialism, almost all cited their own experiences or those of friends, as the primary bases for their opinions. However, it is central to this discussion to note that RFE was cited by a quarter of the Czechs/Slovaks, and a third of the Poles and Hungarians, as significant in influencing their views on the workings of socialism.

Do the peoples of East Europe believe the propaganda of the regimes and see the West as an exploitative unjust regional bloc, or do they see western countries as having viable, well-functioning societies? This question is of interest, in that the ability to influence the opinion-formation process of a group is related to the perceived credibility of the external source, in this case, a western broadcaster.

Not surprisingly, in contrast to the negative evaluation of the performance of socialism in the Eastern Bloc, western democracy was considered to be functioning 'well' or 'very well' by the great majority of respondents. Of particular interest is the increase in positive evaluations over the four-year period. Hungarian perceptions of the desirability of western democracy greatly increased, although nearly 15% of the Hungarian respondents remained critical of how democracy works in the West. There was a strong relationship between the great affinity expressed for western democracy and listening to RFE, and RFE was cited as important in influencing opinions about the functioning of western democracy by approximately a third of the respondents. As a surrogate national communicator, RFE serves to set the record straight concerning how both socialism and western democracy perform.

Serious US-USSR Conflict
Of potential interest to both the East and West is the issue of East Europe's support in the event of a major conflict between the two superpowers. The USSR, as the theoretical spiritual leader and ideological ruler, would expect East Europeans to support its position. In contrast, East Europeans share with their continental cousins a common tradition and heritage which, compounded by the inaffectual economic systems of the East and an affinity for democracy among East Europeans, implies an inclination to support the West.

In the interest of ascertaining how East Europeans would react to a crisis in US-USSR relations, respondents from Czechoslovakia, Poland and Hungary were asked: 'If a serious conflict should develop between the US and the Soviet Union, would your sympathies lie with the US, with the USSR or with neither?' Gallup International asked West Europeans to express a favourable/unfavourable opinion about the US and the Soviet Union, which is roughly comparable to the question RFE asked of East Europeans (Table 13.9).

Table 13.9: Serious Conflict - US vs. USSR

	Western Europe %	Eastern Europe %
Favourable to/ would side with		
US	57	61
USSR	14	10

This table shows that East Europeans were slightly more pro-American than were the West European societies. Three-fifths of the combined East European samples sided with the US, as against one-tenth who sided with the USSR. The remainder were neutral in their support, siding with neither power, or did not respond.

The theoretical willingness to support the US instead of remaining neutral or siding with the USSR, might suggest that the peoples of the East tend to believe that internal change is not likely to be the product of domestic forces, but it intertwined with the balance of East and West power. Thus, the occurrence of a serious conflict from which the West stands a chance of gain, could appear to the majority of East Europeans to be a precondition for a better future.

Positive attitudes toward the US, and negative attitudes towards the USSR in East Europe, are strongly associated with listenership to RFE. Cross-nationally, RFE listeners sided with the US in a serious conflict with the USSR at a ratio of 82 to 1 (per cent).

Further insight into the attitudes and opinions of East Europeans is evident in responses to the question: 'The leaders of the socialist countries say that they are in favour of detente or peaceful coexistence. Why is this so?' (Table 13.10).

Table 13.10: Detente/Peaceful Coexistence

	Czechs/Slovaks %	Hungarians %	Poles %
It's a lie/hypocrisy; a stratagem to fool everybody, the Soviet line	53	55	69
They want peace/ everybody needs peace; do not want war	25	50	11
Other answers/ no answers	27	26	29

Since respondents were allowed to choose more than one answer, totals may exceed 100%.

If the peace policy is judged to be hypocritical and deceitful, this might be perceived as yet another reflection of the lack of confidence in, and denial of legitimacy of, the Socialist regimes by the people.

Based on the data presented above, there appears to be a generalised distrust of whatever the regimes say in Czechoslovakia and Poland. The Hungarian findings show a more trusting, less alienated stance toward this government policy. The general proclivity of Poles and Czechoslovaks to dismiss as a lie whatever the regime has to say, makes impacting these groups with western broadcasts easier. By the

Public Opinion Assessment

same token, a more differentiated view of the regime and its pronouncements by a significant segment of the basically anti-communist Hungarian society, makes impacting it a more difficult task if the Kadarist compromise is widely felt to depend on at least some form of detente.

Political Change
General lack of support and belief in the East European regimes raises the question of what might be feasible in terms of political change, because abstract criticism of a government is not necessarily concomitant with a willingness to engage in political change.

This issue will be addressed from two perspectives: the role of RFE as an agent of change, and the role of the people in domestic change. Table 13.11 illustrates the question, 'Should RFE foster gradual changes in your country, should it foster a different system there, or should it do neither but simply report developments?'

Table 13.11: RFE's Role in Change

	Czechs %	Slovaks %	Hungarians %	Poles %	Romanians %	Bulgarians %
Should foster gradual change	26	47	48	46	40	45
Should foster a different system	27	30	15	21	30	28
Should simply report developments	42	19	35	30	29	22

Almost half the RFE audiences questioned wanted RFE to pursue a policy of urging gradual change, except the Czechs, who displayed an unexpected preference for an inactive reportorial role for RFE. The unsuccessful 1968 reform experiment in Czechoslovakia may be responsible for this lack of faith in the potential for gradual change. A greater desire for RFE to play an active role in fostering a different system was noted among the regular listeners, as opposed to the less regular listeners, who tended to prefer the role of inactive observer or reporter.

Thus, it is important to recognise that the majority of its listeners would like RFE to serve as an agent of change, and to do this more by actively taking part in the processes by which pressures from below may force those in power to make concessions, than by actively fostering a different system.

The question reflected in Table 13.12 addresses change that originates from within the system, such as acts of open opposition by dissidents: 'In your country, as in all countries, there is opposition to the government. Those people openly opposing the government are usually labelled dissidents. Do you think that this kind of opposition is a good thing?' The data were gathered during the pre-martial law period, when the hopes kindled by Solidarity's drive for a share of the political power base were reflected in a heavy endorsement for open acts of political resistance.

Table 13.12: Open Opposition to the Government.

	Czechs/ Slovaks %	Hungarians %	Poles %	Romanians %	Bulgarians %
Yes	38	43	63	56	41
No	22	27	16	20	25
Undecided/ No answer	40	30	21	24	34

These data revealed that acts of open defiance were least often approved of among the Czechs/Slovaks. A relatively large percentage of those who were not strong supporters of dissidents (Hungarians, Bulgarians and Czechs/Slovaks) refused either to approve or disapprove of such behaviour. Acts of political resistance found the strongest support among RFE listeners, followed by listeners to other western stations. Those who did not avail themselves of western radio least favoured resistance.

An understanding of why some support open dissidence and others oppose it, is important. Two main reasons were cited by respondents who supported open political opposition: first, that it was necessary and not without at least some effect on the

Public Opinion Assessment

regime; second, that overt dissidents echo the feelings of the silent majority and demonstrate that there are still people of courage left.

The view that open political opposition was not also crystallised around two arguments: that such acts of defiance 'upset things' and jeopardised progress already made (this was heavily stressed by Hungarians); and that such actions are bound to fail, and that they are too dangerous (stressed by Czechs/Slovaks and Romanians).

These findings suggest an interplay between satisfaction derived from seeing the communist regime defied, and fear that a vindictive regime might retaliate, thereby halting progress towards change.

As final consideration of the issue of political change (in this case, one of the consequences of that change), the results of a question which sought to assess East European views about appropriate US reaction to the Polish crisis are presented in Table 13.13.

Table 13.13: Approve/Disapprove Sanctions by US

	Approve %	Disapprove %
Czechs/Slovaks	88	12
Hungarians	70	30
Poles	92	8
Romanians	86	14
Average	84	16

The majority were strongly in favour of US retaliation against martial law in Poland. Poles, Czechs/Solvaks and Romanians were most in favour of US sanctions. Hungarians, who were probably concerned about potential repercussions of a severe East-West crisis, were markedly less in favour of US sanctions. As the following table shows, economic sanctions were preferred to diplomatic ones:

Table 13.4: Economic Sanctions/Diplomatic Sanctions

	Economic %	Diplomatic %
Czechs/Slovaks	59	41
Hungarians	64	36
Poles	72	28
Romanians	61	39
Average	64	36

The preference for economic sanctions was particularly strong in Poland's case, where the possibility of overt Soviet intervention makes the Polish people more conscious of the risk of severe US counter-measures may entail.

The most important point of this study is that the sanctions chosen were most often aimed only at the USSR. This suggests that East Europeans blame the Soviet Union for the military coup in Poland and feel that the Soviets should suffer the consequences. Because of the effects on the people involved, sanctions that were aimed at one's own country had the least appeal.

Summary
It is apparent that the communist regimes of East Europe, have failed to gain the support of the masses. While the level of acceptance and perceived success of socialism is, in large measure, a function of historical experiences in each of the various countries and the present socio-political condition, it is still a fact that even in Hungary, the relatively most progressive of Socialist states, only 7% of the population stated they would vote for the Communist Party in 'free elections'.

Radio Free Europe, as an effective communicator, serves the people of East Europe by providing both domestic and international news and information, which the regime-controlled media either distort or fail to report. It, therefore, serves to motivate its listeners away from political stagnation, and allows those who wish to, to maintain their contact with the West, its traditions and values. RFE not only reaches a majority of the adult population of East Europe, but has a reputation as an objective, credible source of information. Its broadcasts have been documented to be effective in both opinion-formation and reinforcement.

BIBLIOGRAPHY

Books
David Abshire, <u>International Broadcasting: A New Dimension of Western Diplomacy</u>, Washington Papers, Center for Strategic and International Studies, Georgetown University, (Sage Publications, Beverly Hills, 1976).
Anon, <u>Radio Free Europe, an Instrument of Propaganda Aggression</u> (n.p. Warsaw, 1983).
F.C. Barghoorn, <u>Soviet Foreign Propaganda</u> (Princeton University Press, Princeton, 1965).
Edward W. Barrett, <u>Truth is our Weapon</u> (Funk & Wagnalls, New York, 1953).
Donald R. Browne, <u>International Radio Broadcasting</u> (Praeger Publishers, New York, 1982).
F. Gayle Durham (Hollander), <u>News Broadcasting on Soviet Radio and Television</u> (MIT Press, Cambridge, Mass., 1965).
F. Gayle Durham, <u>Radio and Television in the Soviet Union</u> (MIT Press, Cambridge, Mass., 1965).
F. Gayle Durham, <u>Soviet Political Indoctrination: Developments in Mass Media and Propaganda Since Stalin</u> (Praeger, New York, 1972).
Julian Hale, <u>Radio Power: Propaganda and International Broadcasting</u> (Paul Elek, London, 1975).
Allen C. Hansen, <u>USIA, Public Diplomacy in the Computer Age</u> (Praeger, New York, 1984).
John W. Henderson, <u>The United States Information Agency</u>, Praeger, New York, 1969).
R.T. Holt, <u>Radio Free Europe</u> (University of Minnesota, Minnesota, 1958).
Mark W. Hopkins, <u>Mass Media in the Soviet Union</u> (Pegasus, New York, 1970).
Mauray Lisann, <u>Broadcasting to the Soviet Union</u> (Praeger, New York, 1975).
Thomas L. McPhail, <u>Electronic Colonialism: The</u>

Future of Broadcasting and Communication (Sage Publications, Beverly Hills, 1981).
Gerard Mansell, Let the Truth be Told: Fifty Years of BBC External Broadcasting (Weidenfeld and Nicolson, London, 1982).
James W. Markham, Voices of the Red Giants (Iowa State University Press, Ames, Iowa, 1967).
Cord Meyer, Facing Reality: From World Federalism to the CIA (Harper & Row, New York, 1980).
Allan Michie, Voice through the Iron Curtain: The Radio Free Europe Story (Dodd, Mead & Company, New York, 1963).
Sig Mickelson, America's Other Voice, Radio Free Europe and Radio Liberty (Praeger, 1983).
Robert W. Piersein, The Voice of America: A History of International Broadcasting Activities of the United States Government, 1940-62 (Arno Press, New York, 1979).
Paul Roth, Cuius regio - eius informatio: Moskaus Modell fur die Weltinformationsordnung (Verlag Styria, Vienna, 1984).
Thomas C. Sorenson, The World War (Harper and Row, New York, 1968).
James L. Tyson, US International Broadcasting and National Security, National Strategy Information Center (Rampco Press, New York, 1983).
Gerhard Wettig, Broadcasting and Detente (C. Hurst & Company Publishers, London, 1977).
Arthur Williams, Broadcasting and Democracy in West Germany (Bradford University Press, Bradford, 1976).

Articles
Vladimir Artyomov and Vladimir Semyonov, 'The BBC: History, Apparatus, Methods of Radio Propaganda', Historical Journal of Film, Radio and Television (vol.4, no.1, 1984/March, pp.73ff).
Douglas A. Boyd, 'Broadcasting Between the Two Germanies', Journalism Quarterly (vol.60, no.2/ summer 1983, pp.232ff).
Douglas A. Boyd, 'The Pre-History of the Voice of America: US Short-Wave Broadcasting to 1942', Public Telecommunication Review (vol.2, no.6. December 1974, pp.38ff).
Donald R. Browne, 'The International Newsroom: A Study of Practices at the Voice of America, BBC and Deutsche Welle', Journal of Broadcasting (vol.27, no.3, summer 1983, pp.205ff).
Donald R. Browne, 'RIAS Berlin: A Case Study of a Cold War Broadcast Operation', Journal of Broadcasting (vol.10, no.1, spring 1966, pp.119ff).

Rolf Geserick and Arnuld Kutsch, 'Möglichkeiten und Behinderungen des Informationszuganges für westdeutsche Korrespondenten in der DDR seit 1972', Publizistik (no.3/4, 1984, pp.455ff).
Thomas Gubak and Steven Hill, 'The Beginnings of Soviet Broadcasting and the Role of V.I. Lenin', Journalism Monographs (December 1972).

Reports
BBC Annual Report and Handbook (British Broadcasting Corporation, London).
BBC Monitoring Service: Summary of World Broadcastings, 1939-83 (Ann Arbor: UMI-microform publication).
BBC Monitoring Service: Summary of World Broadcastings: ongoing publication.
The Board for International Broadcasting, Annual Report, 1973- (BIB, Suite 1100, 1201 Connecticut Avenue, Northwest, Washington, DC, 20036).
James R. Price, Radio Free Europe: A Survey and Analysis, (Washington, DC: Congressional Research Service, Library of Congress, 22nd March, 1972).
Report of the Presidential Study Commission on International Radio Broadcasting, The Right to Know, (Washington, DC: U.S. Government Printing Office, 1973).
The Media Institute, Voice of America at the Crossroads: a Panel Discussion on the Appropriate Role of the VOA (The Media Institute, Washington, DC, 1982).
Paul Roth, 'Die neue Weltinformationsordnung. Argumentation, Zielvorstellung und Vorgehen der UdSSR(I)', Berichte des Bundesinstituts für ostwissenschaftliche und internationale Studien, no.44, 1982.
RFE/RL, Soviet Area Audience and Opinion Research (SAAOR) Periodic Reports.
Joseph G. Whelan, Radio Liberty - A Study of its Origins, Structure, Policy, Programming and Effectiveness (Congressional Research Service, Library of Congress, Washington, DC, 22nd March, 1972).
World Radio TV Handbook (Watson Guptill Publications, New York, annual publication).

Periodicals
London Calling (BBC World Service).
Voice (Voice of America, 1984-, bi-monthly).

CONTRIBUTORS

Donald R. Browne
Has written extensively in the area of comparative and international broadcasting (see Bibliography) and his research has been supported by numerous grants from the Ford Foundation, NATO, and the Fulbright-Hays Programme, among others. He was a foreign service officer for the US Information Agency in Africa in the early 1960s, and since 1966 has been a professor in the Department of Speech-Communication at the University of Minnesota, Twin Cities.

William A. Buell
Senior vice president of RFE/RL, a graduate of Princeton University and George Washington University. He served as a pilot in the US Marine Corps during World War Two and subsequently flew for a Chinese civilian airline before he entered the US Foreign Service in 1951. He served in a variety of roles in Warsaw, Taipei, Hamburg, Brussels, Lome, Togo and Paris before attending the Naval War College in Newport in 1964. The following year he was made director of the Polish language service of the VOA, later taking charge of Polish affairs in the State Department, and then, until his retirement in 1975, he was director of the Office of Northern European Affairs. Following two years as legislative assistant to Senator Adalai E. Stevenson, he assumed the position of director of the Radio Free Europe division of RFE/RL in Munich in 1977, moving to his present position as chief of the Washington office in 1979.

Kurt Carlson
Formerly a member of the staff of the Voice of America's European division, is editor of The Law of the Sea Treaty: Current Choices (World Without War Publications, 1982).

Peter Fraenkel
Born in Breslau (Wroclaw). Started broadcasting in 1952 with the Central African Broadcasting Service, Lusaka moving to Reuters, London as a sub-editor in 1958. Joining the BBC External Services as a feature writer three years later, he was subsequently attached to the Malawi Broadcasting Corporation as head of programmes. From 1967 to 1972 he was Greek programme organiser for the External Services, moving on to become assistant head, Central Talks and Features. Between 1973 and 1979 he was assistant head and head of East European Services before being appointed to his present position in 1979. He still writes occasional radio plays and features and is the author of two books.

Alan Heil
Director of broadcast operations, Office of Programs, VOA. He joined the Voice in 1962 as a news writer, and served subsequently as a regional editor for Africa, as chief of the Arabic branch subcentres in Beirut and Cairo, and chief Middle East correspondent from 1969-71. He was chief of VOA news and current affairs from 1974-81 and was appointed director, VOA broadcast operations, in 1983.

Botho Kirsch
Head of the Eastern service of Deutsche Welle. After World War Two, he studied in Berlin and Heidelberg before becoming a newspaper correspondent in Moscow in 1960-1. He was then foreign editor and eastern expert for Der Speigel before coming to his present position in 1966. He is author of several books, including most recently Zwischen Marx und Murks (Edition Interfrom, Bd.123, Zürish, 1980).

Helen Koshits
Born in Yugoslavia in 1931, of White Russian stock, Helen Koshits was raised and educated in Belgrade in French, Russian and Serbian schools and studied physical chemistry at the University of Belgrade. She

left the country in 1950, and, following a stay in Italy, emigrated to Canada in 1954. After some years of laboratory work and a break to raise a family, Mrs Koshits joined the Russian production team of Radio Canada International in 1963. Some of her more important assignments were coverage of the Royal tour of the North-West Territories and Manitoba in 1970, Prime Minister Trudeau's visit to the USSR in 1971 and Marshal Tito's visit to Canada in the same year. She became supervisor of the Russian section in 1976.

Mary McIntosh
Chief of the Statistics, Analyses and Attitude Research section of East European Audience and Opinion Research, Radio Free Europe in Munich. She was educated at the University of Oklahoma and North Texas State University and worked in educational research before teaching at the Texas College of Medicine in the Department of Medical Humanities.

Edward Mainland
An American Foreign Service officer, currently chief, European division, Voice of America, a unit that broadcasts in 15 languages to about 40 million people in West, Central and Eastern Europe. Formerly chief of the VOA's Romanian service, his Foreign Service career has included Bucharest, Moscow, Guinea, Paris and Brussels.

R. Eugene Parta
Graduate of the School of Advanced International Studies of Johns Hopkins University, has been director of Soviet Area Audience and Opinion Research (SAAOR) at Radio Free Europe-Radio Liberty since 1981 and has been working on audience and opinion measurement in the USSR since 1969. As a visiting research associate at the Massachusetts Institute of Technology he worked with the late Professor Ithiel de Sola Pool on computer simulation models in mass communications research, with special attention to the problem of projecting incomplete survey data onto the population of the USSR. Mr Parta is the author and co-author of numerous studies in western radio communications to the Soviet Union and on public opinion and attitudinal patterns there.

Mark Pomar
Currently chief of the USSR division of the Voice of America, graduated from Tufts University in 1972 and received his doctorate in Russian literature and history from Columbia University in 1978. From 1975 to 1982 he taught Russian and Soviet studies at the University of Vermont; in 1981 he was a Fulbright research fellow in the USSR. After a short stint at Radio Free Europe-Radio Liberty in Munich, he joined the VOA in 1983. Dr Pomar has published numerous articles and reviews on subjects ranging from Pushkin and Dostoevsky to problems of contemporary Soviet ideology.

Jürgen Reiss
Born in Berlin of Christian-Jewish family and member of the resistance group Ernst during World War Two. Beginning as a reporter on the newly founded newspaper Der Kurier in 1946, he worked on several newspapers before becoming the editor-in-chief of Der Kurier from 1959 to 1966. He was awarded a PhD by the Free University of West Berlin for his research on George F. Kennan's policy of containment. In 1968 he was appointed director of European services at Deutschlandfunk in Cologne and, in recognition of his services, was awarded the Federal Service Cross in 1985 by the Federal Republic of Germany's President Richard von Weizsäcker.

Barbara Schiele
Senior programme analyst at the Voice of America, editor-in-chief of its annual report to the American public and Congress. She joined VOA in 1958, has served as research assistant to the director, production assistant in the American Republics division, and as aide in the Office of Public Information. She is well known in the international broadcasting community as the long-established 'corporate memory' of VOA.

Frank Shakespeare
Recently retired first chairman of the Board for International Broadcasting (1982-85), has served as director of the United States Information Service (USIS) from 1969 to 1973. He is the vice-chairman of RKO General, Inc and holds Honorary Doctorates from the Colorado School of Mines, Pace University and Delaware Law School.

K.R.M. Short FRHisS
Senior Lecturer in History at Westminster College, Oxford. Formerly secretary general of the International Association for Audio-Visual Media in Historical Research and Education (1979-85), editor of Historical Journal of Film, Radio and Television. His publications include Feature Films as History (Croom Helm/University of Tennessee, 1981) and Film & Radio Propaganda in World War Two (Croom Helm/University of Tennessee, 1983).

Frank Ward
Spent nearly nine of his 27 years with Radio Canada International as editor in charge of newscasts beamed to Iron Curtain countries. He recalls it as an experience totally unlike any other in a career which started in 1944 with the Montreal Gazette and, later, the Montreal Herald. In 1956, he became an editor in the English newsroom of the international service of Radio Canada and a year later transferred to the Eastern European desk. He became senior news editor, news feature producer, head of the English news service, and originated a central talks programme. The last years of his career were spent in Ottawa as head of news and current affairs. He retired early in 1985 and now lives on a farm in Eastern Ontario.

Gerhard Wettig
Studied at the universities of Freiburg, Tübingen, and Leeds, receiving his PhD from the University of Göttingen on 'The Role of the Russian Army in the Revolution of 1917'. He was a research fellow of the German Society on Foreign Affairs concerned with the demilitarisation and rearmament in Germany after World War Two, before his appointment in 1966 to the Federal Institute for Eastern and International Studies in Cologne. In charge of the Institute's foreign and security studies, he has published extensively on Soviet policies and East-West relations. His works include Broadcasting and Detente: Eastern Policies and their Implications for East-West Relations (C. Hurst & Co, London, 1977) and most recently, Umstrittene Sicherheit: Friedenswahrung und Rüstungsbergrenzung in Europa (Berlin Verlag, West Berlin, 1982).

INDEX

Afghanistan, war in 104, 108, 118, 127, 236-38
Aksyonov, Vasily 122
Aylen, Peter 28, 31

Bailey, George 11
Ball, George 167
Board for International Broadcasting (BIB), see also Radio Free Europe/Radio Liberty (RFE/RL) 64, 69, 76-8
    BIB Act (1973) 75-6
Bonner, Yelena 118
British Broadcasting Corporation (BBC) External Services 9, 12
    audience, Poland 152
    criticisms by emigrés, 147-51; Communists 145-7; The Spectator 151-3
    listeners' opinions 247
    origins 139-40
    policies and practices of Eastern Service 144-7
    typical transmissions 143-4
Brown, Alan 43, 45
Brown, James 11, 17

Central Intelligence Agency 9, 75
Chancellor, John 102
Charter 77, 109
cross-reporting 74, 92, 96

Delafield, Charles 28-9, 33, 36, 38
Desy, Jean 28, 33, 36

Deutsche Langwelle 174
Deutsche Welle, Russian Service 3, 9, 172
    Federal Radio Law and Mission 160
    German 'revanchism' 167
    listeners 163-4, 247
    origins 159
    output 158, 161
    transmitters 162
Deutschlandfunk 3, 9
    European service 180-3
    German language service 177-80
    listeners' mail 183-4
    listeners' opinions 247
    organisation and legal mandate 175-7
    origins 172-5
Deutschlandsender 173-4
Dilworth, Ira 28, 30

East European Audience and Opinion Research (Radio Free Europe) 183-4, 243
    audience characteristics 244
    opinion on political orientation 250-6; US-USSR conflict 256-258; political change 258-261
    propaganda and western broadcasts 246-50

Federal Republic of Germany, broadcasting
    basic issues 219-20

Index

Basic Law 173-4
Basic Treaty on the Relationship Between the Two German States 209-12
   development 214-6
   impact on German Democratic Republic 204-5
   legislation and organisation 175-6
   resistance of GDR 205, 215, 216
Foreign Information Service 98

Genscher, Hans-Dietrich 168
German Democratic Republic (see also Federal Republic of Germany)
   problem of West German broadcasts 212-14
   restrictions on western reporting 217-18
Giddens, Kenneth R. 111
Goldberg, Anatol 148, 152-3
Gorbachov, Mikhail 1
Görner, Gunter 206-7

Heil, Alan 10, 13-14
Helsinki, Final Act 1-3, 17-18, 45, 104, 212
Hibbitts, Bernard 43, 46
Holocaust 168
Honecker, Erich 198, 211-2, 214
Hungarian Uprising, 1956 37, 101, 129

Ionesco, Eugene 123

Jacob, Sir Ian 151
jamming (see USSR)

Kennedy, President John F. 120, 170
Kirkpatrick, Jeane 16-17
Korean Airliner (KAL 007) disaster 74-5, 104, 233-6, 245

Lerner, Professor Aleksandr 16, 167-8
Ley, Simon 154
Loomis, Henry 102, 126

Mansell, Gerard 106, 108, 150
Medvedev, Roy 164
Mickelson, Sig 10

Nekipelov, Viktor 4, 166
Neues Deutschland 158-9
New Information Order 15
nuclear threat, Soviet opinion 238-9

Orlova, Raisa 166

Phelps, Arthur 28
Pipes, Richard 147
Pomar, Mark 110
Public Diplomacy; Report of the United States Advisory Commission (1982) 15, 22-3

Radio Canada International (formerly International Service of the Canadian Broadcasting Corporation)
   broadcast hours to Europe, 1970 42
   broadcast language and times 48-9
   change of name 43
   East European Department Staff and Programming 49-54
   jamming 37, 39-40
   listenership 53
   mandate 46
   origins 27-46
   target area selection 36
   technical facilities 54
   threat of closure 9, 38-42
Radio Free Europe/Radio Liberty 3, 9, 15
   audience opinion 244, 247-50, 258
   audiences 67, 95-6
   broadcast effectiveness 73-5
   budgets 71-3
   funding 10, 153
   mission of ... 85-7
   Pell Amendment 77-8
   policy guidelines 88-97
   programming 82-3
   'soft sell' versus 'hard sell' 78-80

Index

targeting audiences 84
West European Advisory Committee 64
Radio In the American Sector (RIAS) 3, 9
    audience response 189, 191-2
    East German radios 202
    funding and control 195-99
    origins 185-89
    programming 193-4
    special status 201
    staffing 194-5
    target audiences 190
Radio Marti 73
Radio Moscow 11, 60, 150
radio sets, Eastern Europe 134; USSR 135
Ralis, Dr Max 225
Reich, Walter 16
Reinhardt, John 61, 107
Rostropovich, Mstislav 67, 121-2

Sakharov, Andrei 4, 108, 118
samizdat 4, 92, 94, 162, 164
saturation broadcasts 104
Schapiro, Professor Leonard 151-2
Shakespeare, Frank 9, 106
Shultz, George 1, 2
Sola Pool, Professor Ithiel de 227
Solzhenitzsyn, Alexander 4, 63, 67, 108, 121-3, 147-9, 169
    Gulag Archipelago 104-6, 108, 110, 162, 168
Solidarity Movement in Poland 74; Soviet opinion of ... 239
Soviet Area Audience and Opinion Research (SAAOR) 164
    attitudes and western broadcasting 230-3
    audience ratings, weekly 229
    case studies: Afghanistan 236-8; Korean Airliner 233-6; nuclear threat 238-9; Solidarity 239-40
    demographic composition 228
    methodology 227-8
    origins of 225-6
Spectator, The 151-3
Suez Crisis 129

tamizdat 162
Tomlinson, Kenneth 60, 115-7, 125

United States Information Agency 16, 57, 61, 101
Universal Declaration of Human Rights 88
Urban, George 11, 16
Urban, Jerzy 245-6
USSR 63, 65-8
    censorship 4-5
    jamming 5-8, 37, 39-40, 103-4, 127-8, 162-3
    post communist period 63
    radio sets 135
    view of East-West relations 219-220

Voice of America 9, 57, 85, 98, 136, 166, 202
    audiences 113-4, 116, 127
    East European service 130-2
    future developments 126
    listeners' opinions 247
    modernisation 110-12
    Munich Programme Centre 101
    origins 98-103
    Religion 123
    representing American Society 119-124
    source of news 113-19
    Soviet service 121, 132-33
    VOA Charter 102, 106-7, 109, 114-15, 119
    VOA editorial 124-6

Wiles, Professor Peter 151-3

Zaslavskaya, Academician Tatyana 169